WITHDRAWN

I appreciate Mark's kind words *in The Multiplier Model* about the businesses I have grown through franchising (Massage Envy, The Joint, Redline Athletics, and Amazing Lash). As Mark teaches in this book, growth through multiple units or even multiple brands is very much about multiplying the systems that work. If you have the passion and desire to build something that's enduring, Mark's advice will help you lay the foundation.

—John Leonesio, CEO, Redline Athletics Franchising

Insightful and pithy! *The Multiplier Model* is a must-read for any business looking to grow.

—Tom Ryan, vice president of franchise development, CD One Price Cleaners

Developing a systems mindset is key! Another great business expansion book from Mark Siebert.

—P. Allan Young, chairman and partner, FranBridge Capital

A captivating read on how systems impact everything from operations to marketing to sales to company culture. Mark generously shares his knowledge from 30 years in the business, including compelling stories from the companies he has met along the way.

—Scott Lehr, managing partner and CEO, GT&S Franchise Executive Search, Former IFA executive vice president

Creating repeatable and teachable systems and processes has been so important to our success. This is a must read for any business owner!

—Seth Brink, president of Arete Food Group

When we chose to franchise Sky Zone, we learned a tremendous amount about duplicating our business in working with Mark. And much of that wisdom is imparted here. *The Multiplier Model* is a valuable guide for the start-up franchisor or for anyone considering expanding their existing business.

—JEFF PLATT, CO-FOUNDER, SKY ZONE FRANCHISE GROUP

At Vessel Technologies, we think hard about the role our systems play in allowing us to scale our business and meet growth objectives. *The Multiplier Model* is right on point!

—NEIL RUBLER, FOUNDER, CANDLEBROOK PROPERTIES AND VESSEL TECHNOLOGIES

At Auntie Anne's Pretzels the systems we developed for sales tracking, forecasting and site selection were integral to our success for both franchised and corporate locations. Having solid, dependable systems in place benefits employees, franchisees, and the ultimate customer. Mark's book will show you how successful businesses can harness the power of strong systems to replicate their success.

—SCOT CRAIN, RETIRED VICE PRESIDENT OF FRANCHISE RELATIONS, AUNTIE ANNE'S PRETZELS

Mark Siebert has scored another home run with *The Multiplier Model!*

—PAUL ALTERO, CO-OWNER/FOUNDER, BUBBAKOO'S BURRITOS

When we worked with iFranchise Group to franchise College H.U.N.K.S. Hauling Junk and Moving, they helped us streamline and systematize the whole process. In *The Multiplier Model,* Mark shares his expertise on streamlining for every business owner with expansion goals.

—NICK FRIEDMAN, CO-FOUNDER AND OWNER, COLLEGE H.U.N.K.S. HAULING JUNK AND MOVING

Mark's third book provides intelligent strategic advice for anyone looking to replicate their business! The stories he shares from successful entrepreneurs make this a very engaging read.

—DAVE PAZGAN, CO-FOUNDER, 101 MOBILITY AND DIRECTOR OF FRANCHISING, KIDOKINETICS

Whether you are trying to grow your business or just looking to improve existing operations, you will come away from this book with a deeper understanding of the power of systems in helping businesses prosper and evolve.

—PATRICK WALLS, COO, FRANCHISE BUSINESS GROUP, LEISURE POOLS AND SPAS MANUFACTURING NORTH AMERICA INC.

Everything you need to know about replicating your business the right way is in this book. For over 30 years Mark has helped people realize the American Dream working with them to turn their small business into a franchise.

—PAUL ROCCHIO, VICE PRESIDENT OF DEVELOPMENT AND MEMBER SERVICES, INTERNATIONAL FRANCHISE ASSOCIATION

We looked to Mark and his team at iFranchise Group to design our expansion strategy and it was one of the wisest decisions we made. Mark is a great teacher, and he shares some of his best lessons in *The Multiplier Model.*

—Scott Jewett, CEO, Pinspiration Franch ise Group

Mark demonstrates again why he is one of the foremost thought leaders in the small business space. His book shows how you can apply the lessons learned in franchising to small business strategy in a way that is both informative and compelling.

—Debra Shwetz, Co-Founder, Nothing Bundt Cakes

the multiplier model

HOW SYSTEMS CAN CREATE EXPONENTIAL BUSINESS GROWTH

Mark Siebert

Entrepreneur Press®

Entrepreneur Press, Publisher
Cover Design: Andrew Welyczko
Production and Composition: Eliot House Productions

This publication is designed to provide accurate and authoritative information
in regard to the subject matter covered. It is sold with the understanding
that the publisher is not engaged in rendering legal, accounting, or other
professional services. If legal advice or other expert assistance is required, the
services of a competent professional person should be sought.

Entrepreneur Press® is a registered trademark of Entrepreneur Media, Inc.

Library of Congress Cataloging-in-Publication Data
Names: Siebert, Mark, 1955- author.
Title: The multiplier model : how systems can create exponential business
    growth / by Mark Siebert.
Description: [Irvine] : [Entrepreneur Press], [2021] | Includes index. |
    Summary: "Franchise expert and consultant Mark Siebert knows that the
    key to duplicating success is a solid system that's easy to follow. Taking a
    page from successful franchises, The Multiplier Model delivers a step-by-
    step process to creating a business with systems and processes for
    exponential growth and profits"-- Provided by publisher.
Identifiers: LCCN 2021025415 (print) | LCCN 2021025416 (ebook) |
    ISBN 9781599186672 (trade paperback) | ISBN 9781613084243 (epub)
Subjects: LCSH: Franchises (Retail trade) | Small business--Growth. | Success
    in business.
Classification: LCC HF5429.23 .S56 2021 (print) | LCC HF5429.23 (ebook) |
    DDC 658.8/708--dc23
LC record available at https://lccn.loc.gov/2021025415
LC ebook record available at https://lccn.loc.gov/2021025416

Printed in the United States of America

25 24 23 22   10 9 8 7 6 5 4 3 2 1

contents

chapter 5

marketing your money machine 87

chapter 6

competing with the internet. 109

chapter 7

selling 129

chapter 8

operations

chapter 9

people

foreword

by peter ross, ceo and
cofounder, senior helpers

I have always felt there are two kinds of people in the world of business. Those who will follow the norms, and those who never saw a norm they did not want to challenge. For the first 20 years of my career, I was part of that first group. For the second 20, I was a part of the latter.

On the high seas, that second group would be called pirates. On the highway systems, they would be repeat offenders. In the art world, we might call them geniuses. But in the business world, they might be called unemployable—or they might be called entrepreneurs.

If you are reading this book, my guess is that you are in that second group.

In the U.S., that means you are either a part of the 10.6 percent of the working-age population who owns a business or that aspires to. The other 90 percent or so are likely content to work for others or are hoping that they, too, will be able to become a part of the great American Dream one day.

But that second group can be broken down further. According to U.S. Bureau of Labor Statistics, roughly 50 percent of new businesses will have failed within five years, and 65 percent will have failed in ten years. And of the remainder, if I had to guess, less than 10 percent end up making the kind of money that one would call life changing.

If these statistics scare you off, I am guessing this is the wrong book for you.

But for those of you who have not been scared off, ask yourself what is the difference between those who made it and those who did not?

Having stood in your shoes and having taken the plunge on more than one occasion, I think I know at least one small part of the answer.

I did not start out in life as an entrepreneur. In fact, before I became an entrepreneur, I had been very successfully running the corporate treadmill and was on the "fast track" to career success. I started my career with ADP as a sales representative, worked my way up through sales, was promoted to sales training manager, then was promoted again to National Director of Sales Promotions and Telemarketing in their corporate office by the ripe old age of 25. After a couple of years, I leapfrogged the "normal" career path, which would have seen me become a sales manager next, to become the youngest regional Vice President of Sales and ultimately their Vice President of Marketing.

From there, I was recruited by Ernst & Young to head up their marketing on the west coast. And while I had learned a lot about sales and marketing at ADP, it was at EY where I really began to learn about business. And the more I learned about business, the more I got the "entrepreneurial itch." Private equity then hired me in management positions for a couple of startup companies and I was later lured me back into the corporate world, where my next move was to become the Vice President of Corporate Sales at Intuit.

Now I tell everyone who will listen that once they have gone out on their own, they should never return to the corporate world—because once you have been your own boss, you will never again be satisfied working for others. But at the time, I did not take that advice, and fortunately learned more valuable lessons before realizing that the corporate world was no longer for me. As it turned out, all the people I met at Intuit were Jack Welch disciples and in my tenure there, I became an expert in Six Sigma. And like many of the principles Mark has espoused in this book, Six Sigma is focused on taking a systematic, data-centric approach to process improvement.

When I left Intuit, I went into business with Tony Bonacuse. Tony and I had worked together at one of the companies I worked for in between my corporate stints and we had become good friends. Over the years, he and I had talked about starting a senior care business together, and by the time I joined him, Tony had already started the first Senior Helpers in Baltimore in 2002. In 2004, we became partners and I started up a Senior Helpers in California so that we could demonstrate that our business could be duplicated. We figured if we could duplicate it once, we could franchise it.

Tony and I always knew we wanted to franchise. And by 2005, we were ready to go.

The problem was that while both of us knew business, both of us came from the corporate world and neither of us had any experience with franchising. That is when I met Mark and his team at iFranchise Group. We knew from our experience in the corporate world that the best way to shortcut the learning curve is to hire outside experts who have hands-on experience doing what you are attempting. And we were only going to get one shot at doing it right.

In early 2005 we hired the iFranchise Group to develop our strategy, operations manual, training programs, and our franchise marketing plan and materials. By September 2005, we had sold our first franchise and we were off to the races. Honestly, we sold too many multi-unit territories in the early years and did some of the things that iFranchise had advised us against. But at the same time, a light bulb had gone off.

Build a business. Refine the business. Systematize the business. Then duplicate the business repeatedly, in our case, using franchising.

In 2007, one of Tony's former roommates from college, Dr. Scott Burger, had the idea that we could do a franchise of urgent care. So just as we were getting successful in Senior Helpers, we started an urgent care center across the street from our Senior Helpers office. We wanted to see if we could franchise urgent care, and by 2008, we were ready to launch our second franchise—Doctors Express. And because it had worked so well in the past, we hired the iFranchise Group again.

The good news was that we were building the systems for franchise marketing, sales, and for onboarding new franchises. So while many new franchisors look at the franchise growth process as an unknown, our systems told us that if you start with a good concept, spend an adequate amount of money on franchise marketing and spend it in the right places, franchise sales will be the inevitable result. And Doctors Express grew to 80 units in a very short period, and by 2012, we were the third-largest urgent care in the country and were doing quite well.

In 2010 we launched a third company, Assisted Transition, which competed with A Place for Mom in the marketplace—helping people identify appropriate long-term care facilities for seniors. Once that model was working, we just hit repeat once again. We hired the iFranchise Group, grew the brand quickly, and had opened about 75 or 80 units by the time we sold the company to CarePatrol in 2012, which is now part of ComForCare/Best Life Brands.

At about the same time, we completed the first private equity sale of Senior Helpers. We sold Doctors Express right after that. It was rebranded as American Family Care and now has about 200 franchises operating across the U.S.

Tony and I stayed involved with Senior Helpers and brought in Altaris Capital as a second round of private equity in 2016. Tony decided to exit the business and focus on other business investment opportunities, at the same time continuing to sharpen his golf game.

Then in 2018, I started Town Square, a unique adult day center providing an enrichment experience for seniors using design elements and themes from a 1950s small town. And, of course, once we had perfected the initial prototype, we went back to the well again and hired the iFranchise Group to help expand that business through franchising. Lather. Rinse. Repeat.

In early 2021, we sold Senior Helpers to Advocate Aurora Health, at which point I had to give up the rest of my equity in the business, as I could not hold equity in a nonprofit.

Altaris and I still own Town Square, which is my fourth brand. Despite the pandemic, we have 14 franchises awarded and, as of early 2021, we expect that we will begin to see some substantial growth from here as the country moves beyond the Covid-19 pandemic.

The fact is, just as Mark has laid out in this book, growing each of these businesses has been very much a repeatable process. And while I never spent much time thinking about it before, Mark has teased out the details of the process in a manner that will allow you as a would-be entrepreneur to systematically approach the growth of your business from idea to plan, from plan to testing, from results to refinement, and ultimately from Money Machine to expansion.

When I lay out the history of my last 20 or so years above, it seems like a straight path to the top. But it wasn't. We made mistakes along the way. Tony and I have had a few different ideas that we rolled out but never moved forward with. We were going to add medical staffing to the Senior Helpers model. We tried it. Calling it Staffing Helpers, we rolled it out in California. And when we ran the numbers, we thought that as a stand-alone, the franchisor would have been rolling in dough, because the model got to very high levels of revenue in no time. But because the business had very low margins, the franchisee would have had a very hard time making money—so we pulled the plug on the concept.

Ultimately, the key to our success was constantly measuring the results that we were achieving, recognizing the need for change, and making those changes while measuring again—sometimes throwing out the wild-hair ideas that we could not make work—while constantly refining both our core business models and the franchise business model with which we were expanding our business.

As an entrepreneur, you cannot expand before you know why you succeeded the first time. You need to understand what you're getting into, vet it completely, and not be afraid to fail. You're going to make some mistakes.

While not the sole focus of this book, I love franchising, too. My favorite term is OPM—other people's money. I think there is no way in any business world that you can grow exponentially as well as you can in franchising—especially when you are talking about brick-and-mortar. I tell people all the time that having a franchisee instead of a branch manager is like the difference between dedicated and committed—like ham and eggs—the chicken is dedicated but the pig is committed.

A lot of new franchisors think they've already perfected their model. I can tell you for a fact that's just not true. I learn something new every day. And I try to use that learning to improve the business. As a franchisor, you must control the brand. You must have brand standards. But you also must be open to change because the world is moving too fast for any of us to stand still. But you cannot change for the sake of change or just because an idea sounds good. You must let people think, you must let people be creative, you must let people know you are listening, and you must be willing to adapt. People want to be a part of the process. But adaptation without measurement will only drive chaos.

If you are going to go the franchise route, you need to know the business so that when you sit across from a franchisee who is putting their hard-earned money into a franchise, you know what you are talking about. That's why we needed to run each of our own businesses before we started to grow. We needed to be sure that the model worked and we could transfer a business concept from one market to another successfully before making the decision to expand.

So that's my story. Four brands over 16 years of franchising. And, of course, I have a couple more ideas for additional brands that I plan to launch one day, but I'll leave those ideas for another time and place.

The fact of the matter is, I so very much love the process. And, while this book was not out when I got started, the process described here is the same one we have been coached on over the course of years—and the same one that has helped contribute to our success.

Now I just need a process to convince Tony to stop playing golf so much. I need to get him back to work again. We drank the Kool-Aid with Mark and his team at the iFranchise Group back in 2005 and I think we have been very blessed. I am hoping that for us, the process will not stop any time soon.

It has been one heck of a ride. And a ride that I would encourage anyone with any entrepreneurial spirit to join me on.

introduction

I do not expect it happens very often that a book teaches its author a lesson about its subject. But in this case, that is exactly what happened.

As I began writing this book, I wanted to capture the essence of what distinguished those businesses that had achieved great success through franchising. And it occurred to me that over the years, many of my clients had told me they intended to franchise from day one—even before they opened their doors for business. Those lessons, I reasoned, could be applied to all types of businesses—even those that did not franchise—allowing business owners to use the systems that worked so well in franchising to maintain quality, grow faster, and control their growth better.

After all, while the iFranchise Group is the world's most prominent franchise consulting firm, much of what we do extends well beyond franchising. For example, we created the food-service operations manuals for the U.S. Navy's nuclear aircraft carriers, where they feed 5,000 sailors three meals a day aboard the only carriers in the world that are capable of resupplying at sea. That's clearly not a franchise, but we used what we knew about franchising best practices to help create a model the Navy could use.

I started writing with the idea that creating a business that was designed to grow was really a question of creating a system that could be readily replicated. Every successful franchised business is built on such a system. I thought if systems were the key, the secret to success in business was creating a system for creating those systems.

But then I began wondering if it could really be that simple. Could someone just read a book and then build a business by creating, implementing, and refining a system, and then reap the benefits years later? I realized that I was missing something.

Over the course of my career, I have been involved in far more than my share of home-run success stories. And when you combine those with the stories shared by others on my team, the list reads like a who's who of franchising: 101 Mobility, 1-800-Flowers.com, Amazing Lash Studio, Auntie Anne's, Board & Brush, Buffalo Wild Wings, Clean Juice, College H.U.N.K.S. Hauling Junk & Moving, Culver's, Einstein Bros. Bagels, Fuzzy's Taco Shop, Häagen-Dazs, i9 Sports, LINE-X, Massage Envy, McAlister's Deli, N-Hance, Newk's Eatery, Nothing Bundt Cakes, Office Evolution, Oreck, Pearle Vision, Pinkberry, Senior Helpers, ShelfGenie, Sky Zone, Teeth Tomorrow, Teriyaki Madness, Tommy's Express, Which Wich, and many others.

But scattered among the many home runs were a number of base hits: the companies that might award 10, 25, or 50 franchises before stalling out.

Of course, many of these companies were not interested in aggressive growth. Some got into franchising to take advantage of "walk-up" inquiries or to provide opportunities for friends, family members, or employees. Others had such narrow market niches that their franchisees needed very large territories to survive, so selling more than a few dozen franchises would saturate the market. And for many, aggressive growth was simply not needed to meet their more modest financial goals. In fact, the majority of franchise systems in the United States are regional rather than national brands.

And, unfortunately, as much as we worked to avoid them, there were also occasional strikeouts. Some of those, like the ultimate collapse of Blockbuster Video, could be attributed to obvious changes in the marketplace combined with a failure to rapidly adapt. The cause in other cases may be less obvious. In an effort to help you learn from those experiences, I will be referring to some of them throughout this book, although I will change enough details to be sure no one can recognize them, in order to maintain confidentiality.

In thinking about how to write this book from that perspective, I decided to go back to the drawing board. It occurred to me that by the time I met my clients, they had already achieved a measure of success in their own right. At the iFranchise Group, we receive literally hundreds of inquiries every month, mostly from business owners who would like to franchise their business. We have a team of four consultants who screen these inquiries—so only ones who are particularly well-qualified end up meeting with me or one of our senior consultants. I was basing my experience on the finished product. If I wanted to understand what it took to build a company for aggressive growth, I needed to step back in time, not to when I first met these folks but to when they were setting the foundations of their business.

So I started racking my brain for other clues as to what I might be missing. And one came to me from one of my more recent success stories, one that has taken a more measured approach to their growth—a great company called Bubbakoo's Burritos.

I knew Bubbakoo's was going to be a winner almost from the moment I met partners Paul Altero and Bill Hart at one of their New Jersey locations in August 2013. At the time, they had six locations and were seriously investigating franchising. Both Paul and Bill had a background in franchising; they had previously worked with Johnny Rockets, and Paul had also worked with Friendly's. My first impression as I drove up was that it was bright and well-lit, and the guacamole-green sign really popped.

When Paul and Bill arrived, they were not "dressed to impress" in suits and ties, which people still wore on occasion back then. They were regular, down-to-earth guys, which was fine by me. As they showed me around their locations, it was clear they had a great rapport with their managers and employees. The décor was unique, recognizable, and consistent. The units were spotless, well-run, and nicely systematized. And when I tried the food, I was thrilled: fresh, made-to-order, and sold at a price point that was affordable. Not only was the food delicious, but these guys knew their numbers down to the decimal. Food, labor, paper, and every other line item expense. They had their operation down to a science.

But when I commented on all this, Paul looked at me like I had three heads. I had totally missed the point. What they really had going for them was their culture—and their people. For them, well-run locations were the cost of entry in a competitive marketplace. What set them apart, and what they were proudest of, were their employees, who translated into great service and great operations. I knew right then that Bubbakoo's would be a home run. This was a company that was built to franchise!

As of this writing, Bubbakoo's has sold some 60 locations in seven states in less than five years, having grown to ten times their initial size. More important, because they have been growing their infrastructure along the way, they are now in a position to accelerate their growth, and they have been signing more and bigger deals in the past year.

After thinking about that story, it occurred to me that perhaps what I was missing was the "soul" of the brand. Or, as Jeff Goldblum put it in the 1986 movie *The Fly*, it was the "poetry of the steak." I could see the science of the business, but I was missing its poetry.

I then thought about my friend John Leonesio. When I first got to know John in 2002, he had just opened his first Massage Envy location and was looking to franchise. He and his brother Frank had previously built and sold a successful chain of health clubs, so John took the membership model common to athletic clubs and applied it to his new therapeutic massage company. When John retained us to franchise Massage Envy, the prototype location had been open only three months.

Today, Massage Envy is a success story for the ages—growing the company to some 800 locations before selling it in 2008 (today it is twice that size). And since that time, John has taken that same formula and successfully franchised The Joint, Redline Athletics, and Amazing Lash Studio—in which we were also involved.

So perhaps John more than anyone was my role model when I first thought about writing this book. But as I continued to think about the many entrepreneurs I have had the privilege of working with over the years, the pattern began to change. While some of these entrepreneurs had built their businesses with the intent to franchise, many more of them seemed to have stumbled into franchising almost as an afterthought.

Instead, I found that many of these entrepreneurs had an intense passion for their business—and that passion led them to obsess on the ways in which the business could be improved. They would tinker with the business model and tinker some more, but as they got closer to their vision to "perfect" their business, the incremental challenge posed by their tinkering and the incremental improvements that it brought were no longer enough to keep the entrepreneurial fires burning. And expansion grew out of a compelling need to climb the next mountain.

My first encounter in 1991 with Jim Disbrow and Scott Lowery, the founders of Buffalo Wild Wings, was very different from my Bubbakoo's meeting. At that time, they too had about six locations, although they were not nearly as geographically concentrated. But that was where the similarities seemed to stop. Jim and Scott wanted me to try every single item on the menu, so we went to the biggest table in the house and began ordering. I don't remember how many different levels of heat they had on their wings at the time, but I am fairly sure they were enjoying my pain as I worked my way up the thermometer. All kidding aside, though, they took an extraordinary pride in each of their recipes and went into a great deal of detail as to how each was created and why.

The chief thing that struck me was the level of buzz and excitement in the restaurant. It was clearly a place where people wanted to be. But while their unit level financials were great given their revenue levels, their command of some of the key restaurant operating metrics reflected their lack of experience. Still, it was clear that they were on to something, and we developed a strategy in which franchises would be sold in college towns during the initial years while internal controls were put in place so that they could attract area developers as they grew.

When I met Frank Fiume at i9 Sports, it was yet another story. Frank had recently quit his high-paying job to pursue his passion for youth sports leagues. Some of Frank's story is chronicled in his book, *Running With My Head Down* (Greenleaf Book Group LLC, 2019), which describes how he pursued his dream, often in the face of criticism and reproach from friends and even his father, and continued to put everything on the line for his goal. When he finally achieved what many would consider the pinnacle of their success with ABA Sports, the largest adult sports league on Long Island, he decided to shift gears, move to Florida, and franchise a children's sports league. His only problem was that he needed to sell his one and only successful business to be able to afford the cost of pursuing that dream. And while there were some initial bumps along the way, i9 Sports now serves two million participants in over 900 communities in 30 states and has generated over \$300 million since its inception in 2003.

Not everyone I met with saw franchising in their future. I remember Alan Bush, one of the founders of Fuzzy's Taco Shop, telling me half in jest that he had no interest in growth—that he would rather sit on his porch and drink beer. Today, after beginning to franchise with the iFranchise Group in 2009, there are more than 150 locations open (and far more than that sold), and in 2016 the founders sold a 70 percent ownership interest to the private equity firm NRD Capital.

Dr. Don Newcomb, the retired dentist who founded McAlister's Deli (and later Newk's Eatery), was another entrepreneur who, when I first spoke to him in 1988, was very skeptical about franchising. Today, though, McAlister's has more than 450 locations and is owned by Focus Brands, an affiliate of Roark Capital, which is the largest private equity firm in franchising.

Over the years, I have perhaps personally met, analyzed, and worked with more successful small businesses than all but a handful of consultants around the world. By my calculations, over the past 34 years, I have provided one-on-one consulting advice to more than 5,000 companies—the vast majority of which were small businesses at the time and had been prescreened in terms of the success of their business. Of those 5,000, I have had a more in-depth client relationship with well over 500.

In that time, I have learned a great deal about what these successful companies have in common—and what it takes for them to get from success to superstar. One thing I can tell you for certain is that it isn't about luck. It's about multiplying the systems that work.

multiplying your success

The vast majority of the small businesses with which I have consulted over the decades were already successful, often very successful, in their own right. Yet not all of these businesses had what it takes to grow exponentially.

The ones that did, it seemed to me, had refined their business model to the point where it would work without them. They understood the drivers of the business. They had developed systems surrounding the systems that drove the business so that it could be duplicated. They had developed further systems to continually refine and improve on their business model—knowing that businesses need to adapt to survive. And they had developed controls to ensure that the systems they had developed were being followed—and to correct the situation when they were not.

The companies that could harness this process had something special. And these are the companies that, as a starting point, had the potential to take advantage of what I am calling the Multiplier Model. And those that have used the systematized approach inherent in that model not only to replicate the success of their original business, but also to develop an expansion system for that business, have been able to utilize this Multiplier Model for their growth.

what to expect in this book

This book has several audiences, and as a result, I have used some literary shortcuts to make reading it easier. Some of the people I am trying to address in this book will be looking to open a retail business, while others may want to open or expand a restaurant. Others may hope to open or expand a service-based business that serves either consumers or other businesses, and they may or may not have a physical office outside the home.

I should also note that while systems are vital for any sustainable business, the process of growth for some internet businesses is very different than it is for businesses with a physical market presence. So to those readers who find this hopscotch writing style problematic, I apologize in advance.

Additionally, this book talks about the application of systems to a variety of business topics that have all been covered in tremendous detail and often in far superior fashion elsewhere. There are literally thousands of books on advertising and marketing, purchasing, inventory control, pricing, production, finance, management, and small business topics in general. As a book dealing specifically with systematization, I have touched on many of these areas on a cursory level, not so much in an effort to educate you on these very complex business topics, but instead to point out how any business that hopes to grow needs to develop systems in these areas in order to replicate what works. Finally, this book will also advocate that as you create your business' system, you also create systems to continually test, improve, and refine your systems.

Let's begin by talking about what I mean by "systems."

introduction to systems

Let's start with a simple premise: All businesses have systems. Some of those systems change from minute to minute, and some change depending on who is working that shift. Some are carved in stone, some in clay.

Sometimes those systems consistently deliver profits for the company. Those are the businesses that have it all figured out. They have institutionalized high-performing systems. Let's call these Type A businesses. This is what you want to build.

Sometimes, of course, businesses never become profitable or only return marginal results. While a lot of these folks contact us for help at iFranchise Group, they do not often make it to my conference room, as we have pretty rigorous screening criteria. Let's call these Type C businesses. They need to make substantial changes quickly or they will not survive much longer.

Finally, some businesses do well occasionally, but they do not always meet their goal of consistently driving profitability. Let's call those Type B businesses. All too often, the Type B business owner does not understand why his business model is sometimes profitable and sometimes not. Or, alternatively, why it sometimes delivers strong profits and sometimes only marginal results.

In my many meetings with small business owners over the years, I would estimate that perhaps as many as 40 percent fall into the Type B category. Perhaps they have opened multiple locations and had to close one or two—but when asked why a particular location failed, their analysis goes no deeper than "It just wasn't a good location." Or they may have one location that has a higher cost of goods sold or labor cost than others in the system, but have never quite understood why.

Failures are only failures if you don't learn from them. To do that, you need to recognize both that they are failures and the precise cause of the failure. But more than that, you have to institutionalize the systems that work and find ways to identify and eliminate those that do not if you want to avoid a repeat of those problems in the future.

In this chapter, we'll look at some examples of companies that rely on proven systems to multiply, starting with McDonald's, one of the best-known brands in the world. I will also introduce you to the central quandary I have seen successful business owners face again and again as they struggle to take their company to the next level—especially the pain points involved in going from the first location to the second. I hope to open your eyes to the pitfalls of simply grinding it out instead of first building and perfecting the systems to help your business expand. I want to ease your fears that growth involves losing control of your business, because well-built systems put you more in control. And you can begin to see how the Multiplier Model depends on creating a systems mindset.

how McDonald's does it

McDonald's does not have the most franchise locations in the world (7-Eleven has that honor) or even the most franchises in the food-service industry (that title goes to Subway). It does not have the highest system-wide revenue of any franchise company (Yum! Brands, which has 50,000 restaurants combined between its KFC, Taco Bell, and Pizza Hut brands, holds that title). But when it comes to brands, McDonald's is nothing short of iconic.

In earlier books, I talked about different companies that tried to copy McDonald's concept but failed. Some of their failure, no doubt, can be attributed to McDonald's earlier entry into the marketplace. After all, the first one to market with a new concept often owns the category's "mind space." But that would not account for the later success of Burger King and Wendy's, or the more recent success of companies like Five Guys, BurgerFi, Mooyah, Smashburger, Elevation Burger, and others.

You could also point to their lack of differentiation. Burger King captured market share in the 1970s with "It takes two hands to handle a Whopper!" and "Have it your way!"—campaigns that emphasized their points of difference from McDonald's. Wendy's appealed to an older demographic in the 1980s by touting their "old-fashioned" burgers with an octogenarian spokesperson named Clara Peller, who asked, "Where's the beef?" And, of course, the new generation of gourmet burger restaurants, which likely has not stopped evolving, is returning to the limited-menu roots of their predecessors, and trying to compete on quality.

But if it is not strictly dependent on timing or market position, why did McDonald's succeed so spectacularly while so many of their competitors either stalled or flamed out? What was their "secret sauce"? Was it better execution? Better locations? A better product? Better management? More capital?

While all the above no doubt factored into their rise to franchise superstardom, the overriding factor contributing to its success could be explained in a single word: systematization.

McDonald's succeeded because they built a *system* for delivering burgers faster, cheaper, and with lower labor costs than their competitors. Over the years, their system has evolved to encompass everything. They have a system for selecting a site and measuring the impact on other local restaurants. A system for construction that allows new restaurants to open quickly, efficiently, and at a reasonable cost. A system for their supply chain that results in lower costs and reliable delivery. A system for production that ensures consistency across more than 39,000 restaurants worldwide. A system for testing and introducing new products, and another system for testing new advertising campaigns. A system for adjusting product pricing. A system for determining when and how long to offer limited-time-only menu items like the McRib. And McDonald's systems are executed with the precision of a Swiss watch and multiplied consistently. Again and again.

These systems have made it possible for McDonald's to expand to thousands of locations around the world, while offering their customers nearly identical experiences in each one.

The irony is that McDonald's was originally built by two brothers who had no intention of franchising. It was only when Ray Kroc came along with the idea to franchise that the restaurant's system was put to the test.

Franchising, when executed properly, is like a die-casting machine. Pump the molten metal into a mold cavity, and out comes a nearly identical part, time after time. As long as the machine remains in good working order and the materials used are the same (including capable and committed operators), the outcome is predictable. And while the mold for a franchise business will need to be modified to match changes in the marketplace, the principle remains the same. Consistent inputs lead to consistent outputs.

But before we talk about using systems to build your business, we should look at what holds back many business owners from fully capitalizing on their initial success.

the founder's quandary

Regardless of what type of business you choose to run, it will always have one thing in common—you. So before we talk about the development of your businesses—or any businesses you have yet to open—we should start by better understanding a little about ourselves.

In 1942, Albert Camus wrote a philosophical essay titled "The Myth of Sisyphus," which dealt with the absurdity of life. The essay hearkened back to the Greek myth of King Sisyphus, whose punishment in Hades was to push a giant boulder to the top of a steep hill, only to have it roll back to the bottom, where he would start his task anew, again and again, for all of eternity.

I would not argue that all of human endeavor is absurd, whether it is working for yourself or for someone else. There is always a world outside the workplace that can make your life worthwhile, and that can justify all your Sisyphean efforts. And there are certainly occupations that offer variety and fulfillment.

But a 2017 Gallup poll showed that only 15 percent of employees worldwide and only 30 percent of employees in the U.S. felt engaged at work. Some people who cited that study characterized it as "hating their jobs," but I will not go that far. But many jobs lack the variety, creativity, flexibility, impact, or pleasant human interaction that we desire in an activity that will account for almost one-third of our lives.

If you go to work tomorrow feeling like you have to push that boulder up the hill again, know that there are alternatives that can change your life. And those alternatives, while they may involve risk, can be crafted to be exactly what you want them to be.

If you have already made the leap to small business ownership, you too may feel the weight of that stone on your shoulders every day as you get up to go to your newfound "independence." Only you may feel even worse than your employed colleagues—who can at least walk away from the job they hate. Sure, when you first went into business for yourself, the thrill of business ownership was exhilarating. You could not wait to get to work each day. Each day was a new challenge to overcome, and for the most part, you met that challenge. But you found yourself so busy working on the day-to-day aspects of the business that you were unable to grow the business.

Perhaps you realized that to grow the business, you needed to hire someone to handle the daily tasks. But you also knew that hiring someone as good as you are would wipe out most (and perhaps all) of the profits you were currently enjoying from the business.

I call this the *Founder's Quandary*. Think of it as a wire snare around your leg that prevents you from making any progress. You took a risk and made that initial investment in your business, and now the risk has paid off. But having rolled the dice and won, you realize (or perhaps you don't) that you have to roll them again to get the business to the next level. You must take one step back (hiring someone and reducing your cash flow) so you can take two or more steps forward (working on growing your business).

But it is hard. The tendency when you are caught in a snare is to pull harder against the wire to try to get away—not to back up so that the noose loosens. And this is why the most difficult step for small business owners is often not building the first location (where they can be personally involved and leverage their own time and resources), but building the second one, where they are forced to take that scary step backward, walk away from their profits, and, for a second time, venture into the unknown.

But as an entrepreneur, you have no choice if you want to succeed. Having a single business that relies on you every day is worse than having a job, as you have likely figured out already. Unlike an employee, you cannot just quit, take a vacation, or leave your work at the office when you go home at night. You have to sweat every payroll. If a street closes or a bad story breaks or the wrong ordinance passes or the economy tanks, you could be left holding the bag. If your landlord decides to jack up your rent at the end of your lease, you could essentially end up working for them—or be forced to move on. Any equipment you buy depreciates every day. And your only chance to get out is to hope you can find a willing buyer—which may work out if your business is going well, but if the business is that dependent on you, the buyer will certainly take that into account in the sale price.

Go back to your boulder. Or take that one step backward.

But first, let's look at what most successful small businesses have in common—and how systems helped them to become big businesses.

two steps forward, one step back

When you opened your first location, chances are it was built largely on sweat equity—and had your full-time attention to every detail. If something went wrong, you were there to fix it.

Over time, you became intimately intertwined with every aspect of the business. Instead of hiring an accountant, you worked the books. Instead of hiring a consultant to help you with pricing or managing inventory, you read books and searched the internet to learn how to do it. Instead of bringing a merchandiser or a designer onboard, you relied on your best instincts. And you learned you could save a lot of money by doing all this yourself.

Gradually, you began to realize some profits. Some of those profits you took in the form of a salary, and some of them were beyond the salary you might have taken had you simply gotten a job managing the location. That is the entire premise of opening a small business.

But now you want to expand, and you simply do not have any time. Gone are the 100-hour weeks you may have put in when you were first opening. But you are still working 60 to 70 hours every week doing everything the business needs. You are there to open in the morning and close at night. You are handling the accounting, hiring, managing, buying, payroll, human resources, billing, and collecting, all while developing and refining the business model. You do not have 170 hours every week to devote to everything that must be done to open a second location. And even if you did, your children are just starting to recognize you again, and you do not want to give that up.

In order to grow, you need to hire someone to help you. But when you do the math, between salary and benefits, you will need to spend perhaps two-thirds of your current six-figure income on a qualified manager—and it will take you months just to get them trained. So instead of making a salary and a nice profit, you will be counting only on the profit portion to pay your bills. And that might be *less than you are paying your own manager!* So you would be running the business, taking the risks, and working the longest hours—and you would not even be the highest-paid person on staff.

And this is where many new businesses stall. Instead of making the leap, they put it off indefinitely and go back to their Sisyphean routine. Go to the bottom of the hill. Push the rock up the hill. Go home. Start over. Ultimately, the excitement of the new business fades. You are no longer building—you're grinding.

But if you go that route, you have created an enterprise with all the disadvantages of small business ownership—long hours, risk, stress, sacrificed family time and health—and, other than the financial reward, none of the benefits—independence, time, and the freedom to enjoy those financial returns. You have not built a business. You have created a high-paying job from which there is no escape.

Many entrepreneurs have come to me with "grinder businesses" just like this. And their pitch usually goes something like this: "I have a great business model, but I am burned out. I am not ready to franchise or grow it, but I'm sure that if someone else bought it, they could franchise it and be very successful. Do you know anyone who would want to franchise my business?"

They've all heard the story about how Ray Kroc approached the McDonald brothers, took the successful McDonald's business model, and replicated it worldwide. If only they could find their own Ray Kroc, then someone else could take care of their expansion worries and they could get paid (hopefully better than the McDonald brothers made out with Kroc).

But the Ray Krocs of the world are few and far between. In the 60-plus years since Kroc took McDonald's from a single-location startup to the world's most iconic franchise brand, I cannot think of a single similar story of an entrepreneur who came into an existing business and began duplicating it on behalf of the business owner who ran it—at least not one where the business achieved any significant growth. And I certainly cannot think of any such example where the original owner did well as part of this grand plan.

At this point, many entrepreneurs resign themselves to the grinder existence they have created. They have walked away from the corporate world, with its perceived security, its regular paycheck, its pension plan, and its benefits. But they have their independence! Or as much independence as they can have while working 70 hours a week.

All because they did not understand the importance of taking one step backward to build their business. If these grinders could only take a break from their grinding, they could build the systems they need to get them to the next level. But because they are grinding away at their 70-hour "job," they typically cannot find the time to systematize those things that others could do for them.

Businesses (and profitability) rarely grow in a straight line. They move forward and backward—the key to success is the long-term upward trend of the profit line.

When you invested in that first business, you likely risked a sizable amount of your time and personal wealth to do it, not to mention your career path in the corporate world. But if you are trapped in the Founder's Quandary, you may feel unwilling to do so a second time.

My advice for anyone thinking about getting into business is to start with the understanding that business ownership is not about putting your chips on the table and rolling the dice once. It means you have to stand at the table all day, taking risks again and again. Put your capital on the line to build something, build it, and do it again. The risk doesn't stop with the first win. The first win just gets you another throw of the dice.

The key to growth is your willingness to take one step backward so you can take two steps forward. Sometimes that means hiring a manager or another employee even if it will significantly diminish your profitability, so that you can work on replicating your success through expansion. Or it may mean outsourcing various jobs that you currently handle yourself—perhaps accounting, payroll, advertising, or other functions. Perhaps it means investing the money to create and codify the systems you have developed, so you can better replicate the business. Perhaps it means investing in the development of a formal franchise program.

Building these systems means that you will need to document how various aspects of your business work in enough detail that someone else can learn to perform those tasks. It means you need to develop training programs to teach someone to replicate that process. And it means you need to remove yourself from day-to-day operations to accomplish these tasks.

Each of these steps will cost you time, and none of them has an immediate payback. But if your long-term goal is to grow your business, your short-term strategy must be to make sure that the business can function without you, so you can work on business growth, not just on pushing the rock up the hill.

Unfortunately, that rock waits for no one—so if you don't push it, who will? And so many of us return to the grind, day after day, hoping it will get easier, but knowing, deep down, that the only thing that will happen is that we will get older and wearier.

the trap of day-to-day complacency

As a kid, I used to go to a small grocery store named Santucci's that was comparable to today's modern convenience stores. The guy behind the counter, Mr. Santucci, would make you a sandwich to order and sell you whatever staples you needed. He was behind that counter, every day, for years. But Mr. Santucci did not seem very happy—at least, he did not seem happy to my 8-year-old self.

I expect Mr. Santucci made a decent living—at least one that exceeded what he could have made before he immigrated to the United States. But through the prism of more than 50 years later, it also occurs to me that he was trapped. He had made the decision to go into the convenience store business and, because the business relied on him, he had to live with that decision, essentially forever. And because he was a small business owner, if he ever did escape from the grind of Santucci's, he would be walking away with a skill set and a resume that would have made him largely unemployable outside the convenience store industry.

If he had gotten a job, of course, he could have walked away. But Mr. Santucci had invested his life savings in the inventory on the shelves and signed leases that ran for many years. And (I am guessing here) I do not think he was making enough money to hire someone to run the location for him.

So Mr. Santucci came to work every day for a decade. Maybe two decades. I don't remember him ever taking a vacation. Until one day he sold the business to Bill Basil and Santucci's became Basil's, and Mr. Santucci was never heard from again.

I don't know for certain whether Mr. Santucci loved or hated the grocery business. But I can certainly envision a scenario where he would feel even more trapped than Sisyphus, going to the same "job" again and again, with no way to escape. Every day starting again with his boulder at the bottom of the hill.

A business like that could break a person.

So before you start to build your business, make sure you are not creating a prison from which you cannot escape. Build your business so it can run without you, so that even if you cannot sell it, you can walk away from its day-to-day obligations.

Nick Friedman, one of the cofounders of College H.U.N.K.S. Hauling Junk & Moving, tells a wonderful story about how he realized that he needed to work "on their business instead of in their business" their very first summer. He and cofounder Omar Soliman had a single junk removal truck at the time, emblazoned with their 800 number on the rear door. And, as one of the only two employees of the business, Nick routed the 800 number to his cell phone, so he could respond while driving from job to job. As he put it:

> *Four or five times that summer, I would get phone calls while we were driving complaining about the guys in the truck and their erratic driving. And I would have to tell the caller how I would tell them to be safer on the road. We probably had to fire ourselves three or four times that summer. We were burning out, until someone recommended Michael Gerber's book* The E-Myth Revisited, *which talks about systems and working on the business.*
>
> *After we read it, we just said, "Holy cow. If we are ever going to have another truck, let alone another location, we need to document how we are doing everything." So we literally just started to make checklists: How do we drive the truck? How do we answer the phones? How do we wear the uniform? How do we load the truck? How do we document appointments? And these checklists were the foundations of how we would eventually expand—and eventually led us down the path to learn about franchising and to connect with iFranchise.*

Some of our other clients had been succeeding despite themselves, and ended up finding this out the hard way. One client operated a hugely popular 24-hour diner that generated more than $4 million a year in cash sales. When they decided to franchise, they brought us in to document their operations and begin developing systems. As part of that process, one of our consultants, Joe Bargas, was working behind the "back of the house" during one shift. The restaurant had a line out the door. Over the course of an hour, Joe saw employees clocking in and eating lunch before starting their shifts; he spotted instances in which the cash register was not ringing and where palms were getting greased to get to the front of the line. And the banter that went back and forth about the relatively large lifestyles that some employees were leading left little doubt in Joe's mind that these employees were helping themselves to more than an occasional free meal.

Later, after observing similar behavior on the night shift, Joe told the ownership group, which consisted of a family of six who had not worked a shift in years, that there was massive theft going on in their operation. He estimated they were losing at least $100,000 a year in sales. And because they had virtually no inventory controls, he felt it was likely they were losing more out the back door as well. The owners were almost ready to fire us on the spot, saying that these were some of their oldest and most loyal and trusted employees. But Joe challenged them to have just family work the restaurant for a week to see what would happen.

A week later, Joe got a call late one night from one of the owners. "You were wrong about the $100,000 figure, Joe," he said. "It's way, way more than that." Their weekday average had increased by $1,000 per day, and their weekend average increased by $7,000 per day. By the time inventory losses were accounted for, their total losses were probably close to $1 million per year, without even accounting for the labor "theft" that was going on.

Needless to say, all the employees were let go and they began developing systems to keep close track of inventory and sales. They were lucky; the vast majority of businesses would have gone under, but the immense popularity of this location helped it survive despite itself. One other note: Six months after being let go, the store manager of the restaurant invested several hundred thousand dollars to open a competing location less than half a mile away. Some time later, a fire consumed that business, which was destined never to reopen—leaving one to wonder whether karma was at play or whether the new owners were simply happy with their insurance settlement.

And that story, perhaps as much as any I tell, reflects some of the fear that many entrepreneurs feel when it comes time to give up control. But the lesson is not that you cannot delegate. You have to give up control if you want to grow. But delegating does not mean simply hiring someone and letting them take charge. You need to take the time to develop your systems, checks, and balances before letting go, so you can ensure that your systems will achieve the desired end results. Only then can you delegate without fear.

freedom from fear

I remember having a wonderful dinner at Remi on 53rd Street in Manhattan with one of the founders of medical giant Medco in the 1990s and asking what it took to achieve his spectacular success. "Success in business is not about doing one thing right," he told me. "There are a thousand things that influence your success in business. A thousand choices. And success is about making more of them right than wrong."

That conversation struck me as being particularly insightful at the time. Here I was talking with someone who had made a fortune growing a corporate giant. And his recipe for success was basically to make more good decisions than bad decisions.

But over the years, I saw that pattern repeated again and again. Some of the greatest entrepreneurs I met would tell me stories not about how they had thought everything through and how everything had worked like clockwork from day one, but instead how they had learned from their mistakes and made fearless choices on the fly that ultimately worked for them.

I remember, for example, the stories that Fred DeLuca, the founder of Subway, was fond of telling, such as the time his car broke down and he was forced to hitchhike home. When he was picked up by someone who liked his restaurant, there was a certain sense of pride, but before he could mention that he was the owner, the driver told him that the really nice thing about Subway was that they kept their drinks in a cooler up front. And while your sandwich was being prepared and their backs were turned, it was easy to grab a soda for free. Needless to say, he had the cooler moved the following day.

You never know where that idea for the next business improvement will come from, so it's important to overcome your fear of failure. The fearlessness of the entrepreneurs I have known has manifested itself in their ability to make decisions quickly and often based on imperfect information. While I have, on occasion, met entrepreneurs who analyzed everything within an inch of its life, most of them were more likely to follow in General George S. Patton's footsteps, who famously said, "A good plan, violently executed now, is better than a perfect plan next week."

If you are the kind of person who loses sleep over a $3,000 purchase, you may want to give some thought as to whether entrepreneurship is for you. To be an entrepreneur, you need to be as comfortable with losing as you are with winning. As Ray Kroc once said, "If you are not a risk taker, you should get the hell out of business."

it's about systems

But simply being willing to make mistakes and having a fearless confidence in your decision making is clearly not enough to distinguish the successful from the "also-rans." The business graveyard is littered with the bones of the bold and venturesome. So what distinguishes many of the winners from the losers? Systems.

Consider the story of Allan Young, one of the cofounders of our client ShelfGenie. While ShelfGenie has been an extremely successful franchise, with more than 150 franchise territories currently operating, Allan actually learned his lesson the hard way.

In the mid-1990s, well before his current success, Allan started an air-purification company called Puratech. In his first year of business, he generated more than $1.3 million in revenue while putting close to 37 percent to the bottom line! Every day, Allan would get up early, work late, and close accounts—and he was well on his way to becoming wealthy when fate intervened. In 2005, his Army Reserve unit, in which he served as a commander, was called up to serve in the Middle East. With only six months' notice before he deployed, he knew he had to sell his business.

Given its healthy financials, he felt he should be able to command a reasonable selling price—and he got a lot of initial interest. But as the buyers did their due diligence, every one of them came back with virtually the same answer: "This business only works because of you." And as he began to examine the numbers, he realized that it was largely true. While he was closing 74 percent of his prospects, the best salesperson he employed was only closing about 39 percent of theirs—and his employee turnover rate was close to 300 percent. He had not figured out a system for transferring his skills and dedication to his employees.

Up until 2020, when ShelfGenie was sold to Neighborly, Allan would tell that story when he first met with prospective franchisees. At the end of the story, he would ask them what kind of earnings multiple they thought he got when he eventually sold the company. The prospects would usually guess somewhere in the one to three times earnings range. But the correct answer is zero. He ended up selling the company on an "earnout," but the company, without his direct involvement, went out of business six months later, before he could collect a dime.

"So when I started with ShelfGenie, I was determined not to make that mistake again," he said. "And we started building systems for everything from day one. When I was in the Middle East later that year, I was having trouble with my feet and had to see the doctor. The podiatrist diagnosed the problem in about 15 seconds: I was trying to put my size 12 feet into a size 10 combat boot." She asked if he hadn't been in constant pain for years. "I was," he replied, "but they are Army boots. I thought they were supposed to hurt."

He said he came to the realization that he felt the same way about business. Getting up at six every morning and working until eight each night was just part of the pain one should expect in small business. But years later, he realized that a small business, like his boots, did not need to be painful if it were systematized in a way that would allow the business to run without him. Today, he leads three companies—Noble Brands (which has three companies under its umbrella), Art of Drawers, and FranBridge Capital—and still finds time for his family while training for pentathlons, free diving, paragliding, skydiving, and backpacking with his son.

why franchising depends on systems

By this point, you've probably noticed that many of the examples in this book come from franchising. Because that's the world in which I live and work every day, I must admit that I have a bias toward franchises. But there are two very good reasons to take business lessons from successful franchisors.

First, in order to succeed as a franchisor, you need to build a successful core business. You cannot expect to franchise a failing business and find success.

In fact, to succeed as a franchisor, your business model needs to be so successful that it can produce a good return on investment (ROI) even after the franchisor strips out a franchisee's royalty, which can range between 4 and 10 percent (or more) of revenue. On top of that, the franchise needs to pay a "manager"—who might be an owner-operator franchisee—a market-rate salary.

Second, systems lie at the heart of franchising. There are very few other types of companies in which systems are so closely integrated into every aspect of the business. The core of every franchise is its franchise operations manual, which documents virtually every aspect of how the business should be run, from unlocking the door in the morning to turning out the lights when you leave. Ideally, if you follow the systems in that manual, the business will virtually run itself.

In fact, the typical franchise operations manual starts telling you what to do before there is even a door in which to turn the key. It often begins by describing the site selection process and then moves on to negotiating the lease, working with the architect, hiring contractors, obtaining permits, overseeing the build-out, and working through punch lists until the unit is ready to open.

And the best franchisors go far beyond that. They take their new franchisees through a thorough training program to get them up to speed as quickly as possible. They expect the trainees to accomplish defined goals over the first 30, 60, and 90 days—all of which are laid out in exacting detail in the operations manual and in the franchisor's onboarding process. Nothing is left to chance. And while not every franchisee will achieve each milestone, those who do have substantially improved their chances of turning a profit more quickly.

The best franchisors also assign field consultants to their franchisees. In some franchise systems, these consultants are seen as policemen. They will walk through a location with clipboard in hand, sternly writing down anywhere the franchisee failed to meet expectations, best practices, and brand standards. But ideally, these field consultants act as brand ambassadors, providing ongoing training and active coaching to their assigned franchisees at every step of business development and sharing with them the best practices that other franchise owners are employing throughout the system.

And, equally important, the best franchisors understand that their business model and their processes need to constantly evolve. When McDonald's launched in the 1950s, its menu had nine items: hamburgers, cheeseburgers, milkshakes, fries, cola, root beer, coffee, orange drink, and milk. It had no indoor seating or drive-thru lanes. It had no Big Macs, Filet-O-Fish, Chicken McNuggets, Egg McMuffins, or Happy Meals. It had no TV advertising. In short, while it had a system in place to grow, it also had a system in place to evolve.

So what exactly is this system? The theoretical literature in the space talks about inputs being processed to create an output. But in plain English, a system is simply the process you go through to get a result. By that definition, every business has systems. And, in fact, they do. Sometimes these systems change from one minute to the next and sometimes they are employed consistently—but every business has them.

The difference between a franchised business and most non-franchised businesses is that in non-franchised businesses, those systems often exist only in the business owner's head, while in a franchised business, they are carefully documented in a franchise operations manual that can run for hundreds of pages.

But the mere act of documenting these systems is not enough to make a business successful. If you document a system that is broken or suboptimal, you will be institutionalizing underperformance—and perhaps creating the thing that ultimately kills your business. So you must constantly be on the lookout for ways to improve performance by developing or refining your systems.

every problem is an opportunity

In the day-to-day operation of any business, things will go wrong. The key to improving your business is your ability to ask "Why?"

As a business owner, you need to encourage your people to share with you, openly and honestly, why the desired outcome was not achieved. This means that they must not be afraid to own up to their mistakes.

But once you have created that kind of culture, each problem provides two opportunities. First, it gives you the opportunity to prove to your customers what a great company you really are. After all, even good companies make a few mistakes. But what distinguishes the truly great companies is how they respond when they do occasionally disappoint.

And second, the problem itself provides an opportunity for introspection that may allow you to avoid that type of mistake in the future. When something does not go as planned, ask yourself if it is systematic or if it is a fluke. Was the error caused by the *way* in which something is done?

There will certainly be situations in which the circumstances that caused the problem were so unusual that they are unlikely to occur again—or if they did, it is unlikely that the situation would be handled in the same manner. In that case, there would be no need to change the way you conduct business.

But there are also situations in which a simple change of procedure would eliminate the problem. Perhaps a second person should do a quality inspection before you leave a client's premises. Or you need to ask a client to sign off on the work. Maybe you need to repeat the order back to the customer when you enter it into the POS system or review the contract with the client before they sign.

Whatever the problem is, if you believe it is systematic, build a system to resolve it.

Sometimes those problems end up being solutions on their own. Tommy Clark, a former senior executive with Snap-on Inc. and a current senior consultant with iFranchise Group, told me about one such situation at his old company.

Snap-on has a worldwide network of mobile franchisees selling tools and equipment to mechanics, repair shops, automotive dealerships, and other professional tool users. Their more than 3,200 U.S. franchisees offer more than 22,000 products, including hand tools, power tools, diagnostic equipment, tool storage, and shop equipment. The prices on this diverse product line range from a few dollars to several thousand.

But when selling to some customers, Snap-on franchisees found that some of the bigger-ticket items were difficult to move. To assist franchisees with selling the more expensive items in the product line and help support their cash flow, Snap-on developed a division called Snap-on Credit to offer their end-user customers long-term financing for big-ticket purchases. Once the customer is approved and signs the credit agreement, Snap-on Credit pays the franchisee for the sale and assumes the debt directly from the customer.

Snap-on Credit has become a hugely successful division, generating almost $340 million in revenue for the company in 2019, which represented 7 percent of Snap-on's total revenue that year.

the systems mindset

One of the keys to creating a successful business is your ability to look at every aspect of your business as a system. The business itself is one giant system, which is made up of smaller systems, which are made up of micro-systems.

As someone who is looking to grow your business, you should constantly be looking for ways to do things more effectively. "More effectively" can mean many things: more cost effectively, with fewer errors, with higher customer satisfaction, with higher employee morale and lower turnover, with higher levels of sales but lower margins, or with fewer sales but to better customers. And that means you must keep an eye out for patterns that might indicate you need to add a new system or refine an existing system.

Scot Crain, the former vice president of franchise relations at Auntie Anne's, still remembers overhearing a conversation one February, only a few months after he joined the company in the early 1990s. Two members of senior management were discussing sales trends, and one expressed concern that "our average store sales have dropped to half of what we were seeing during the holiday season—I wonder what is going on?"

While Scot was new to the company at the time, he had a strong sense that the sales decline was simply the result of a mall-based business experiencing less traffic after the end of the holiday shopping season. But since no one had yet explored the company's seasonality, he took it on himself to better define their sales trends using historical sales data and later presented his findings to company leadership.

Once the company better understood their seasonal highs and lows, they began to build their first sales tracking and forecasting systems for both their franchisees and their corporate operations, which allowed them to better project cash flows, inventory requirements, staffing needs, and so on throughout the year. Those systems have evolved and improved over the past 25 years, but they are still an integral part of Auntie Anne's sales forecasting.

The occasional error or unexpected result you encounter in your business should not be looked at as an error, but instead as an opportunity to learn and perhaps create a system to avoid a similar problem in the future. When something goes wrong, your first reaction (after you have fixed the immediate problem) should be to ferret out the root of the problem and determine if the underlying cause could have been corrected by systematizing the process in a different manner.

Admittedly, it's not always as simple as instituting a system at every step of the process. A former restaurateur I knew once told me his first employer knew that his employees were occasionally stealing some of the leftover food from him at the close of business every night rather than paying for it as they were supposed to. As a young employee eager to impress his boss, he had told him that he could end the theft, to which his boss laid down the challenge: "If you can do it without increasing the costs more than the money you save, I would be happy to institute the system."

Sure enough, every new system he tried to implement added too much time and costs to the process. Physically counting the inventory before and after each shift hiked the labor costs. And the inventory in question would have found its way to the garbage in any event, so it wasn't worth much. No matter how hard he tried, he always ended up spending more money than he saved in the process of avoiding the minor shrinkage. Lesson learned. Sometimes the best systems are no new systems after all.

The problem with thinking in terms of a system for everything is that ultimately it turns your company into the kind of bureaucracy that big government is known for. And systems that exist for their own sake rather than for the sake of streamlining and improving the business model can all too easily become an "end" in itself instead of the "means" to achieve a desired result. Long-term, the mantra of "that is how we have always done it" can easily become the death knell of the innovator.

So while every problem is an opportunity to question whether you need a new system, it should also pose the corollary question of whether you currently have a system in place that is not working. The goal should be to streamline, simplify, and improve operations— not to complicate. So as you are creating and documenting systems for your business, be sure to question the need for their existence. Do they save time or money? Improve the customer experience or the employee experience? Provide actionable data? Improve consistency? If not, why do you have the system? Can you live without it?

Likewise, as part of the systems mindset, you need to continually ask yourself what it takes to produce the various things that land on your desk. If you get a report once a month that you no longer read, ask yourself whether someone really needs to keep making it. Unfortunately, we are all creatures of habit, and our systems can easily get the better of us if we do not proactively manage them.

Several years ago, we worked with a national franchisor with more than 500 locations across the country. Our task was to undertake a comprehensive evaluation of their systems and processes for supporting franchisees. As part of that task, we sat down with their management team and challenged the thinking behind some of the systems documented within their franchise operations manual. As we went through that exercise, it became apparent that the management team was not aware of several of the systems in the operations manual and that many of these systems had not been used for years. This is something we often see in more mature companies that have experienced a high level of management turnover or that have been acquired one or more times. Systems must constantly be revisited to ensure they are as relevant to the business today as they were in the past.

As businesses grow, bureaucracies can also begin to emerge. And if senior management does not encourage everyone throughout the organization to constantly challenge existing systems and explore better paths, creative people within the company have little incentive to question systems they know could be improved. In many cases, these are the staff members who are most engaged with the end users of the company's products or services. They see the trends where it counts, but their voice is not heard.

The last part of the systems mindset is to make sure that the systems that *should be* implemented are *actually* implemented. All too often, employees, managers, and franchisees try to do things their own way to save time or effort. If nothing is lost, that may be an indication that the system needs to be refined. But if the failure to implement that system has hurt the business in some way, you need to have a process in place to ensure that your systems are implemented correctly.

a system without controls is a doorstop

The systems you create are only of value to the extent that they are actually implemented and monitored. If your 500-page operations manual is never used, what you really have there is a very expensive doorstop.

I cannot begin to count the times I have been asked by my clients whether anyone ever reads the operations manual. I must admit that there are some sections of a typical manual that are included simply to protect the franchisor from liability. And while in an ideal world these sections would be read, understood, and implemented, they are often less about communicating systems to the people who will be using them and more about communicating them to potential litigants after the fact.

In the best businesses, however, these systems do mean something—and they are followed. And while much of it may go unnoticed by the customer, that is likely because the system ensures that everything goes right every time. Take McDonald's again. If you order a hamburger, do you notice that the same condiments are applied in the same proportion every time because there is a tool that ensures the mustard is applied first in five small "kisses" that go evenly around the toasted crown of the bun? Or that the onions are diced consistently each and every time? Or that the pickles are placed on the burger last so they will remain cold while the rest of the burger remains hot? Or that when it is wrapped and placed in a bag, there is a yellow line on the bag where the employee folds the top before turning and handing it to you fold down? Probably not. But would they notice if their hamburger tasted different? Absolutely.

I also find it amusing that people sneer at the quality level at McDonald's. Sure, it's not serving filet mignon, crab legs, and Dom Perignon on a white tablecloth, but in my book, quality is about consistency. And I can think of few organizations in the world in which consistency is maintained at a higher level than McDonald's. And when you consider that McDonald's has more than 39,000 locations in more than 100 countries serving nearly 70 million people a day, there is simply no organization in the history of the world that can compare.

Of course, McDonald's has had more than 60 years to refine and integrate their systems into their day-to-day operations. And, thanks to the internet, these systems have been further pushed down to every level of the organization. Through the use of learning management systems (LMS), franchisors and other businesses can now easily control which parts of their systems are shown to which employees. So the system on how to wash dishes can be demonstrated on video, shown to the dishwasher, and then the dishwasher can be tested for competence—without showing them irrelevant information about cooking hamburgers or using the cash registers.

As a current or future business owner, you should focus on developing systems that generate value for your customers or clients in a way that is superior to the value provided by your competitors. And to do so in a manner that will allow you to compete based on some combination of price, quality, marketing, service, assortment, style, product, or delivery.

When you first create these systems, they will be based on your personal experience, the experience of the team you recruit, and, to some extent, your best guess combined with your business intuition. From there, many people think about the process as one of trial and error. And it is.

But it is also about understanding how your particular business system works at a macro level, understanding the underlying business metrics at a micro level, and then applying an organized and repeating system of testing, results, and refinement that will continually shape each of your internal systems at a micro level.

By creating systems surrounding every aspect of your business that influences profitability, you will turn your business into a virtual "Money Machine" that will work with or without you. And that Money Machine can be multiplied again and again if it relies on repeatable systems.

Now that you've been introduced to the basics of systems, let's explore what I mean by the "Multiplier Model."

creating your money machine

I have consulted with literally thousands of small businesses in my career. Some of those businesses were run by entrepreneurs who stumbled into business ownership without quite knowing why. Others were built by businesspeople with a specific purpose. Maybe it was to spend more time with their families, or to become more independent—or maybe it was just because they saw an opportunity and they took it.

But the entrepreneurs who were most successful typically had one thing in common. While they may have had a passion for what they did, they all understood that a business is ultimately just a Money Machine.

What is a Money Machine? It is a business that provides a reasonable return on investment (ROI) for its owner regardless of whether they ever even set foot in an individual operation. Unlike the grinder businesses we discussed in the previous chapter, all the labor costs are factored into your Money Machine—so you can measure returns just as if you were investing in a publicly traded stock. You can pay yourself dividends or reinvest in your future growth. But ultimately, your Money Machine should provide you with an ROI that is commensurate with the risk you are taking by going into that business.

the heart of your money machine

At its core, we can say that a business is just a complex system designed to provide value to its customers. As such, it needs to begin with the customer in mind and end by providing that value to that customer.

That brings us to a paradigm for understanding the nature of most small businesses that I call the Small Business Success Cycle, which you can see in Figure 2–1 on page 29.

Let's start by agreeing that there is no universal model of business success. But there are commonalities that will hold true for most businesses that are striving to create a Money Machine. Each of the elements of the cycle is subject to its own need for system ization. And each element of each system can best be refined and improved by developing feedback mechanisms and key performance indicators (KPIs) that will allow you to measure the effectiveness of what you are trying to accomplish.

In looking at the cycle, I hope there is an apparent logical flow. Start at 12 o'clock with a business model that meets a sustainable and ideally repeatable consumer need. You then need to find ways to convince prospective buyers why you are a better choice than those currently serving that need through your marketing and sales

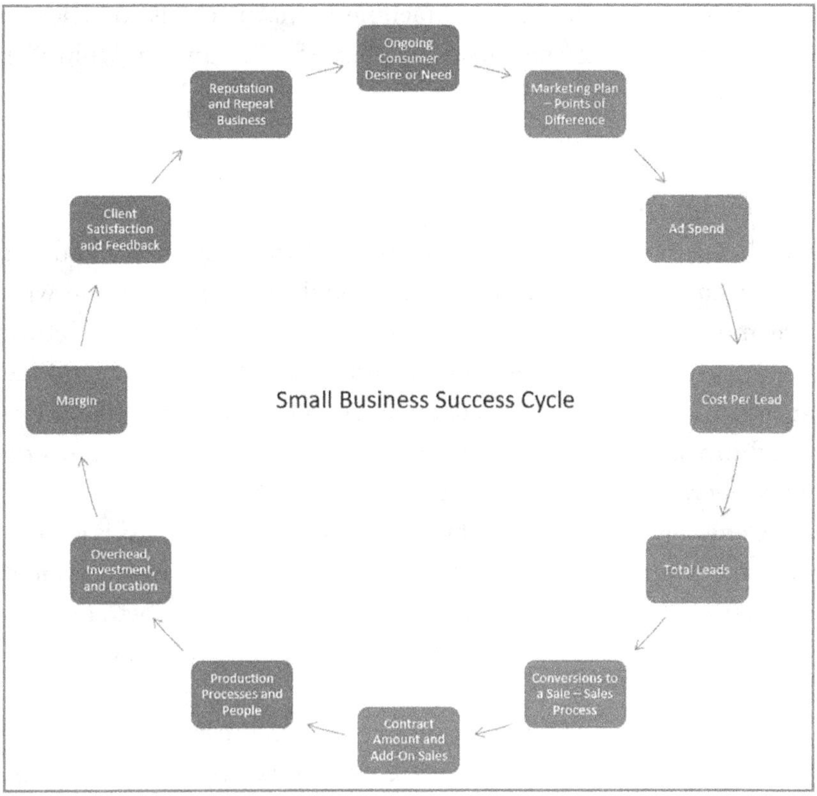

FIGURE 2–1—**SMALL BUSINESS SUCCESS CYCLE**

efforts—all of which can be readily measured using your KPIs. From there, you need to actually fulfill your brand promise at a price and margin that provides you adequate profit and ROI; different KPIs will let you measure your effectiveness here. And circling back around to the top, you must maintain that relationship with your client/customer through communication and using that feedback to alter the system as needed to provide further value going forward. Again, you can and should measure your progress in these areas using KPIs as part of your systematized approach to business growth.

Before we get to the fun stuff of figuring out what business you want to grow, let's get some of the basics out of the way. There are a few basic principles you will need to understand as you go forward with your planned business endeavor. One of the defining characteristics of our Money Machine is that it needs to generate enough return to make subsequent investments in our Multiplier Model worthwhile.

return on investment

So what is a reasonable ROI? Think of it this way: If you did not choose to invest in a business, you could do something else with that money. You could invest in the bond market and get a return of perhaps 4 percent. You could invest in the stock market and see an average long-term return of about 10 percent annualized. Or you could invest in real estate and get a higher compound return over a longer period of time by leveraging your investment.

Generally, we assume that the risk of a startup business is greater than the average risk associated with any of the above investment strategies. Why go into business at all if you can make a better return just by putting your money into a mutual fund and sitting back on the sidelines?

And, of course, if you are going to work in the business yourself, you will need to include a market-rate salary as one of your expenses. After all, if you invested in the stock market, you could go out and get a job—adding a return on your time to the ROI.

So where does that leave you? Ideally, you want that return to be north of 20 percent annualized (plus a market-rate salary if you plan to work in the business)—although, with many small businesses, you may not be able to achieve that kind of ROI in the first couple of years. And you should adjust that number up or down based on the perceived risk associated with your desired startup. So, for example, if your Money Machine required a sizable capital investment in an unproven business model, your risk would be substantially higher, and thus your required ROI should also be higher.

It may sound cynical to discuss business simply as a means of making a return on investment without mentioning "the common good." After all, many businesses have started as altruistic ventures or in direct response to the frustrations encountered in the consumer marketplace. Anne Beiler, the original Auntie Anne, opened her first pretzel stand in a farmers market to help make money and fulfill her husband's dream of becoming a crisis counselor.

But regardless of why they were founded, in order to grow their businesses, these entrepreneurs knew that they needed to start by turning each location into a Money Machine.

Henry Ford envisioned his business that way from the start. While Ford's politics and personal views were nothing short of abhorrent, when it came to business, there is almost universal agreement that he changed manufacturing forever by systematizing and simplifying the process of building an automobile. In 1913, the Highland Park Ford Plant introduced what many have claimed to be the first moving assembly line. By dividing the production of a Model T into many different steps that occurred at various points on a conveyor belt, Ford was able to reduce the production time of the car from 12 hours to only five and a half hours—and after further improvements, down to an astounding 93 minutes. What Ford had done was to develop a system that, with some polish provided by time and motion experts, was a highly efficient means of producing cars. And while people can certainly argue about exactly who invented the assembly line, the concept of a business as an assembly line that creates money is what I would like you to hold in your head.

Of course, Ford's business model was much more complex. There were raw materials and parts to source. There was advertising to create demand in an age where the automobile was more of a luxury than a necessity. There was engineering and design work. Labor management and finance. But what Ford had built when he created that first motorized assembly line was a virtual Money Machine.

And while your inputs and outputs are going to be very different today, if you want to achieve the kind of success that can be replicated by franchising—or by any other kind of widespread growth—you need to create your own virtual Money Machine. Thinking about your business as a money assembly line will help you understand what the best franchisors try to accomplish.

✳ ROI vs. ROE

A simplified way to calculate return on investment (ROI) is to divide the anticipated profits (returns) in any given year once the business has matured by the amount of the total investment (profits / total investment). And of course, when calculating your return, be sure you have included a market-rate salary for yourself as an expense, if you are working in the business.

In some businesses, you will have the opportunity to use leverage (loans or leases) to reduce the amount of your initial investment. Because you will ultimately be responsible to repay that capital, I would normally advocate for a return on total investment approach.

However, if you want to measure your returns based on your out-of-pocket investment, do a return on equity (ROE) calculation. In that case, divide your returns by only the amount of equity you invested. Keep in mind the returns would also be reduced because you would need to subtract loan and lease payments. Generally, you would anticipate a higher ROE than ROI, as increased leverage carries increased risk.

In the franchising world, we have different names for the parts and subassemblies. We call them *systems* and *processes* and we measure how well they are accomplishing their individual tasks using what we call key performance indicators (KPIs). In the next section, I discuss in greater detail the role of KPIs for different types of businesses.

determining your KPIs

One of the most important things you can do to help ensure the success of your business is to determine your key performance indicators. Think of these KPIs as the inputs into your business' system. Each of them has target ranges that, if achieved and combined successfully, will allow you to manufacture the output of profitability.

KPIs vary substantially depending on your industry. For restaurants, a few of the many important KPI measurements include your sales-to-investment ratio, your food costs, your labor costs, your average ticket, your table turns, and your occupancy costs. If you are in the hotel business, some important KPIs include your overall occupancy rate and your average revenue per occupied room. If you are a manufacturer, you will certainly want to look at things like your product return rate and perhaps your net promoter score. If you are in the business of selling advertising, like Valpak or Money Mailer, you may want to focus on sustaining your customer base—so KPIs like customer retention rate, customer churn, and repeat purchase ratio might make your list. And if you are in a membership-based fee-for-service business, like a massage or fitness business, you might add to that list things like revenue growth per customer and time between purchases.

Moreover, the target numbers for each of these KPIs will likely be different even within the same industry. For example, in the restaurant industry, a steakhouse might aim for food costs in the range of 35 percent, while for a pizza restaurant that number might be closer to 30 percent. But shoot for those numbers at a pretzel shop, where 20 percent would be considered high, and you would have a disaster on your hands.

Different types of businesses in the same broad category (in this case restaurants) can have very different target KPIs because of other changes in the business model. A pretzel shop, for example, generally has much lower sales than a typical steakhouse and, because it relies on impulse purchases in a high-traffic location, does not need to spend the same amount on advertising. In addition, because its footprint is much smaller, it pays less in rent (although it's often higher when calculated on a per-square-foot basis).

The other thing to be aware of when identifying your KPIs and target ranges is that any changes you make may have implications in other areas of your business. Going back to our restaurant example, the logical assumption is that we want to keep our food costs down. After all, each percentage point saved on food costs, all else being equal, will translate to a significant increase in profitability. But everything is not always equal. If you can reduce your food costs by eliminating waste, improving portion or inventory controls, or establishing better systems for pricing or purchasing, that could improve your Money Machine. On the other hand, if you had to sacrifice quality, raise prices unreasonably high, or make your portions so small that your customers left dissatisfied, your reduced food costs KPI could have a severe negative impact on your overall profitability. After all, anyone can decrease food costs to 2 percent if they charge $50 for a burger. But how many will they sell?

Likewise, you could reduce your labor costs in your restaurant simply by hiring fewer people. But if that results in poor service and unhappy customers, you may have missed the point of the exercise. So as you start identifying the KPIs and target numbers that will ultimately drive your business, bear in mind that changes to your KPIs may have unintended consequences.

Generally speaking, the KPIs for a small business can be grouped into several major categories: marketing metrics, sales metrics, production and financial metrics, and client satisfaction metrics. And these KPIs generally occur in that approximate order. Marketing drives sales. Sales drive production. Production drives client satisfaction. And client satisfaction (and the word-of-mouth it delivers) drives repeat and new business. I showed this in the Small Business Success Cycle (in Figure 2–1 on page 29), but first let's talk a bit about the importance of sequencing when assembling your Money Machine.

look at it sequentially

In considering how to create your Money Machine, think about your business as if it were that car going down the assembly line. There are certain things you need to think about first and other things that will come further down the line. And different inputs to your assembly line will occur at each step of the process.

You must make the right moves at each step of the assembly process to end up with the best possible result. And just as Ford had many potential suppliers from which to source the parts for his automobiles, you will have a similar number of choices to make at each step of building your business.

But don't worry about making the optimal choice on every single decision. All businesses make mistakes—even some of the best:

* Ford famously introduced the midsized Edsel in 1957 to much fanfare, only to find that the consumer market had moved toward compact cars, causing it to pull production just two years later.
* In 1985, Coca-Cola introduced "New Coke" after taste tests revealed that customers preferred the sweeter taste of archrival Pepsi. Needless to say, Coke fans nearly rioted in the streets and the New Coke experiment was quickly pulled.
* During the 1960s, both NBC and CBS passed on the opportunity to bid on a new idea proposed by the NFL—Monday Night Football. (Third-place ABC jumped at the chance.) Today, ESPN pays more than $2 billion per year to the NFL for the rights to air the games.
* In 1962, a young group called The Beatles was looking for a record label. Decca Records gave them an audition but declined to sign them because, as they famously told their manager, "Guitar groups are on their way out, Mr. Epstein." The Beatles went on to sell more than two billion records.

You just need to make better decisions than your competitors do—and avoid the catastrophic ones. Like the old joke about two campers running from a grizzly: You don't have to run faster than the bear. You just need to run faster than the other camper. And make sure you don't run down a dead-end canyon.

If you make good choices at every point along your assembly line, you will build a Money Machine that runs. It may not run like a Ferrari (or a GT40 for those of you who are fans of the American cars), but it will at least provide you with the basic transportation you need to get going.

From there, assuming that you understand your inputs and how they impact your ultimate output (money), you can start refining your process—improving each step until you get to the point where your business runs like the proverbial well-oiled machine.

So start with the basics: customers. You need to determine who they are, what they need, and what message will drive them to your door. And you need to figure out how to find them in the most cost-efficient way—and at an acquisition cost that will allow you to make money. Knowing your customers is the first step toward building any business.

As part of your customer knowledge, you then need to establish what price they are willing to pay for your product or service and how you can differentiate it from your competitors enough to capture some of those customers. Essentially, you need to create a reason for your customers to buy from you (and not your competitors) at a price point that allows you to make a profit. And, like all aspects of your system, you want that customer acquisition element of your process to be simple (so you do not have to do it yourself) and repeatable (as much as possible in today's rapidly changing world).

Finally, determine how to produce the product or service that you will be delivering at a cost that allows you to make a profit while making your customers happy. Do that, and you are well on your way to creating your Money Machine.

Now, while laying out the process sequentially is helpful here, that is often not how things work in the real world. Often entrepreneurs start with the product or services they plan to provide, believing they have found that better mousetrap. But if you fail to think about your business holistically and sequentially, you may build a business that cannot be repeated.

customize your paradigm

While a general paradigm like the one I outlined above is useful for many businesses, every business will have unique characteristics that may alter the flow of the business model. So as a business owner, take the paradigm above only as a starting point for creating your own business model.

But before you begin to customize your business paradigm, make sure you understand why you are creating it in the first place.

The purpose of this paradigm is to provide you with a simple set of analytical tools that will give you performance benchmarks. As such, your paradigm should be equally simple. If your business model paradigm looks like the schematics for building a 747, you will never be able to use the many data points in your analysis to course-correct.

Essentially, your business paradigm needs to be actionable— which means that you will want to limit it to only the data you need to alert you when you start to go off course. The primary KPIs you will want to be sure to measure are lead generation, sales, production, and client satisfaction. Under each of those broad categories, you will probably want to have three to five more granular KPIs that you will want to further monitor to help you understand what has caused the performance of your primary KPIs. This will leave you with a maximum of perhaps 20 different measures you will want to monitor on a regular basis. Some of these KPIs can be found in your profit & loss statement (P&L) statement, the standard accounting document that periodically measures revenue, expenses, and profits. But many of these KPIs will be measurements you need to create yourself, based on your own assessment of what drives your business.

Beyond that, of course, it is not enough to just know the numbers—you need to understand the numbers and what causes them to change. And that means all of them. If you cannot glance at your P&L and understand each line item (and whether you are performing with appropriate efficiency), you simply do not fully grasp the nature of your business. Likewise, if you do not fully understand your KPIs, you are much more likely to find yourself mired in an unanticipated crisis.

it has to work without you

One of the key qualities of a machine is that it is not dependent on one specific individual to operate it. And while there may be particular skills needed to run a machine, no engineer would take the trouble and expense to design a machine that only worked for one person.

Likewise, the assembly line has to work without you operating it. If you are integral to the performance of your business, you have not built a Money Machine. You have, in fact, simply built a job.

When the plant turned on the conveyor belt, Ford did not need to run the welder or stand over his workers to see that things were done correctly. He simply turned the key and let the assembly line run. And, as predictable as clockwork, cars came out on the other end.

When entrepreneurs come to me looking to franchise, one of the telltale signs that they may not be ready is their inability to break away from their work, even for a day. They are often so tied up in their business that simply scheduling a 90-minute phone call is a chore. And when it comes to implementing their expansion programs, their primary concern is often their ability to devote the time and effort to the program—and an unwillingness to delegate either their existing role in the company or their new role as a franchisor to anyone else.

One of the most difficult lessons for many entrepreneurs to learn is that if they want to grow, they need to give up control. If they can't, they will usually fail. Success in business expansion requires you to not only create systems, but also recruit and trust talented people to implement them.

apply the multiplier model

Once you have built your Money Machine and it works without you, now you have something you can simply turn on and watch it print money. It can run while you are on vacation, at your children's athletic events, or on the golf course.

Or you can take the money from your Money Machine and reinvest it in a second Money Machine. If your Money Machine runs consistently, as you hope it will, it will bring you a consistent ROI. So the formula for your growth becomes relatively easy to predict, barring a Covid-19-type disaster.

Use systems to create a duplicatable Money Machine, measure its performance, and harvest the returns. Reinvest those returns in another Money Machine, continue to monitor performance, and harvest the returns. Reinvest in another Money Machine. Lather. Rinse. Repeat. That's the Multiplier Model.

Let's assume that your Money Machine requires an investment of $180,000 in equipment, build-out, and signage. Let's further assume that you need another $90,000 in working capital until your Money Machine breaks even at the end of the first year. And let's assume that at the end of year two, your Money Machine will generate revenue of $600,000 and will throw off a profit, after paying the salaries of everyone involved, of 20 percent (maybe 15 percent after taxes), giving you $90,000 in returns. Let's further assume that you can live off the manager's salary while you build the business and can reinvest all the profits in growth.

If you were to reinvest all your profits, you could open a second Money Machine in year four. And at the end of year four, you would have two Money Machines, generating 15 percent returns on $1.2 million in revenue. Your timeline now gets cut in half, although at some point you will need to add overhead. In year six, you have enough capital to build a third Money Machine. But here is where it starts to get interesting. In year eight you could open a fourth unit, a fifth in year nine, a sixth in year ten, and two more in year eleven. By year 20, if you had the fortitude to continue reinvesting at that pace, you would have 65 units in operation, $39 million in revenue, and nearly $5 million in annual profits, with 17 additional locations scheduled to open the following year.

Of course, that does not account for your need for incremental overhead to support your growth. And it assumes that the business model does not change or evolve over the years—which is unlikely. And, of course, it also assumes that there are no major recessions or other setbacks along the way. So there is some optimistic thinking baked into this analysis.

But it also did not account for any bank financing or tenant improvement allowances that might have been granted. It did not account for any purchasing economies that might have improved margins or increased buying power on advertising and stronger name recognition that might have driven higher revenue. And it did not account for faster growth strategies such as franchising that would allow for more aggressive market penetration.

But the point remains the same. If you build a successful business model that works without your direct involvement, duplicating that business model over time will multiply those profits substantially. And that is the Multiplier Model.

And while things like franchising, outside investors, and bank financing can accelerate your growth (and each of those strategies comes with their own costs and risks), the first step remains the same: Develop a Money Machine that can run without your day-to-day involvement and then stamp them out like clockwork. That's the key to successfully multiplying your business.

understand how to measure success

I f this book were written strictly chronologically, this chapter would come toward the end. After all, you cannot begin to measure success until you have built the business and the systems that you are measuring.

But from the standpoint of the Multiplier Model, it is imperative that you know how to measure success before you try to create your first Money Machine. Trying to run a business without an understanding of what it takes to succeed is certain to end in disaster. Moreover, if you do not know what it takes to succeed, you will not know if you have the capital or the skill set to achieve that success.

The measurement tools you will need vary from business to business, but in broad terms, you need to know how to measure how well your inputs create outputs. This might be as simple as understanding the basics of accounting or as complex as some branched A/B testing of marketing messaging. So in this chapter, we will explore some of the ways you will need to monitor the systems that make up your Money Machine to determine if they are operating at peak efficiency and decide what tweaks you should make to optimize the business.

finance matters

You need a basic understanding of finance if you want to succeed in business. Oddly, in many books on starting a business, the idea that you will need to understand finance is often not discussed—or perhaps is simply assumed. And frankly, it is too big a topic to handle in this book as well. But if you are absolutely lost when it comes to these vital issues, be sure to educate yourself. One book you might want to consider reading is *Accounting for the Numberphobic: A Survival Guide for Small Business Owners*, by Dawn Fotopulos, which is designed to show how these basic tools can be used as a financial dashboard for your business's health.

Unless you are "buying yourself a job," which is not what this book is about, you need to be able to understand where your systems are working and where they are broken. And you cannot do that without understanding the basics of finance.

The good news is that you do not need an accounting degree— you will hire accountants and bookkeepers to take care of that for you. What you do need is to know how to read and understand a P&L statement. Hopefully, all this information is very basic to you. But over the years, I have seen plenty of Type B business owners who have only a marginal command of this vital business tool.

Several years ago we worked with a casual dining chain that had more than 30 locations throughout the Chicago area. They had been in business for more than 20 years, and their average unit generated more than $1 million in revenue. But they did not know their numbers and they didn't have separate P&Ls for each of their locations. As consumer dining trends evolved and the market matured, they lacked a sufficient understanding of their numbers to make good business decisions. Today they have three locations remaining.

measure with your income statement

When I hold exploratory meetings with clients, I typically ask about various items on their P&L—which is also called the income statement—without actually referring to the document itself. I ask what their cost of goods sold is or what their labor cost is or for some other expense item. Type A business owners can usually give me a very specific number—often down to the decimal point. Type B owners usually give me a range—sometimes narrow and sometimes not so narrow. Type C owners usually give me a shrug.

The P&L is essentially broken into three component parts: revenue (or sales), expenses (or costs), and profits/losses (or income)—which equals revenue minus expenses. In looking at the sample P&L shown in Figure 3-1 on page 44, you will see it contains some pretty basic but very important information.

Essentially, your P&L will help you understand several important principles that you need to grasp from the start of opening your business.

On the revenue side, you need to understand how you will generate your sales. Will some of them be from repeat business? Will some be from add-on sales? Will there be a membership component? Will your revenue grow over time? Will you run into capacity issues?

More important, on the expense side, you need to understand the relationship between your fixed expenses and your variable expenses. Your fixed expenses—like your rent and the salaries you pay staff—represent the costs you will have every month,

Mark's Money Machine		
Sample Profit & Loss (Also called an Income Statement)		
	For the year ending 12/31/2021	
Revenue		
Sales of Product	$1,000,000	
Sales of Services	$500,000	
Other Income	$500,000	
Total Revenue		$2,000,000
Cost of Goods Sold		$400,000
Gross Profit/Gross Margin		$1,600,000
Operating Expenses		
Advertising	$200,000	
Automobile	$20,000	
Bank Charges	$30,000	
Depreciation	$50,000	
Insurance	$25,000	
Labor & Related Expenses	$850,000	
Office Supplies	$15,000	
Rent	$120,000	
Utilities	$20,000	
Other Operating Expenses	$15,000	
Total Operating Expenses		$1,345,000
Net Operating Income		$255,000

FIGURE 3–1—**SAMPLE P&L**

regardless of whether you make a sale. Your variable expenses represent the costs you only incur with a sale. And by subtracting your variable expenses from your selling price, you get your contribution per sale.

Once you understand these two elements, it is easy enough (at least in theory) to calculate a hypothetical break-even point for your business by making certain assumptions about pricing and variable costs. Simply divide your fixed expenses by your contribution per sale, and you will have a feel for how many sales you will need to make to break even. If you want to achieve a certain level of profitability, add that profit to your fixed expenses and recalculate, and you will know what level of sales you will need to achieve to get there.

Of course, it will never be quite this easy.

The vast majority of businesses do not sell just one product or service, and each product and/or service will have its own associated price. And the price for each product or service will not have a consistent margin, either. Just look at a fast-food restaurant, where you can buy a burger for $1 and a large soft drink for $1.50, and you'll see that the cost of different products is not consistent across every product sold. So the "product" you sell and the "price" of that product will actually depend on your product mix, and perhaps on value pricing or discounting as well.

Then there are questions of labor costs. In some businesses, where labor is hired on an as-needed basis to complete a job, production labor is all variable cost. In other businesses, some labor functions are overhead and some may be partially overhead and partially variable. Again, using a food-service operation as an example, during the slowest times of each shift, you can never have fewer than one employee in an open restaurant. But you will need to increase your staffing to meet your service requirements at different parts of the day, on different days of the week, or even depending on different weather patterns. So while you will treat restaurant labor as a variable cost, at least some portion of it is essentially "fixed."

And that is even before you begin to account for some of the minutiae like credit card processing fees or shipping and handling costs.

This may all sound incredibly daunting if you have not done it before, but once you get used to it, the process becomes second nature and you will soon learn how the decisions you make on a day-to-day basis impact your bottom line.

the balance sheet: your other scorecard

The other side of your financial statement—your balance sheet—is essentially a scorecard of what you own and what you owe—your assets and your liabilities, combined with the accumulated equity you have invested or built in the business over the years. As you will see in Figure 3–2 on page 46, this side of your financial statement lets you know how much money you have to work with. It will tell

Mark's Money Machine
Sample Balance Sheet

As of 12/31/2021

ASSETS		LIABILITIES AND EQUITY	
Current Assets		*Current Liabilities*	
Checking Account	$150,000	Accounts Payable	$50,000
Savings Account	$50,000	Short-Term Portion of Loan	$25,000
Accounts Receivable	$125,000	Payroll Liabilities	$25,000
Inventory	$25,000	*Total Current Liabilities*	$100,000
Total Current Assets	$350,000		
		Non-Current Liabilities	
Non-Current Assets		Long-Term Portion of Loan	$175,000
Building & Land	$200,000	*Total Non-Current Liabilities*	$175,000
Office Furniture	$50,000		
Equipment	$100,000	*Equity*	
Accumulated Depreciation	($150,000)	Owner's Capital	$50,000
Total Non-Current Assets	$200,000	Retained Earnings	$225,000
		Total Equity	$275,000
TOTAL ASSETS	$550,000	TOTAL LIABILITIES AND EQUITY	$550,000

FIGURE 3–2—**SAMPLE BALANCE SHEET**

you how much you have in the bank, how much you can expect to come in, and how much you have in hard assets that, while you may not be able to use them to make your next payroll, represent value in your company (all of which might help you get financing from a lender, if needed).

The purpose in providing this brief overview here is not, in two short pages, to give you enough of a financial education to be able to run a business. It is instead to warn you that if you do not know at least this much about finance, you are jumping in with a significant handicap. It is as if you are going to a foreign country where you cannot read the street signs and trying to find your way to your destination. You can do it, but if you don't understand the language, it's going to be a lot harder.

The street signs you will use to get to your profitable destination are all found in your financial statements. If you can't read them, it will be impossible for you to know whether you are making progress toward that goal. So if you don't understand finance, one of your first tasks must be to recruit someone who does.

measure with comparative testing

The other premise we are going to be discussing a lot in this book is the need to introduce alternatives in order to continually strive for improvement. In the marketing world, we call these A/B tests. In an A/B test, you try to isolate two variables to determine which one works better.

For example, let's assume you are running a pay-per-click (PPC) ad for a home-service business, and you want to know whether an ad that touts same-day service is more effective than one offering a money-back guarantee. By running both ads and measuring the results against similar audiences, you could see which message resonates better.

Then you could try two more ads with two completely different messages and measure their results against the winner of the first test—or go head-to-head in a real-time matchup—and you can significantly improve how well your message resonates with your customers. Do this again and again, and ultimately you will have statistical evidence as to which message (or messages) work best to attract your targeted buyer.

There are all kinds of variants and refinements you can try. Perhaps B won your first A/B test, and now you need to decide between B and C. (This process of incrementally improving your messaging can—and should—go on virtually forever.) If you are testing PPC ads, you could send the respondents to different landing pages, creating two sets of A/B tests with your messaging—one that measures the drawing power of the initial message and one that measures the power of the message on the landing page. Now your testing process begins to look like a decision tree, as you can see in Figure 3–3 on page 48.

What we are talking about here is creating a system that you have tested, measured, and refined until each element of the system works. Now imagine that the system you have built for your advertising message can be extended beyond just the message to the media that carries that message. Of course it can. Each form

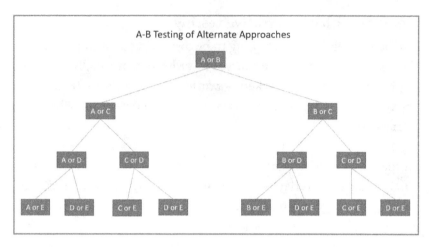

FIGURE 3–3—**A-B TESTING DECISION TREE**

of media can produce different leads for you, at a different cost per lead. And each of those leads will have a different value to you in terms of cost per sale. So you need to measure these variables during your testing process as well.

But if you can do that across the entire marketing spectrum, you can refine your media mix and your advertising budget along with your message, allowing you to optimize your marketing and create a true system for the entire marketing process. Keep in mind, though, when you measure this system against your financial performance, you should only keep it if it generates revenue for you at a rate that allows you to provide your service (or your product) profitably. If your marketing costs are so high that it becomes impossible for you to turn a profit, you need to go back to the drawing board and find something (different marketing, hopefully, but perhaps different products or services) that will allow you to make money.

This is how successful marketing systems are created. But these systems are not just limited to marketing. In the best businesses, they are incorporated in almost every repetitive function of business operations—from site selection to build-out to hiring to training to grand openings to purchasing to pricing to production to delivery to follow-up to communications.

Some of these systems also lend themselves to A/B testing and statistical analysis. For those, you need to understand, at least on a general level, how statistics work. For the ones that don't, you need to know when to rely on your gut and when to use other predictive tools for decision making.

ask the right questions

Of course, if you start with a poorly defined message, A/B testing can result in only slow, incremental improvements—and before you achieve profitability you may find that you have run out of cash. So the key is to start with the right questions.

To begin, think back to the game of "Twenty Questions" that you may have played as a child. The object was for the questioner to try to guess what their opponent was thinking in 20 yes/no questions or less. And the opponent was allowed to think of virtually anything. Before the questioning began, the one clue that was provided was the answer to "Is it an animal, vegetable, or mineral?"

But a skilled questioner could almost always guess the answer simply by starting with generalities and building their answers on each other. One of the common questions, at least back in the day when people had them, was "Is it bigger than a breadbox?" If the answer was yes, the next question might be "Is it bigger than a car?" An animal question might start out with "Is it living or dead?" to determine if the player was thinking of a historical figure.

So when you set your testing premises, start with broader tests, and work your way toward more specific measurements. For example, instead of testing ads with similar headlines, like these two:

A. Free widget with your first purchase

vs.

B. 20 percent off your first purchase

Instead, test:

A. Free widget with your first purchase

vs.

B. Our widgets have a lifetime guarantee

That way you can determine if your buyers are more likely to value price or dependability. From there, you can further refine your message.

the problem with statistics

As you go about your testing, however, you must be able to judge how meaningful your results are. Obviously, a treatise on statistical analysis is also beyond the scope of this book. But as a business owner, you should understand the basics of statistical analysis when you are using the results of these tests to make decisions about your Multiplier Model.

The first issue you must deal with is bias. Statistical bias occurs when the results of your test are different from the true underlying results you are attempting to estimate. There are many ways bias can creep into your tests:

* If you own a restaurant and decide to test menu pricing for a new product rollout at a college campus or in a market with a large senior population, your test sample might have a much higher price sensitivity than your actual customer base.
* If you plan to test a new PPC ad using A/B testing on Google, you may find that you have excluded segments of the senior population who do not use Google for their shopping.
* If your ad is only written in English, you may have left out the roughly 15 percent of the U.S. population who primarily speak a different language—and you will have certainly eliminated the 8.6 percent of the U.S. population that is considered limited in English proficiency.
* If you're a national brand and only test consumer responses in one region, your decisions may ignore how consumer perceptions and tastes vary from one region to another.

Beyond these issues, there is also the bias that can find its way into your test design. For example, you might believe that your product's advantages so far outweigh those of the competitor's that when you write the ad, that enthusiasm shows in your copywriting ("the world's absolute best widget"). But the copy for the discount ad has far less conviction ("a fairly decent discount").

Another problem with statistics is that often the size of the samples you are measuring is simply too small to provide you with any meaningful data. The sample size required varies based on the size of the population you are trying to measure and on the number of observations within the sample. So, for example, if you are expecting to draw business from the entire population of the country, you might need close to 2,000 observations of any given test to gain statistically significant data.

Another issue you will face using statistics in business is that the quality of your data degrades over time. If you are looking at advertising data, for example, a single medium will begin to lose its effectiveness as it is "mined" of its most likely buyers, so the cost per lead may go up over time—reducing your effective advertising spend to attract readers, new subscribers, or readers whose situation may have changed. Likewise, your consumers' behavior may change over time.

building a business plan/financial model

Let me start by saying that I am not a big fan of business plans—at least not for their own sake. When you build a business plan, it should be with a purpose. There are four basic purposes for making a business plan:

1. As a tool for good decision making and planning
2. To provide you with a framework for judging progress and success
3. To attract investors
4. To convey your thoughts about the specifics of the business to others who will have a role in helping you build it

But when it comes to initially building your business, your primary concern should be on the first two of these criteria. And, as a part of that, you should focus on building a financial model that can work and be replicated, and then using that financial model to understand the success measures that will dictate your returns.

When businesses fail, it is universally because they ran out of money. The reasons for that may of course vary widely. Their underlying assumptions about revenue and margins may be wrong. Their ideas about demand may be off. Their assumptions about client acquisition costs may be inaccurate. But ultimately, they run out of money before they fix whatever the problem is with their business model.

With that in mind, it is essential to create a financial model when planning on opening or expanding a business. When developing a financial model like this, the tests you conduct on different models are called *sensitivity analysis* instead of A/B testing, but the process is largely the same, with the exception that you are substituting your hypotheses of various future events for the historical performance statistics you would use for an A/B test. But in essence, you account for all costs, whether they be fixed costs or variable, under various levels of growth to understand how you will make more or less money under each scenario, to allow you to make an informed decision about how to structure your business. This kind of "what if" financial modeling should be used when making many different business decisions, and you may want to measure the impact of decisions including everything from speed of growth to hiring to advertising to pricing to outside factors like price increases.

With this in mind, use a program such as Excel to create your financial spreadsheet, which will allow you to easily test your model under a variety of assumptions. It is probably best to have one page with any key variables that you will subsequently challenge. So if you have various drivers that will ultimately determine your success (average ticket, customers per day, etc.) and those might vary based on how long you are in business, set those up as a table on an assumptions page under headings for Year One, Year Two, and so on, so that you can use those inputs to calculate averages for each year. If you want to get more complex and calculate by time of day (called "daypart" in the restaurant industry) or by product line, you can do so.

You can then figure out profit margins for each product, treating them as variable costs that might reduce with volume purchasing. Work in fixed costs (such as rent) and other fixed costs that might stairstep up at certain points (such as labor) to get a more complete set of assumptions surrounding the growth of a single business unit.

On a separate page, have the actual cash-flow statement for the single business unit, all of it driven by the numbers on the assumptions page. And then, on still another page, would be your growth plan (franchised, licensed, manufacturing, or corporate), again based on your assumptions page.

Then, once you have completed all the core modeling, begin altering your assumptions by subjecting your core growth scenario to increasingly difficult situations in terms of growth, margins, or overhead so that you can begin to plan based on various worst-case scenarios. In this way, you will have a system that has prepared you to respond to any of the situations that may arise in your business rather than simply reacting to them.

The U.S. Small Business Administration website has more information on business plans, including some sample plans that you can review at https://www.sba.gov/business-guide/plan-your-business/write-your-business-plan.

don't confuse metrics with strategy

The underlying metrics that you measure are meant to provide you with insight into a premise that is central to your strategy, and while they can influence your tactics, they should not be confused with strategy.

Say, for instance, that your business adopts a premium pricing strategy. Your pricing metrics may tell you consumers perceive that your price is too high. The tactical response to such a finding might be to lower the price. But that response might be counter to your overall strategic approach.

You may instead want to use that same feedback to refocus your marketing message on your premium value proposition. Or you may be marketing to the wrong target audience, and you need to alter the underlying media mix of your marketing campaign. Or you may need to do a better job of differentiating your product or service by adding incremental value to your offering.

So while the metrics are a measure of your success, without the underlying business strategy, they cannot move the ball forward. The key is being able to distinguish between the metrics telling you that you are failing to execute on a strategy and the metrics telling you that you are executing a failed strategy.

Sometimes the answer to that question lies in your ability to use the metrics to alter outcomes. If your examination of the metrics tells you, for example, that you cannot achieve your desired profitability because your cost of goods sold is too high, those metrics can lead to both tactical and strategic alternatives.

Tactically, you might look at finding alternate suppliers for your raw materials. You might enter into longer-term purchasing agreements with suppliers to reduce the selling price. You might look at warehousing some of your goods, again to allow for bulk purchasing to reduce prices. You might even look for substitute products.

But there are strategic alternatives, too. You could raise your prices to the consumer, potentially changing your brand positioning from a value brand to a premium brand. In that process, you might need to alter your service model to accommodate the premium positioning you are looking to achieve. And you would likely need to alter your marketing to reflect the changes in your brand strategy— and potentially change the nature of your target audience.

So in looking at your metrics, and the alternatives they offer you, be sure you understand the implications of any changes in processes at a strategic level.

leverage outside expertise

One of the ways you can make up for the deficiencies of your data as you build your business is to accelerate the learning curve by working with consultants, advisors, and others who have the benefit of more experience (and perhaps their own data) in the field. So by hiring designers, architects, professional marketing firms, small-business consultants, supply-chain consultants, demographic experts, site-location specialists, time-motion specialists, franchise consultants, and others, you can significantly improve the knowledge base on which you build your business.

Each of these specialists brings their own database of experience to the table—and if they have taken a quantitative approach to the analysis of that data, they can give you a significant head start on developing your business model. Moreover, they can refer you to others in their network who can help you get off to a fast start.

Using outside experts to help build your business can offer substantial benefits and greatly reduce the amount of time you spend in development. That said, there are a couple of things you should keep in mind. First, remember that outside experts often have a very narrow focus—in fact, the more broad-based knowledge a consultant claims, the less depth of expertise they may have in any one area.

At the same time, remember Abraham Maslow's old saw: "When your only tool is a hammer, every problem is a nail." So if you retain a highly specialized expert, you may find that they will promote only solutions that are relevant to what they are selling—giving you a strong motivation to manage them closely.

From your perspective, there are two primary reasons to hire outside expertise. First, if you do not have the time, resources, or ability to develop in-house expertise, an outside expert can provide substantial benefits and knowledge. Second, an outside expert is of substantial value when serving as "arms and legs" on a project—where they will provide a service of limited duration (or requiring less than a full-time effort).

Almost certainly, two of those first experts should be an outside accountant and a business attorney. And like employees or franchisees, interview them to be sure they are a good fit for you and your organization when you get started. Make sure they are willing

❋ THE SPANISH SUBMARINE AND THE DECIMAL POINT

While centuries ago the Spanish Navy was one of the most powerful forces on the planet, in recent years, it is no longer the superpower it once was. And while the Spanish Armada of 1588 is considered a case study in poor planning and ineffectual leadership, my personal preference is for a more recent story: the Spanish submarine that would not float.

Sometime after the contract for the S-80 submarine was first approved in 2004, they discovered a "serious design flaw" that made it too heavy to resurface after diving. Apparently, someone, somewhere, had misplaced a decimal point. And while I am not an expert in submarines, I am fairly certain this is not a good thing. After spending €14 million, they solved the problem by making the sub longer, at a massive increase in cost and a delay of several years.

Then, in 2018, they discovered that the increased size of the vessel meant the docks at Cartagena could not accommodate it. So once it went out to sea, it could never return to Spain.

Oops.

So the base had to be dredged and reshaped at significant expense so that the new submarine would have a home. As Spain's defense minister put it, "There have been deficiencies in the project."

I guess.

From a planning standpoint, the conventional wisdom is that things will take twice as long and cost twice as much as you expect. And while it's not always true, it often is. So when you plan,

✳ THE SPANISH SUBMARINE AND
THE DECIMAL POINT, CONTINUED

"measure twice and cut once," and make sure you account for anything that might go wrong. Ask yourself what could possibly happen that might derail your efforts. Don't let your enthusiasm for your new venture blind you to the potential problems that could occur down the road.

to stay in their lane while being proactive in providing you with advice on important issues for your business's growth.

Ultimately, once you know how to measure your success, you will be in a better position to begin to form your corporate identity and the value proposition of your Money Machine, which we will address in the next chapter.

know
who
you
are

I always smile when someone starts to tell me how some overnight sensation got lucky. He was just at the right place at the right time. He just happened to invent the Pet Rock. The person in front of me had the exact same idea a decade earlier—but this overnight sensation managed to capitalize on it before they could. The "if-onlys" of life.

But you need to be honest with yourself if you hope to ever achieve the same "dumb luck." The difference between the overnight sensation and the person telling the story is that only one of them went out and did it.

There is an old saying, "See a penny, pick it up, and all day long, you'll have good luck." Today, maybe that penny is a Bitcoin, but either way, it represents opportunity. But how many times do you walk past that opportunity because your head is occupied worrying about all the little things that bog down your day. Maybe you even see the penny but are too damn busy thinking about what you have to do in the next hour, grinding away. Or perhaps it is fear. Fear that if you stop to pick up that penny—or that Bitcoin—there will be a cost associated with the effort.

When you talk about the lucky break the other guy had, consider that it was because he saw that penny when no one else seemed to recognize it for what it was—found money. Like whoever the person (or people) who goes by the name of Satoshi Nakamoto, who invented Bitcoin, you have to "pick it up."

People are constantly saying how they had come up with some idea long before it became popular. Yet it takes someone special to see the opportunities that others might later see as "obvious" with 20/20 hindsight.

First they had to see that penny. That opportunity.

Then they had to pick it up. They had to be willing to take the chance.

Of course, if it were just about taking that chance, the world would be overflowing with billionaires.

But it's not. You have to understand what is involved in taking that opportunity from vision to sustained profitability. And to do that, you should start with an understanding of how you get from the starting gate to the finish line—or at least something that approximates a finish line.

In this chapter, we will focus on how to identify a business that is a good fit for your skill sets and how to begin developing your value proposition.

start with passion

Any business you build will have one thing no other business in the world has—you.

As a franchise consultant, I am first and foremost about creating systems. But in order to create those systems, you will need to be relentless in refining your Multiplier Model and idiosyncratic in your attention to detail. That drive for perfection simply does not come without the kind of passion that can keep an entrepreneur motivated for years and perhaps decades.

Because you're an entrepreneur, there are several things I know about you without even asking, just based on my experience.

First and foremost, you have a very strong belief in yourself. You believe you can do things better than the next person and that you are very unlikely to fail at anything you put your mind to. More than most, entrepreneurs share a combination of two of the tenets of tae kwon do—perseverance and indomitable spirit. And, like martial arts practitioners, they are not averse to a little hard contact. In fact, many relish the fights that might make the timid turn away.

A corollary to this belief in yourself is decisiveness. Because you believe in yourself, you are willing to make the hard decisions necessary to run a business without overthinking them.

A second corollary to this is that you are a risk taker. Starting a business requires an investment of time, capital, and emotional energy. Entrepreneurs could easily get a job elsewhere and take a dependable salary. But they would rather bet on themselves, even if the time they spend out of the work force may make them less marketable in the corporate world. Entrepreneurs could be spending their capital on a nice home or a retirement portfolio, but they would rather risk that capital on a destiny that puts them in control. And they could focus their emotional energy on a 9-to-5 job where they would be free to focus on family or other pursuits after-hours. Yet they choose a path where they are constantly thinking about their business—sometimes to the detriment of their personal relationships.

As an entrepreneur, you will constantly be faced with decisions that must be made quickly, and without regret or hindsight. If you cannot make big decisions and sleep well at night, the entrepreneurial road might not be for you. Entrepreneurs see mistakes not as a flaw, but as a part of the learning process.

Entrepreneurs want to be in control. They relish that "the buck stops here" in their business lives, even if they are collaborative in the decision-making process. For many entrepreneurs, working for others is just not an option if they have other choices.

The second main thing I know about you is that you're a rule breaker and an independent thinker. Given the choice between a "sure thing" business opportunity where there would be little risk and a predictable return but would have to follow someone else's rules (such as buying a franchise) and a more speculative venture with higher risks and higher potential returns where they would make the rules up as they go along, most true entrepreneurs would choose the latter. My shorthand definition of an entrepreneur is "someone who never saw a rule he did not want to break."

(If you see yourself in the former camp, that does not negate your entrepreneurial spirit—it simply means you have a lower risk tolerance than most entrepreneurs. So the best path toward business ownership for you may actually be buying a franchise, as opposed to starting a business of your own design.)

Third, you're a self-starter. Entrepreneurs don't need someone to get their heart started every morning. Instead, they are extremely self-motivated individuals who look forward to every day as a new challenge, not as drudgery. Some say that entrepreneurs are willing to work hard. I believe, on the other hand, that entrepreneurs simply look at things differently. For them, hard work isn't work. It's doing something they love.

Fourth, you have vision and foresight. Whenever entrepreneurs see problems, they see opportunities. If something is broken, they have a solution that often involves creating a new product or business. While many of us look at solutions in retrospect, saying "What a great idea . . . why didn't I think of that?" an entrepreneur is more likely to be thinking "If they just made this change, it would be better."

Ultimately, successful entrepreneurs have passion. Passion turns hard work into play. Passion makes you see problems in a new light and provides a vision of the future. Passion fuels your belief in yourself. Passion gives you the fearlessness to make decisions, make mistakes, and move on. And finally, passion keeps you in the game.

While your business may not be yours (or involve your direct participation) forever, to make it successful, you have to plan to be committed to it for years. After the initial headiness of the startup phase wears off, will it be something you continue to enjoy on a daily basis? Will you be able to maintain your passion?

The problem, of course, is that you may not know exactly what your day-to-day routine will look like before you start your business. Some franchisors, like Domino's Pizza and McDonald's, have solved that by requiring prospective franchisees to first work in their stores. If your business is being started on familiar ground, then perhaps you are already mentally armed for the grind. But if it's new territory, be sure to investigate the nature of the business, perhaps by observation or by speaking to similar business owners, to decide whether your passion aligns with the reality of the business you are creating.

Often, when I meet people in a social setting, they ask me "What is the best franchise?" or "What industry is hot right now?" The underlying assumption to these questions is almost always "Where can I make the most money?" What these people are missing is that you can make money in almost any business if you execute well. So as you start building your business, it is imperative that you don't try to follow the latest trend. Don't follow the money. Instead, follow your passion—and let it lead you to something you can make great.

Of course, passion alone doesn't make for long-term, repeatable business success. Building your business requires focus.

beware of entrepreneurial deficit disorder

While passion often drives an entrepreneur's success, passion (which most of them have in abundance) can also be their undoing. Passion without focus can lead an entrepreneur into jumping from one "great idea" to the next. I have met many entrepreneurs with clear "grand slam" concepts who, instead of trying to improve their existing operation, have decided to start something new from scratch.

The problem is that many entrepreneurs are easily bored. They are constantly looking for the adrenaline rush that comes from creating something new. So after they have built their business, they either want to completely remake it (in an effort to perfect it) or, even worse, decide to start a new business instead.

I've also seen many entrepreneurs who struggle after franchising their business, once they realize that being an effective franchisor requires constant training and monitoring of the systems they created. Their passion comes from creating rather than implementing.

To avoid this, you need to identify the source of your passion and then determine where that best fits within the organization. Many times that entrepreneurial spirit works best as the company visionary or the face of the brand rather than as the day-to-day leader of the franchise organization. In that case, you need to trust others to implement and monitor what you have created.

Ideas for the next business venture come at entrepreneurs a mile a minute, and sometimes these symptoms can seem like attention deficit disorder, with the business owner jumping from one plan to the next. If you are afflicted with this entrepreneurial deficit disorder, you must learn to keep it under control or it will cause you to lose focus.

Remember that one of the basic principles of the Multiplier Model is to start by building a Money Machine that provides a reasonable rate of return and then replicate that business. You will need sustained focus on the same business for years to make this model work.

That's not to say you won't refine and change your business model as you grow. You will *need* to do so for your Money Machine to remain viable. But if your business is providing strong and reliable returns, you cannot allow yourself to get sidelined by your next great idea.

I tell people who are considering franchising that the hardest part of creating a successful franchise is almost always coming up with the concept to be franchised. But once that concept is working successfully, your focus, from a purely growth perspective, should be on duplicating that concept, again and again, and reinvesting the returns into your business.

keep your concept simple

Let's start with a basic premise: Almost any business can be franchised. There are franchised medical practices ranging from urgent-care clinics to optical centers to dental practices. Entrepreneurs have franchised businesses as complex as the high-end restaurant Ruth's Chris Steak House and hotel chains like Hyatt and Sheraton, which sometimes operate almost like small cities, with separate systems needed for reservations, security, maid service, food preparation and delivery, spas, entertainment, and business service centers complete with catering, light shows, and audiovisual services for groups that can number in the thousands. And then again, there are carpet-cleaning and lawn-care businesses like Chem-Dry and Spring-Green with much simpler operations and lower startup costs.

So a business certainly does not need to be simple to be franchised—but it helps.

A key premise behind the Multiplier Model is that your business needs to provide returns without your direct involvement. So as you begin replicating your Money Machine, you will need to have people other than you operating the new locations. And because chances are that those people are less qualified and less motivated than you are, simpler systems will always be easier to follow and will allow less room for improvisation.

A major drawback of more complex franchise models is that they shrink the target market of franchisees who could be recruited to run the business. Medical franchises, for example, need to recruit licensed health-care professionals as franchisees or employees. High-end restaurants need restaurateurs with extensive experience in order to run the business profitably. Hotels, especially larger and more complex ones, must often be run by management companies rather than by owner/operators.

By contrast, think about Subway. An average restaurant might be 1,200 square feet. It does not have any grills, deep fryers, or grease traps. It is basically a simple assembly line for making sandwiches to order and serving drinks. A Subway restaurant can literally go into just about any strip mall in the U.S.—and sometimes it seems as if they have, with some 22,000 U.S. locations (and a total of about 40,000 locations in more than 100 countries worldwide).

Aside from the issue of the franchisee selection process, the simpler the business model, the easier it is to control quality. If a 20-foot sandwich prep line has 40 different ingredients in its drop-in dividers, there are only so many things that can go wrong in the food preparation process. And if the customer is watching every step of the way, presumably those issues can be resolved before they have a bad experience with the product.

Keep in mind that more complex restaurants like McDonald's are among the most successful franchises in the world, and even more complex restaurants like Ruth's Chris are highly successful. But take, for example, traditional Greek restaurants with their extensive menus that run for many pages, and you see few players that have successfully franchised in that space.

Outside the restaurant industry, you can see the same trends in many different markets, with franchised businesses dominating industries with simple business models:

❋ *Janitorial-services businesses.* Between ServiceMaster Clean, Jan-Pro Cleaning & Disinfecting, Coverall, Vanguard Cleaning Systems, CleanNet USA, Anago Cleaning Systems, Stratus Building Solutions, and Buildingstars, there are more than 27,000 franchisees in this industry—and more join the market every year.

* *Carpet-cleaning companies.* Companies like Chem-Dry, Oxi Fresh, Stanley Steemer, milliCare, Rainbow International, and COIT have sold thousands of franchises in this space.
* *Lawn-care businesses.* This is another simple business model that is dominating the market by franchising, with companies like Lawn Doctor, Spring-Green Lawn Care, and Weed Man leading the way.

As you fine-tune your concept, it helps to keep your end game in mind, as I discuss below.

creating your value proposition

One of the most important concepts to keep in mind when building your Money Machine is the need to provide value to your customer. Of course, there are many ways to do that. You can provide a comparable product at a lower price than the competition. You can create a product or service that is superior to those already in the market. You can provide a higher level of service or convenience. But ultimately, you need to start with a vision of how you will provide value and where that will take you.

Our client Daniel Stanton, the founder of My Eyelab, is one such visionary. His original company, Stanton Optical, was a highly successful business. But he recognized that to mass-produce that success, he had to make the business economics more appealing, so he set out to deliver on his vision of making eye care easy.

The first problem was that the cost of entry was simply too high, as having an on-site lab required a huge investment in equipment—not to mention the incremental rent and labor costs of maintaining a lab at each location. The other issue impacting labor costs was the need to employ an ophthalmologist on-site to conduct routine eye examinations.

Stanton realized that by manufacturing their own frames and other parts, they could significantly lower costs. Each store was given a relatively static inventory to allow for trial, and with the company manufacturing everything off-site and shipping it to them once it was done, the store became more of a cash-and-carry business than an optical dispensary, while allowing Stanton to invest only in one centralized lab rather than a lab in every store.

Finally, Stanton realized that if he could create a workable telehealth solution, the store would no longer need to employ an on-site ophthalmologist or optometrist. Instead, using their custom software and videoconferencing, the patient could just do a remote eye exam with Stanton's doctors at a significantly reduced price. That eliminated the financial commitment of hiring doctors for each location.

With those changes, the business was essentially transformed. The average footprint for a My Eyelab location was about 2,500 square feet, which was less than half the footprint of a traditional Stanton Optical location. The initial investment to open a location was cut in half, and both rent and labor costs were substantially reduced. Now My Eyelabs could go into smaller locations in high-traffic areas, further improving the economics of the business. And because the medical exams were performed via telehealth, the My Eyelab concept could now be franchised not just to eye doctors, but to businesspeople and entrepreneurs.

As I write this in 2021, there are about 185 locations, but by the time this book is published, I expect that number to be out of date, as parent company Now Optics opened 66 locations last year and expects to grow even faster this year. By systematizing some of the more complex processes involved in running an optical retailer, Stanton has helped the company grow much faster and opened the doors to people who normally could not have owned such a franchise.

start with the end in mind

Over the course of my career, I have met with thousands of business owners. Generally when I ask them about their plans for the future, I am met with a vague response. Sometimes they tell me they want to pass the business on to their children, or they say they want to eventually sell it. But when asked for specifics, they invariably stumble.

How much do they want to earn at some point in the future? How much will their children want to earn? How much do they want to sell the business for and when?

When I ask them how fast they want to grow, the usual response is "As fast as I can without sacrificing quality." And when I ask how much they want to sell their business for, the answer is usually "That depends . . ."

Of course, these are platitudes, not answers.

So start by asking yourself if you want to be in this business forever or whether you want to sell it at some point. As part of that process, ask yourself specifically what your end game looks like.

If you want to sell the business, how much do you want for it? And when do you want to sell it? Start by setting a timeline on your goal. Are you willing to devote the next ten years of your life to the business? Five years?

Be careful here that when you say how much you want to sell your business for, you do not get trapped into trying to value the company. Instead, choose the minimum amount of capital you want to realize from the sale, regardless of what you think it may be worth. The best Multiplier Models are those that grow not just for the sake of growth, but instead according to a logical plan designed to achieve specific goals.

When I work with clients, I tell them to imagine I am willing to write them a check right now that I will postdate and put in an envelope. They get to tell me how much to make the check out for. That number would be the absolute lowest selling price they would accept for their business at some point in the future.

But as soon as I seal the envelope and they put it in their pocket, they will forget all about the check until the day of the sale arrives. Until then, they will make all the decisions, endure all the sleepless nights, and work all the endless hours that are needed to get to that number. In essence, I'm asking them how much they are willing to sell their investment and the next five to ten years of their life for.

Use this exercise to work backward from your future selling price into a plan that will allow you to achieve that goal.

As an example, if you wanted to sell your business for $10 million in five years, start by trying to estimate what your business would need to look like to achieve that selling price. One obvious measure, of course, is an earnings level. Businesses are often valued based on a multiple of earnings. Different industries, different rates of growth, different companies (and their associated "sizzle" factor), different sized businesses, different management teams, and even different points in time (strong vs. weak markets) will impact the earnings multiple that a business might be able to command when it sells. A single unit restaurant, for example, might sell for four or five times its earnings, while a midsized fast-growth franchisor in a dynamic market might sell for 14 times earnings. So an obvious first step might be to try to estimate the kind of multiple you might achieve based on comparable sales in the market.

But before finalizing on that multiple, ask who your likely buyer might be.

While your first option might be a sale to private equity, you could also consider whether there is a strategic buyer who might have a deeper interest. For example, if you are purchasing $500,000 worth of widgets annually from XYZ company, XYZ might view your business as a particularly important acquisition because, in addition to buying the earnings of the business as it stands, they would be securing the channel of your $500,000 wholesale account and the profits that result from those sales. So for XYZ company, this acquisition would have more value than it would for a disinterested third party.

Moreover, if XYZ competes with ABC for your widget business and the products are easily substituted, then both ABC and XYZ are potential buyers—perhaps creating a bidding war between the two companies. Of course, in planning for this kind of sale, it is important to retain absolute control over your supply chain (even if you are growing through independent franchisees or licensees) in order for the wholesale sales revenue to have value to XYZ and ABC.

Once you have determined to whom you might sell the business and a reasonable earnings multiple you can apply to your business, simply divide by the earnings multiple to determine the amount of earnings you will need to show to be worth your desired selling price. And once you know that, you would simply subtract any existing profits you might be achieving, on the assumption that your profits will remain constant, to determine the incremental profitability you need to create to achieve your goal.

Going back to our example, if you wanted to sell your business for $10 million in five years and you felt that someone would pay you seven times earnings for your business, you would divide the $10 million by 7 to understand that you would likely need to be earning about $1.43 million to command that selling price. If your business, after normalizing salaries, was throwing off a stable profit of $230,000 per year, you could then plan around the need to achieve $1.2 million in incremental earnings to reach your desired selling price.

Then, estimate the profits that could be generated in an individual market (or from an individual store) to determine how fast you would need to grow to meet that goal. From there, it is a simple math problem. Figure out what it costs to open a single market/location and how much of your current capital you are willing to risk. Determine the cash flow of each location—how quickly it should achieve break-even, how soon and how much it will contribute to the bottom line over time, and how much of that cash flow you can reinvest in further growth.

At that point, you can begin testing various growth models. If you open company-owned locations based on your projections of the per-unit investment and returns, how many can you open in your given time frame? And will the resultant earnings from this plan get you to a point where you can achieve your desired selling price?

If your plan indicates that you will get to your desired selling price, you can begin to execute against that plan. Again, looking at our hypothetical, if the amount of capital that you have and are willing to put at risk allows you to build out six additional company-owned locations that you are confident will each generate $200,000 in profits, and if you could reasonably add that many stores in a five-year time frame without increasing your overhead, then the company-owned growth strategy appears to be an easy choice.

But what if company growth doesn't get you there?

At that point, you have three options:

1. Change the aggressiveness of your goal
2. Change the timing of your goal
3. Change your strategy

Changing the aggressiveness of your goal might be as simple as being willing to "settle" for a $5 million goal instead of $10 million. And changing the timing might be as simple as a concession that you are willing to devote ten years to achieving your goal instead of your original five. And if your financial modeling gets you close to your goal, these alternatives might pose the most logical choices. But if your goal is so distant that these options do not get you close, you may need to look at alternate growth strategies.

If you choose to change your strategy, you might start by continuing to explore corporate growth. In that case, you might make some assumptions about the more aggressive use of leverage (by taking out bank loans) in your growth plan. Or you might be willing to risk more of your nest egg or bring in an equity partner. If you choose to explore any of these options, run the financials again, making sure you take into account the impact of things like increased interest payments or, if you bring in a partner, the dilution of your equity to determine if these changes impact your ability to reach your goal.

Another option is some form of third-party distribution strategy, such as franchising, licensing, distributorships, or joint venturing. In each of those instances, a third party takes some responsibility for opening and operating a market or a location and shares in the benefits from the business.

So the implications for planning here are significant, but the underlying assumption is that your Money Machine can be duplicated from one market to the next and similar levels of returns can be achieved.

stay true to your brand promise

I have been fortunate enough to be able to travel the world extensively. I have been to every state in the U.S., almost every province in Canada, and dozens of other countries.

When I travel abroad, one way to judge how "Western" an economy is involves looking at how many international franchises you see on the street. When I tell people I am a franchise consultant, they often lament how these companies are robbing some countries of their culture.

And while I love to immerse myself in the local culture of any country I visit, I never feel any regret at the global success of franchising.

The reason franchises thrive in these cultures is that they do a better job of meeting their customers' needs than the businesses they supplanted. They bought their products more efficiently and passed those savings along. They experimented with different products to find out which ones the consumer liked best. And, most of all, they provided the customer with a consistent brand experience from one market to the next. They delivered on their brand's promise. The systems they developed and adapted to the local market led to their success.

That's not to say that they remain entirely consistent across borders. There are always adaptations. In fact, one of the things I enjoy when traveling abroad is to visit McDonald's to see how they have adapted to the market.

Some of the things you may find at McDonald's around the world that you likely will not find in the States include:

* Australia—Gourmet Angus Truffle & Cheese
* Austria—McNoodles
* Belgium—Wacko Guaco (chicken patty with guacamole)
* Brazil—Pão de Queijo (cheese bread)
* Canada—Poutine; McLobster (lobster roll)

✳ Chile—Guacamole 2 Carnes (double beef with guacamole); Empanadas Con Queso (empanadas with cheese)

✳ China—Taro Pie; Mashed Potato Burger (burger topped with bacon and mashed potatoes); Bacon, Macaroni, and Cheese Toastie; Black and White Burgers (twin burgers with white and black buns)

✳ Costa Rica—McPinto Deluxe (breakfast meal with gallo pinto, a traditional beans and rice dish)

✳ Denmark—Pepper Strips (fries seasoned with black pepper and onions)

✳ Egypt—McFalafel (vegan falafel wrap)

✳ Finland—Chili Cheese Tops (fried dough stuffed with chilies and cheese)

✳ France—Macarons

✳ Germany—McNürnburger (made with bratwurst); Beer

✳ Greece—Greek Mac (burger in pita bread)

✳ Hong Kong—Rice Fantastic (burger with rice patties instead of buns)

✳ India—McCurry Pan; BigSpicy Paneer Wrap; Maharaja Mac (chicken burger); McAloo Tikki (veggie burger)

✳ Italy—Spinach and Parmesan Nuggets; Sweety Con Nutella

✳ Japan—Ebi Filet-O Shrimp Burger; Melon McFloat; McChoco Potato (fries with chocolate sauce); Shaka Shaka Chicken (fried chicken patty with a spice packet); Idaho Burger (burger with bacon and a hash brown patty); Gracoro Burger (macaroni patty, shrimp, and white sauce)

✳ Korea—Shrimp Beef Burger (beef patty plus shrimp patty)

✳ Lithuania—Aštrūs sūrio gabalėliai (fried spicy cheese with Chapala hot peppers in a crispy crust)

✳ Malaysia—Prosperity Burger (long beef or chicken patty with a black pepper sauce); Bubur Ayam McD (a local rice porridge)

✳ Mexico—McMolletes (local version of the McMuffin, with refried beans and pico de gallo)

✳ Middle East—McArabia (grilled chicken in pita bread)

* Netherlands—McKroket (fried beef and cheese burger)
* New Zealand—NYC Benedict Bagel; Kiwiburger (burger topped with an egg and beetroot)
* Norway—McLaks (salmon burger)
* Oman—Smokey BBQ; Jalapeno Cheese Bites
* Philippines—Chicken McDo With McSpaghetti (fried chicken leg with spaghetti and meat sauce)
* Poland—Cordon Bleu Burger (beef patty, chicken patty, and bacon)
* Qatar—Chicken Mac (basically a Big Mac with chicken instead of beef)
* Russia—McShrimp
* Saudi Arabia—Halloumi Muffin (Halloumi cheese on an English muffin)
* Singapore—Chicken SingaPorridge (congee with fried chicken strips)
* Spain—Gazpacho
* Sweden—McPlant Burger (McDonald's is testing its first plant-based burger here)
* Switzerland—McVeggie
* Thailand—Samurai Pork Burger
* Turkey—McTurco (kebab meat in a pita)
* United Kingdom—Bacon Roll; Mozzarella Dippers
* Uruguay—Pancake Helado (pancake stuffed with dulce de leche and topped with vanilla ice cream)
* Venezuela—Empanadas
* And the list goes on.

Even within the United States, there are differences in regional offerings:

* Alaska features the McKinley Mac, an even Bigger Mac with two quarter-pound beef patties.
* In some southern states, you can get biscuits and gravy.
* The McLobster, mentioned above, is available in New England in the summer.

- ❋ Hawaii features the Peach Mango Pie and also offers Spam for those who want to partake at breakfast.
- ❋ And bratwurst has been offered in some locations in Wisconsin.

In addition, when visiting McDonald's in other countries, the ingredients used in their products may be slightly different from market to market. Beef, for example, will be locally sourced, and the diet of the cows (grass vs. grain-fed) influences things like marbling and flavor. The same can be said for McDonald's potatoes, where different local growing conditions will produce a slightly different potato (or may even require a different type of potato altogether)— just like growing conditions can affect the grapes that are used for making wine.

And while the McDonald's case study holds some valuable lessons for those looking to adapt their concepts to foreign markets, there is perhaps a much more profound lesson underlying these product offerings: The brand is not the product.

While the product is one component of the brand promise, remember that the brand you are creating needs to stand for something beyond the product itself. McDonald's, which is known for its hamburgers, does not sell beef (or pork, for that matter) in its 350 locations in India (even though some Indian states allow it), where about 50 percent of the menu is vegetarian. Yet the McDonald's brand remains one of the strongest in the world (and in India) despite these product line differences.

No one ever questions the consistency of the brand because McDonald's takes such care in selecting suppliers and preparing their products. But more important, McDonald's knows that its brand is more than its food.

Part of it is the décor—the ubiquitous Golden Arches and the bright red signage. But there are some markets where that is changed, too, like Sedona, Arizona, where the Golden Arches have been replaced by the "turquoise arches" because of local building codes and design regulations. As McDonald's continues to adapt to the marketplace, it is moving away from the cafeteria look of its red-and-gold interior, with chairs bolted to the floors, to a much more

❋ TOP TEN BRANDS

The brand consulting company Interbrand rated the world's top ten brands in 2020. In eight of the ten, the name of the brand made no reference to the products sold by the company. Here they are, just for the fun of it:

1. Apple—no mention of computers or electronics

2. Amazon—no mention of online retail

3. Microsoft—a combination of the words *microcomputer* and *software*

4. Google—no mention of search engines

5. Samsung—no mention of electronics

6. Coca-Cola—refers to two of the original ingredients—coca leaves and the kola nut

7. Toyota—no mention of vehicles

8. Mercedes-Benz—no mention of vehicles or engines

9. McDonald's—no mention of food

10. Disney—no mention of entertainment

Founder Steve Jobs chose the name Apple because he thought it was fun and unintimidating—and it put the company ahead of his former employer Atari in the phone book (back when people still used phone books).

Amazon, which was originally named Cadabra (a reference to the magical term *abracadabra*), went through a series of names before settling on Amazon. Founder Jeff Bezos picked it out from the "A" section of the dictionary because it was the world's largest river and he aimed to become the world's largest bookseller.

❋ **TOP TEN BRANDS,** CONTINUED

Google was originally named BackRub because its algorithm used backlinks to rank sites, but this was changed later to Google as an intentional misspelling of googol, the mathematical term for the number 1 followed by 100 zeros. The name was chosen to reflect the enormous amount of data they were indexing.

Samsung means "three stars" in Korean; its founder Lee Byung-chull chose it to represent that the company would be as powerful and long-lasting as the stars.

The remaining four brands (Toyota, Mercedes-Benz, McDonald's, and Disney) are named after their founders (or their child, in the case of Mercedes).

"fast casual" look—and introducing self-service ordering kiosks to speed traffic and reduce labor costs.

So while design also plays a role in branding, the name and design elements are simply the tools you use to announce to your customer that they have arrived at a place where the brand promise will be delivered—hopefully with consistency.

So what exactly is the brand and the brand promise?

Over the years, I have heard stories of Ray Kroc's visits to his franchisees. He would often start by patrolling the parking lot, picking up each piece of litter, and unceremoniously piling it on the counter while he waited for the franchisee to appear for his inevitable rebuke. His message: McDonald's core values were quality, service, cleanliness, and value. And no franchisee had better forget it.

Ultimately, it's not the product, the design, or the name. The brand is the promise of a consistent experience from one Money Machine to the next. And you need to deliver on that promise if you want the repeat business that will allow your machine to grow.

names don't make businesses

One of the first tasks you will need to consider when starting a business is choosing your name. The name will represent you to your customers and will carry your brand promise. And as such, it is not a decision that should be made lightly.

That said, names don't make businesses. Businesses make names.

Let's go back to our McDonald's example. Today, of course, when many people think of the word "McDonald's," it is synonymous with hamburgers. But that was not always the case. When I was very young—before McDonald's became one of the most iconic brands in history—when I heard the word McDonald's, my first thought was of the song "Old MacDonald." I did not think about hamburgers. I thought "E-I-E-I-O."

But more to the point, nothing in the word McDonald's implies "hamburgers." In fact, on the original McDonald's sign, the company's name was smaller than the word "Hamburgers"—an indication that early on, it had to let consumers know what it sold.

As the brand became well-known (and the product line more diversified), McDonald's dropped the word Hamburgers from much of their signage and replaced it with a much cleaner look. Today, the brand and the logo are so well-known that the shape of the Golden Arches alone is enough to tell the story. In fact, I have seen McDonald's billboards consisting only of a red background, a solitary Golden Arch, and the words "On your right."

When it comes to brand names, trying to be *too* descriptive is often a handicap, not a virtue.

First, from the standpoint of obtaining a trademark (which will allow you to enforce your intellectual property rights), the more descriptive a name is, the harder it is to trademark. Think about the old McDonald's sign again. The word hamburgers, while it appears prominently on those signs, was never subject to trademark protection. Anyone who wants to use hamburgers in their advertising can. So if I wanted to start Mark's Hamburgers, I could. So understand that if you incorporate any descriptive word into your name, you will almost never be able to protect it. Instead, you would have to disclaim its use under trademark law, allowing anyone to use it. Thus, the more prominent the descriptor is as a part of your name, the more easily your brand will be confused with similarly named brands.

Second, because of the common misconception that a brand should mention the product, there are literally thousands of companies that adopt (and fail to trademark) these descriptive names. So if you ever wanted to enforce your trademark rights, you would need to spend a fortune in legal fees trying to get people to stop using "your mark."

That said, even if you avoid a descriptive name, you will want to communicate brand attributes or values as a part of the name, to the extent that you can. One thing you might do is to ask yourself what attributes you want to communicate about your brand and incorporate a word or part of a word that helps convey that attribute. FedEx, for example, which was originally Federal Express, was focused on the brand attribute of speed. PayPal focuses on friendliness and ease by adding the "Pal" appendage. Some more obvious examples from the franchise world might include FastFrame, Sports Clips, HomeVestors, FastSigns, Jiffy Lube, Lawn Doctor, Burn Boot Camp, PuroClean, Merry Maids, Chem-Dry, Carstar, SafeSplash Swim School, MassageLuXe, and Qualicare Senior Care, to name just a few.

Third, by choosing a descriptive name, you will be locking your brand into a market position that you may not want to own at some point in the future. Kentucky Fried Chicken changed its name to KFC at least in part to get away from the unhealthy image associated with the word fried. Likewise, Boston Chicken became Boston Market because the company wanted to promote other menu items like turkey and meatloaf. So choosing a descriptive name will likely hurt you when it comes time to expand. If you absolutely need to use a descriptor to help explain your consumer offering, use it in a tag line, which you may or may not be able to trademark.

Obviously, the process of coming up with a name and a logo can be complex enough to fill a book all by itself. Name derivation using words or parts of words with certain characteristics, testing names and logos with focus groups, and other tools used by consultants on issues such as color may all factor in.

But approaching the issue strictly from the standpoint of creating a cloneable system, make sure that the name is easy to spell, pronounce, and remember. Shorter names are easier to use on signage—they allow you to use bigger letters and make the name more visible. Avoid limiting references in the name— while companies like Kentucky Fried Chicken, Boston Market, and California Pizza Kitchen got away with geographic references, for example, you should usually avoid these types of names unless there is a specific reference that you feel helps your brand. But most important, be sure that the name you choose can be trademarked before you invest any time or effort in promoting it.

I have met with literally dozens of businesses that have been operating under a brand for many years, only to find out when they are ready to expand that they do not own the name—and that, in fact, someone else already owns it in a market in which they want to expand. These issues are not just limited to small companies. Burger King, for example, operates in Australia under the name Hungry Jack's because of a similar trademark problem.

In the U.S., a quick search of the Trademark Electronic Search System (TESS) on the U.S. Patent and Trademark Office (USPTO) website (https://www.uspto.gov) will often get you a quick "no" when considering a potential name. And, of course, search the top-level domains for the name to check on their availability.

But even that methodology is not without its flaws. If, for example, you searched "MacDowell's" as a possible name for your hamburger restaurant, the TESS search would come up empty, but the USPTO might still reject your trademark if it felt the similarity to McDonald's might confuse consumers. So you do not want your name to be similar to any of your competitors'. And if it is close, a slight change in spelling or word order is not likely to pass muster with the USPTO.

On the flip side, the mere existence of a competing name may not preclude you from getting a trademark, either. Trademarks are registered based on various classes in the USPTO's classification system. There are a total of 45 different classes—34 representing product classes and 11 representing service classes. So the fact that you have the same name as another trademark owner is not necessarily a deal killer, if you're in different classes. Again, it comes down to the issue of confusion. No one is likely to confuse an Ace bandage with Ace Hardware. Or Dove soap with a Dove Bar. Or Domino's Pizza with Domino Sugar. Or Apple computers with Apple Records.

Another consideration should be whether you even want to register the trademark. If, for example, you were operating as "Joe's Pizza" and you felt you could trademark the name, you should consider whether that name is more trouble than it is worth. If you searched Google and found 10,000 different Joe's Pizza Parlors (or similar names), all those businesses would have prior rights to the name. So even if you could get the trademark, you would have 10,000 businesses "infringing" on it—and legally, they would have every right to continue to operate under the brand.

Moreover, if you were to register that mark, you would be forced to defend it against every new Joe's Pizza that cropped up. If you failed to enforce your mark against these new businesses, you would risk losing it, and if you did enforce it, your legal bills could quickly become astronomical.

As you can see, while a good name choice may not be the proximate cause of your success, a bad one can certainly contribute to your demise.

Once you have narrowed down your list of potential names, it is imperative to get the input of trademark counsel on your top choice before you finalize your decision. The cost of obtaining an uncontested trademark, even when using an attorney to file the paperwork, is minimal when compared to the cost of having to rebrand your business at some point in the future.

Assuming your attorney advises you to move forward with registration, you will have various decisions to make—which class or classes to file under, what type of mark (character, design, or sound), how you will demonstrate use of the mark, etc. But the one decision that should be a "no-brainer" is where to file: File for your trademark at the federal level (not the state level). That will give you the broadest rights. And, given the age of the internet and your ability to file for a mark with "intent to use," it is relatively easy to demonstrate the use of a trademark in interstate commerce.

Once you file, the USPTO will assign an examining attorney to review your mark. At that point, your application could be rejected (which you can appeal) or it can move through the process of publication—where your application is listed in the *Official Gazette* published weekly by the USPTO. If no one objects to your mark within 30 days (and remember, trademark attorneys are religiously scanning the *Official Gazette* on behalf of their clients), you go to the next step, and your trademark is registered.

If your mark is uncontested, the process can take six months to a year or more. But you can go ahead during that time and start your business under your chosen name—as long as your trademark attorney feels comfortable that you're likely to obtain the mark. Once they've given you the go-ahead, you can begin developing your look and feel— which will be communicated to the public through your logo.

When you first create your logo, don't worry about spending a lot of money on design. There are a number of online resources that can design good-looking logos for you for less than $1,500. One of the resources our clients have had success with is a company called https:// 99designs.com, which encourages multiple designers to compete for your business by submitting logos that you can then choose from. But there are numerous other design options online.

Again, there are some simple rules to keep in mind. First, it should be easily readable from a distance, especially if you will be using it on a sign or on the side of a vehicle. The more artwork people are required to decipher, the more difficult it will be to read. Think about the simplicity of the Golden Arches, the Nike

* NAME CHECKLIST

- ❏ Is your name unique?
- ❏ Is the URL for the top-level domain available?
- ❏ Is your name nondescriptive?
- ❏ Is it timeless and geographically neutral?
- ❏ Is it easy to spell and pronounce?
- ❏ Is it short enough to be easily read on your sign?
- ❏ Are there any "hidden meanings" that could hinder you in some markets?
- ❏ Is it generic enough (including the tag line) that it will allow for product/service line extensions?
- ❏ At the same time, does it communicate some positive attribute about your brand?
- ❏ Does your trademark attorney believe you will get the name if you file?

swoosh, the Apple apple, or the Amazon arrow. You want a logo that can be used in a variety of different ways; you may need to do some different color treatments as a result, but you will want to specify the exact color variants that can be used. And lastly, whenever you use your logo, you should always attach the appropriate trademark designation (either ™ or ® if the trademark has been registered).

take your concept for a test drive

When testing a new product or menu item, it is important to look at it from a holistic standpoint. Take McDonald's, for example. The company is constantly introducing new menu items.

Some of these products get tested, introduced, and ultimately rejected. In 1991, in the middle of the low-fat diet craze, McDonald's introduced the McLean Deluxe to capitalize on the consumer's desire for healthier eating options. The McLean, which was advertised as 91 percent fat free, used a seaweed extract called carrageenan as a replacement for some of the fat in the burger patty. And while the McLean was extensively promoted and did well in pretesting, it was deemed a failure and dropped from the menu in 1996. Today, of course, there are a number of food-service operators in the "healthy" and organic space, including companies like freshii, sweetgreen, Tender Greens, Dr Smood, Veggie Grill, and others that are taking advantage of this trend—even as larger chains begin to focus on more plant-based offerings.

Also in 1996, perhaps sensing the coming trend toward a "better burger," they introduced the Arch Deluxe, a high-end hamburger whose rollout was accompanied by even greater hoopla and an extensive advertising campaign. At the time, their primary competitor in the "better burger" space was Burger King. Five Guys, which today boasts more than 1,700 locations, had fewer than a half-dozen locations and did not start franchising until 2003. And "better burger" rivals such as Smashburger, Shake Shack, The Counter, Mooyah, and BurgerFi had not yet opened their first location. Yet despite devoting more than $100 million to its advertising campaigns, the Arch Deluxe was also pulled in 2000, making it a very expensive failure.

Since then, McDonald's has made several more attempts at entering the gourmet burger space. It introduced the Angus Deluxe and several other variants between 2009 and 2013, and it continues to roll out gourmet burgers to this day. But why do none of them stick? While they may not be bestsellers, they certainly won some followers and made some sales.

Then there are other products, like the McRib, which was first introduced in 1981. It too was a "flop" when it rolled out and was taken off the menu four years later—only to be reintroduced in 1989. It still has a dedicated following online. Some of these products make seasonal appearances in select locations but are never permanently integrated into the menu. Sometimes they are designed to bring in customers who might otherwise have stayed away.

Before any new product is introduced into the system, McDonald's goes through a lengthy testing process that gives them some level of certitude about how it will be accepted in the marketplace. And yet, not all of their products are successful. So it is important to take a dispassionate view of our products and services and be ready to respond to the feedback provided by our customers. And, of course, the same holds true for their marketing process, which I will discuss in the next chapter.

I hope at this point that you agree a lot of planning goes into defining "who you are" as a business. It cannot be based solely on passion. The branding elements go far beyond just a name. The concept must be well-defined and fine-tuned. You will need to keep your end game in mind.

marketing your money machine

Perhaps the greatest, and at the same time the most confounding, thing about marketing is the ease with which you can use systems to measure the effectiveness of your marketing efforts. The good news, of course, is that there are many readily available tools for measurement in the form of cost per lead, cost per sale, close rates, and time to close that will allow you to continually refine the budget, media, and messaging you are using to attract customers to your business.

The bad news is that you are dealing with consumer behavior. And that often changes faster than anyone can effectively measure or implement changes, as we are always looking at our results in the rearview mirror.

Mastering marketing requires an in-depth knowledge of the statistics that measure success and a thorough understanding of consumer behavior in relationship to those statistics. While it may sound strange, your marketing systems will require you to look both forward and backward. This chapter will expand on Chapter 4's discussion of branding and focus on the related topic of your marketing message and staying in your lane. I will also show you how to gather competitive intelligence and determine your marketing budget.

marketing is a moving target

The consumer is faced with an ever-changing environment. One day, you are shaking hands and kissing your old acquaintances when you meet. A month later, you are bumping elbows in greeting. A month after that, you are locked down, keeping a social distance of six feet, and wearing masks in public.

And while the environment is constantly changing, the consumer is being approached by an ever-shifting group of competitors within that environment, all looking to attract the same dollars you are. If the number of competitors in your market is growing, the only way to *maintain* your level of growth, let alone grow your business, is to find ways to expand the market as a whole. If the market is not growing, you will find that these competitors, good or bad, will keep taking little bites out of your business until you are left with nothing but the core.

Add to that one simple truth: If you are starting your business in the U.S., where entrepreneurship is spelled with a capital *E*, rest assured that the more successful your business is, the more likely it is that your business model will be copied. When I was younger, the copycats were easy to spot. They would sit in front of a business or, if they had a bit more audacity, come inside with cameras, pens, and paper, taking notes and photos. I can still remember folks claiming that their businesses were the inspiration for major success stories. There was the hamburger chain out of Texas that said they were the basis for Fuddruckers and the owner of a double-drive-thru restaurant who told me how he once sat on the hood of his car and chewed the fat with the folks who eventually founded Checkers.

But today, in the era of selfies, Facebook, and Instagram, if people *aren't* posting photos of your operation, it could spell trouble. So how do you know if you're about to be knocked off? The only prudent posture is generally to assume that you are, especially if you have lower barriers to entry.

So as you attempt to apply your systems to marketing your business, remember that the system you create must account for a moving target. Your competition isn't standing still.

aiming with a rearview mirror

Another issue adding complexity to the systematization of your marketing efforts is the diminishing returns that may result from exposure in certain media. Consider an example in which you spend $2,000 per month to advertise in a local magazine. Ten months later as you are planning the next year's budget, you determine that your cost per sale from the magazine is $43, a figure you are happy with given the nature of your business. Should you continue advertising in that publication? While you initially might be inclined to cut the check, let's look a little deeper.

If that magazine were primarily subscription-driven, you might expect your ad buy would show diminishing returns over time as most of the subscriber base stays constant (known as "reach") and the incremental returns of increased ad viewership (known as "frequency") loses its impact.

The theory of marginal analysis tells us to examine the most recent data more closely to see where things stand at present. Perhaps when the ad first ran, your business closed 90 to 100 sales per month or more—but then the ad's effectiveness began to decline as it was continuously served to the same prospects again and again. What if, for example, your monthly sales looked like this during the period the ad ran?

$$100, 90, 80, 60, 50, 30, 20, 15, 10, 10$$

Looking at these trends, you can see sales have fallen precipitously over the past three to four months. So while the cost per sale for the past ten months is, in fact, $43, the marginal cost per sale for the most recent three-month period has more than quadrupled to $171—which, depending on the business in question, could make the difference between a profit and a loss . . . and at a minimum would provide a very different perspective on the magazine's effectiveness.

Another problem that can sometimes arise occurs in situations where your business requires numerous leads to sell a big-ticket item with a relatively low close rate. In those circumstances, a business can mistake a high number of leads coming in for effectiveness in the form of sales. In these situations, early successes can create false expectations, while an early lack of success can have the opposite effect, even though it may still be the wrong conclusion.

Statistically speaking, assume for a moment that you are trying to pull a golden marble out of a bucket that always contains only one golden marble and 99 white marbles. Your odds of selecting the golden marble are identical on your first and last attempt. If you took 100 turns at the bucket and drew the golden marble once, you might correctly guess that your chances of success were about 1 percent. But if you drew the golden marble after only ten tries, you might be inclined to believe that you could count on a 10 percent hit rate and invest far too much money in whatever tactic you used. Conversely, if the same bucket held 30 golden marbles (the equivalent of a 30 percent close rate) but your first ten draws came up white, you might never use that technique again.

In statistics, this is called the law of small numbers—the bias that influences people's decision making based on a limited number of observations. Unfortunately, in order to avoid this bias, you first need to recognize that it exists and then eliminate it by gleaning enough data from each marketing effort to reach statistically valid conclusions. Unless you have a huge marketing budget, this is often impossible to achieve.

Of course, consultants and agencies use various research tricks to get around these problems, such as conducting primary research. Interviewing end users or buyers who have worked with competing businesses, talking with sales reps or industry experts at trade shows, and digesting industry-specific research may or may not work. Primary research is one tool that can help refocus your marketing if the numerical analysis is not favorable. Your primary research could show, for example, that while you thought you should market exclusively to a younger audience, a middle-aged audience should also have been a target of your marketing efforts.

Underlying all your marketing success, of course, is the efficacy of your marketing message, which I address below.

embrace your story and tell it memorably

What is there about your brand that would make a customer want to do business with you instead of your competitors, of which there are certainly many? A big part of success is that the customer picks you because of your story. If you are looking to duplicate your business, you need to have a compelling story to tell, and you need to tell it in a memorable way.

One way successful brands tell their story is through their brand slogan. Let's look at one of our nation's most iconic brands—Dunkin' Donuts—which has recently been rebranded Dunkin'.

The "America Runs on Dunkin'" slogan adopted in 2006 speaks to us as fast-moving consumers. The story this conjures up is compelling ("We're here for busy people"), logical ("You need coffee and 'fuel' and we'll get it to you quickly"), and emotional ("We're Americans and we're in this together"). Note that the slogan does not even mention coffee or doughnuts, and I suspect that is because it would change the underlying brand story too much. As Dunkin' has evolved into "a beverage-led on-the-go brand," their core story is the same—fast, accessible, reasonably priced bakery items and beverages for busy people. In their own words, it is "part of our guests' everyday routine." Their story and the way they communicate it is why they are consistently a leader in the quick-service restaurant space.

While this is not a how-to chapter about writing your company tag line, consider the emotions conjured up by some of the best-known slogans. The Walmart story has consistently been about selling more for less, and its slogans have reflected this, including "Always Low Prices, Always" and the current "Save Money. Live Better." Consider some of the examples below and what they tell you about the brand's unique story, its emotional appeal to customers, and its implied call to action:

* Papa John's: Better Ingredients, Better Pizza
* Planet Fitness: Judgement Free Zone
* Jimmy John's: Freaky Fast
* Southwest Airlines: "You're Now Free to Move About the Country" and, more recently, "Low Fares, Nothing to Hide"
* Big Blue Swim School: Life's Big Moments Start Here

The goal is to convey that consumers should choose you because in some way you are the best option. Taco Bell has succeeded at that with its "Think Outside the Bun" campaign.

I expect many of you have never heard of McDonald's early competitors Burger Chef, Dee's Drive-In, Sandy's, Red Barn, and Druther's (which began its life as Burger Queen). How about Geri's Hamburgers or Wetson's? But I'll bet you all know about Burger King and Wendy's. Why is it that Burger King has thrived while the others didn't? One reason is that Burger King positioned itself as the "Have It Your Way" burger. When introduced in the early 1970s, this message was compelling ("Fast-food ordering doesn't have to be so strict"), logical ("Why would I buy something that wasn't exactly what I wanted"), and emotional ("You deserve this").

Instead of following a copycat strategy (which almost never works in business expansion), Burger King's message told consumers they had a choice. As a practical matter, McDonald's could not compete with this at the time, because it would have required a reworking of its kitchen operations.

Wendy's, meanwhile, survived by appealing to an older audience through its Clara Peller ads, which told its story through the voice of an octogenarian with an emphasis on good old-fashioned hamburgers.

✳ CAN YOU COPYCAT?

Presumably as you have begun to develop your business concept, your goal is to serve a consumer need that is not currently being met. That's the story you tell.

Copying a business model that a competitor has already successfully built is generally a recipe for disaster, but there are a few instances in which it can succeed. Specifically, it can work when the competitor has failed to take full advantage of their concept's growth potential.

I have heard two specific stories in that regard, which I have generalized here because I have been unable to verify them with the founders of these chains. But in both cases, the stories and the outcomes were relatively similar.

In the first instance, a restaurant owner told me he noticed people sitting on the hood of their car across the street from his one-unit sandwich shop, taking pictures and making notes, so he walked across the street and struck up a conversation with them. When he asked what they were doing, they told him they were admirers of his operation and were thinking of doing something very similar in their home market. Instead of being angry, the owner was

❋ CAN YOU COPYCAT?, CONTINUED

flattered, sat with them for an hour, and told them all about his business. A year later, he read an article about them in Nation's Restaurant News, and today, more than 30 years later, there are 800 locations of their restaurant chain around the U.S.

In another case, the owner of a small restaurant chain in Dallas told me how a young man had offered to work for six months in the kitchen for free because he wanted to start up a similar business himself. The owner agreed, as long as the young man promised not to build any competing locations in the Dallas market during the owner's lifetime—a handshake deal that was apparently honored. Today, the second company has more than 150 locations around the world, while the original owner's family has expanded their chain, last I heard, to four locations.

Then there is Starbucks, which was opened by three young men who met as students at the University of San Francisco, and, as the story goes, they modeled their store and their product line after that of the coffee-roasting pioneer Alfred Peet. The first Peet's Coffee and Tea location, which opened in 1966 in Berkeley, California, was the predecessor to Starbucks, and Peet himself taught the trio about the business and supplied them with roasted coffee beans when they first started out. Peet's has been a hugely successful company in its own right, with more than 200 locations and retail distribution in some 14,000 grocery stores. Still, Starbucks, under the leadership of Howard Schultz, who acquired the company in 1987, has grown to be the undeniable leader in the industry, with nearly 33,000 locations worldwide as of 2021.

Or consider Pizzeria Bianco in Phoenix. Even before Oprah Winfrey's viewers learned about the pizzeria in the U.S. back in 2006, patrons

✽ CAN YOU COPYCAT?, CONTINUED

faced a wait time of up to five hours to get one of its famous pies. But few people in the rest of the country were eating gourmet pizza at the time, and only one chain of any real size, California Pizza Kitchen, was making artisanal pies. Back then, the pizza wars were being fought by chains like Pizza Hut, Domino's, Little Caesars, and Papa John's, and no one expected that to change. But today, chains like MOD Pizza, Blaze Pizza, PizzaRev, 800°, Pieology Pizzeria, The Pizza Press, SPIN! Pizza, 1000 Degrees, zpizza, and others are crowding the build-your-own artisanal pie market. And while none of them are pure "copycat" concepts, they have all learned lessons from the businesses that came before them.

You can run down a long list of industries where an early franchisor has spawned similar successful competitors. Our client Massage Envy was the first to franchise in the therapeutic massage space, but multiple competitors (like Massage Heights, MassageLuXe, Hand and Stone Massage and Facial Spa, and Elements Massage) filled the void when Massage Envy could not expand fast enough. My partner, Dave Hood, is the former president of Auntie Anne's. Again, they were the first into the market to offer hand-rolled pretzels in a small, largely mall-based footprint. But today, there are a number of competitors that have also succeeded in that space. Bagel shops, frozen yogurt, janitorial services, carpet-cleaning companies, lawn-care businesses . . . the list goes on.

So while I will stand by my original statement that "copycats are a recipe for disaster" when it comes to fully saturated markets, when it comes to markets with room for expansion, it can often be a race to the finish line. And for those of you whose goal is something short of market dominance, a copycat formula can be a reasonable strategy.

pick a lane

During my career, I have had the privilege of occasionally collaborating with the renowned retail consulting firm McMillanDoolittle. Any company looking to create systems for growth and duplication in the retail space (or even outside the retail space) should consider their advice to "choose your EST" and focus on that position. Think of your "EST" as the one area where you will position yourself as the market leader.

As I discussed in my first book and as McMillanDoolittle discusses in detail on their website (www.mcmillandoolittle.com), a retailer should position itself by being the "EST" at two—*and no more than two*—of the following if it wants to be successful:

* CheapEST: emphasizing price
* HotEST: emphasizing fashion
* BigEST: emphasizing selection
* QuickEST: emphasizing speed
* EasyEST: emphasizing service

For many entrepreneurs, limiting their company's positioning feels counterintuitive and painful. Why not try to do it all—and have your marketing say as much? Because no company can be all things to all people, and those that try to do it all end up doing at best a mediocre job. They wind up in what McMillanDoolittle calls the "Black Hole," in the middle of their positioning paradigm, as you can see in Figure 5–1 on page 97.

To outlast your competitors over the long run, decide which ESTs will be yours, do the work of researching and testing your decision, and—this is the hard part—stick to it. You will frequently be tempted to go in another direction. If, for example, your business model is to provide the quickest and cheapest pizza, you probably won't be able to provide the largest selection. You cannot be the cheapest *and* the best—the best costs more to produce.

Will you lose a few customers as a result? Absolutely. That is the choice every business owner must make. If you have done your homework before launching and in the early stages to correctly

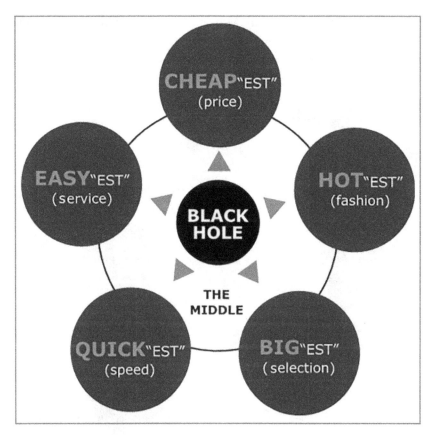

FIGURE 5-1—**THE POSITIONING PARADIGM**

define your position (and you may need outside assistance for this), your chances of long-term success will be better for having intentionally given them up.

When I meet with companies on the verge of expansion, I can often predict early on which ones have defined and are committed to their position—and those with the strongest position are often the ones who are most likely to achieve rapid growth. Some tell me about the times they were tempted to add new distribution avenues, such as wholesale, that might have brought in quick revenue but would have diluted the brand in the long run. They tell me they have turned down offers from buyers in markets that were too far away to ensure consistency of products or service.

As you duplicate your Money Machine, whether through franchising or some other model, and prepare to step back from

❋ CREATE YOUR OWN LEGEND

Many years ago, on one of my first trips to Japan, I was somewhat surprised to see a statue of Colonel Sanders in front of every KFC dressed in a Santa Claus outfit. When I asked my hosts about it, I was told that in Japan, the traditional Christmas meal for many people is fried chicken.

(The Christian population of Japan is minuscule, but Christmas is widely celebrated there as a secular holiday.) As a result, December is by far the biggest month for KFC sales in the country, accounting for almost a third of annual revenue, with sales between December 23 and 25 leading the way. So how did this tradition come about?

Apparently, a savvy KFC store manager heard that Americans traditionally ate turkey for Christmas and came up with the idea that launched the "Kurisumasu ni wa Kentakkii!" (roughly translated, "Kentucky for Christmas") campaign in 1974. It was a huge success, and soon the Japanese began to associate the Colonel with Christmas in America. And this view of KFC, along with the statues of Santa-san, gave it the boost that it needed to launch in the market. After the success of the Christmas campaign, KFC rolled out a new campaign in the mid-1980s where the Colonel is dressed up in samurai garb for Children's Day in May.

The point of this story is to illustrate the way that KFC Japan was able to create a story that has turned into its own "legend." When you are developing your own brand story, think about the legend you are trying to create and what you want to say to your customers.

day-to-day management, you must insist your company sticks with its core values, and make certain those you hire or sell to (in the case of franchising) don't stray from your central positioning.

Once you have determined how you want to position yourself, you need to align your entire business around that position: your employees, operations, marketing, purchasing, merchandising, and customer interaction.

Remember: If you cannot explain your position to your clients, your competitors will be happy to take on this responsibility. And having your competition take charge of your positioning is generally not a formula for success.

a systematic approach to competitive intelligence

One of the greatest things about the internet, and one of its most underused aspects, is its value in conducting competitive research. I remember the method we used to compare pricing across multiple retailers in a particular city when I was a young consultant. You would typically go into competing stores with a list of maybe 20 common branded items and buy them all, checking the prices at each store. When no one was looking, you would try to take photos that would show the store's signage and illustrate merchandising strengths, weaknesses, and techniques. Sometimes you would count traffic or survey customers. The process could take weeks.

Today, you can access all that information from your living room on your cell phone.

The first step, obviously, is identifying your competitors. This is generally as simple as doing keyword searches on the products or services you provide in the markets you serve. Next, you need to decide which factors you want to track from the standpoint of competitive intelligence. Some of the obvious choices would be pricing strategies, product or service offerings, guarantees, promotions, customer reviews, number of locations, and any general news about the company or its owners. Whether you want to record this information in a spreadsheet or some other document, make sure it's searchable so you can use it in your decision making.

From there, the sources of this information are almost endless. Start with the competitor's website and social media pages. And don't just limit yourself to Facebook and Twitter—check Instagram, YouTube, Pinterest, and Foursquare as well. Learn the name of your competition's principals and track them on LinkedIn and Facebook. Then go to the review sites, like Google Reviews (a part of Google Maps these days), Yelp, and any industry-specific review sites such as OpenTable, Tripadvisor, or others, and check for reviews there. Compile all the information you find, being as objective as possible in the process, and include photos wherever applicable.

Lastly, there are subscription services you can use to continue to track your competitors on an ongoing basis. Obviously, Google will give you most of your competitors' plans and activities if you dig deep enough. And setting up Google Alerts will keep you apprised of any news related to companies in your industry sector or any new companies that join the fray.

In addition, for digital marketing in particular, there are a number of free tools such as Google Search Console, Keyword Tool, and AnswerThePublic that can be used for keyword research. Paid tools like SpyFu, Semrush, and Ahrefs can provide you with deeper insight into competitors' SEO and keyword strategies as well. Tools like WhatRunsWhere and iSpionage can help you understand what those competitors are doing from a PPC perspective—from messaging to spend to Google Ads to advertising effectiveness. iSpionage will even provide you with data on when your competitors are doing A/B testing. Others, like Kompyte and Similarweb, provide a broad assortment of analytics in a single package, including analytics of social media metrics. Additional social media measurement tools include Hootsuite, Buffer, and others. And, of course, the list doesn't stop there. Find tools that suit your needs, and continue to use them on a regular basis to ensure your efforts and campaigns are optimized, especially as they compare to what your competitors are doing with their campaigns.

knowing your customer

The goal of any marketing effort is to attract qualified candidates at the top of your sales funnel. But before you start, it's important to know who you are targeting so you can determine how to target them appropriately.

Developing and refining buyer profiles—or, as they're also called, *buyer personas*—is a systematic way to help you clearly identify your target customers and then guide how you effectively communicate with them.

Buyer personas are essentially invented "characters" or profiles of your ideal targeted audiences, which are fleshed out by assigning them a name (we'll use "Calvin Customer" for this example). Start by listing the persona's expected demographics (age, gender, ethnicity, family status, etc.), considering their work experience and job titles, and identifying their values, goals, and primary motivators. Some buyer personas even include a representative photo of the target customer; it can be a stock photo or a picture taken from Google Images to help you visualize who Calvin Customer is.

Developing buyer personas is never a set-it-and-forget-it exercise. Profiles may initially be based on who you think your ideal customers might be, but they can and should be refined over time as you identify common characteristics of your most loyal customers. So Calvin Customer may evolve to become a new persona: Paula Patron, for example. Paula may skew younger or older, and she may have different motivations for considering your brand or buying your products than Calvin does, but it's important to identify and target her as well.

Along those same lines, there's no reason to limit yourself to just one customer profile or buyer persona. Most concepts, across most industries, are likely to have products or solutions that appeal to and serve the needs of different types of customers. Calvin and then Paula may be a solid starting point, but you can expect to add to your collection of buyer personas over time and continue to refine their individual profiles as well.

targeting your customer

Developing a system for generating sales leads in the most cost-effective manner means you must understand exactly who your customers are. Knowing the age, sex, political leanings, and other demographic information of your customers is essential to knowing how you should communicate with them.

Once you know who you are targeting, then you need to decide what to say to your target audience(s). Beyond simply telling them what your product or solution is, think about your brand story, and why it matters to your buyers.

Effective messaging and positioning communicate to a prospective customer what is unique about your brand. Developing relatable, effective messaging and content is the key to building a trusting relationship with your audience. Good messaging should make them feel they have learned something from you, and ideally encourage them to take action.

In addition to conveying the facts about your products or solutions (such as features, pricing, and other details), try to create an emotional connection, so your audience feels good about buying from you. The emotional response consumers have to your product or service often plays a critical part in their buying decision.

An excellent example of emotional advertising is the campaign Dodge created to introduce its retro-designed Challenger in 2010. The campaign was centered on a TV commercial (introduced during the World Cup soccer match between the U.S. and England) showing George Washington leading his troops into battle against the British behind the wheel of a Challenger. Ford had successfully introduced its retro design for the Mustang several years earlier, and Dodge knew consumers would respond well to patriotic messaging combined with America's love for classic cars. And while there were likely other contributing factors, vehicle sales increased by 42 percent in 2010!

Messaging is also not a static element, and while core messaging about your brand, company, and products should be consistent overall, you also need to be prepared to tweak wording based on the marketing tactic or delivery vehicle being used. How you convey features and benefits to buyers will naturally vary based on whether they're being presented in a website or brochure, or if they're being communicated in an email blast with a specific LTO (limited-time offer) or a tweet. Knowing your audience is half the battle, but knowing how to speak to them appropriately based on where they will be most likely to read and learn about you is just as critical.

developing an appropriate marketing budget

Once you know to whom you are marketing and what you're going to say, the next step is to determine how much you want to spend.

One common way to determine your advertising budget is to base it on a percentage of revenue (projected or historical). According to a 2019 article in the *Houston Chronicle*, "The U.S. Small Business Administration recommends spending 7 to 8 percent of your gross revenue for marketing and advertising if you're doing less than $5 million a year in sales and your net profit margin—after all expenses—is in the 10 percent to 12 percent range."

Of course, the percentage of revenue you can reasonably allocate may vary depending on whether you're just starting out, what kind of working capital you have, how competitive your industry or market is, what media you plan to leverage, and other factors. Some companies can get by with word-of-mouth referrals and use only a small percentage of revenue for marketing budgets (1 to 2 percent), while others need to outlay 20 percent to rise above the fray. Overall, though, somewhere around or under the 10 percent mark would generally be considered reasonable as a marketing spend based on revenue.

Another way to set your marketing budget is to look at it as a goal-driven calculation vs. a revenue-driven one. In this case, you should first back out the costs of developing creative materials and any other overhead costs such as salaries, software, etc. To get a true calculation of the effectiveness of your marketing efforts, focus solely on the funds needed for media placements and then use that figure to determine accurate marketing efficiency measurements such as cost per lead and cost per sale (more on this later).

Examine your specific goals, such as how many sales you need to make, or how many customers you are aiming to acquire, or whatever the most appropriate metric would be for your business to reach your financial goals (profitability, growth, maintenance, etc.).

Study historic averages or benchmarks; if you have not yet established a marketing trajectory with sufficient longevity (i.e., a minimum of two to three months, and ideally a full calendar year), look to your competitors' online activities and other media presence to see if you can glean where they are marketing and what they are spending. There are digital/online tools you can use to do competitor marketing sleuthing: some built into Google Ads (such as the Auction Insights report), some via simple Google searches to see where your competitor appears in search engine results, and some via Google Alerts so you are notified when your competitors appear on the internet. There are also a variety of third-party research tools that can help you see what keywords they optimize around, where they are ranked by search engines, and more.

When you have thoroughly researched your market, industry, and competition, you should be able to come up with a reasonable cost-per-sale figure as an initial benchmark or multiplier. Multiply that target cost per sale by the number of sales or customers you plan to acquire over a certain time period (allowing sufficient time for your average sales cycle, whether that's hours, days, or weeks) and determine your marketing budget. For example:

Estimated Cost Per Sale ($500) x 3 Targeted Customers/Week

= $1,500 Needed in Advertising Funds Each Week

x 4 Weeks/Month

= $6,000 Monthly Marketing Budget or

$72,000 Annual Marketing Budget

Then, once your marketing budget is finally set, it's time to look for ways to reduce it. Seek out options to target your ideal customer with a focus on keeping your marketing expenditures under control, such as:

* Maximizing free and low-cost resources, such as referrals, social media posts, etc.
* Geotargeting your marketing efforts whenever possible to avoid spreading your dollars across too wide an area

The overall goal, then, is to make the most of your marketing budget and leverage as much as possible off free or low-cost marketing resources. Let these initiatives run for at least a couple of months and then start measuring your results, as I discuss below.

measurement and refinement

The first rule of evaluating the effectiveness of any business is to track and measure everything, from labor costs and cost of goods to marketing expenditures and results. This is especially important when evaluating the efficacy of your marketing efforts.

In marketing, the rule should be "Measure twice. Then measure again." But when it comes to measuring things, and then the subsequent refining and adjusting based on observed results, don't just focus on what the numbers say about *your own* performance. You need to also leverage competitor benchmarks to ensure you are in line with what other companies are doing, spending, and measuring. There are a wide array of free or low-cost tools that businesses can access to help with this competitive analysis, as we discussed earlier.

Because the digital marketing landscape is constantly evolving, it is a good idea to build into your marketing systems the assistance of outside experts in digital marketing, if you cannot hire in-house staff in this area. This can be accomplished through a retainer engagement or a regular audit of your marketing efforts. For example, a Google PPC review by someone who understands the nuances of that ad engine could uncover that you are bidding against yourself in the Google auction and wasting precious resources.

Beyond a tactical analysis, content strategies—which are often more qualitative than quantitative—can impact performance just as much as the reach and frequency of advertising. Knowing why certain messages perform better than others plays a critical role in determining your marketing effectiveness.

Consider the "Rule of Seven," for example—the idea that a prospect must encounter your marketing message seven times before you can expect them to act. But when does the frequency of your advertising message diminish its effectiveness by burning out your potential customers? At some point, the repetition becomes predictable background noise that fails to attract attention.

A simple way to avoid this type of burnout is to change up the message and the creatives of your online and real-world ads. Consider testing alternative messages and designs with your target audiences. But while A/B testing is a tried-and-true method for optimizing messaging, you should exercise caution when using different messages to avoid brand confusion. The overall presentation of your brand shouldn't stray too far from your core concept and approach—coming out of left field with a campaign that is a total disconnect from how you've previously presented your brand can backfire.

From a marketing perspective, it's also important to optimize the mix of lead generation sources within the confines of your budget, as well as specific media within each lead generation source. You can measure the success of these efforts using cost per lead and cost per sale.

Keep in mind that significantly higher cost-per-lead numbers generally indicate problems such as a poor media mix, inappropriate media selection, incorrect targeting, unexciting message or ad design, or poor timing. A significantly higher cost per sale may indicate a breakdown of the sales process or an offering that is not competitive in the marketplace.

Similarly, significantly lower lead costs can indicate poor-quality leads, which can usually be corrected relatively easily by altering the media, media mix, message, and response format. A significantly lower cost per sale, however, could indicate an overly aggressive sales force or an overall lack of qualification in the sales process.

Thus, the key to successful marketing must always be to *optimize* these key measurements—not always to minimize costs. Use cost per lead and cost per sale as your primary criteria, along with any other metrics (cost per appointment, for example) that are applicable to your business model. Maintain the appropriate media mix within your budget parameters; don't put all your marketing eggs into one media basket. Try to keep a well-balanced set of optimally performing marketing vehicles running at appropriate times, and be cognizant of any seasonality factors.

As your business cycles through the calendar year, and depending on the nature of your business (lawn and pool care, tax services, or holiday decorating, perhaps), you will learn how to adjust your marketing based on seasonal business cycles. The approach is twofold. First, don't overspend on marketing campaigns that are likely to fall flat when consumers are not focused on or in need of your services—especially higher-cost campaigns that require a direct response, such as a magazine ad that invites potential customers to "call today." And second, some out-of-season marketing and special offers can help combat any seasonal downturns in your business. Does your retail business typically slow down after the holiday rush? Does your kids-and-family-focused business see a difference depending on whether kids are in school or on vacation? Then craft and promote a limited-time offer or discount to draw people in during your slower times.

All that said, it's key to maintain a baseline brand presence, especially online, throughout the year. Website optimization, including content posting, for example, is something that can and should be done year-round.

In the next chapter, I will discuss in greater detail how the internet impacts marketing and consumer behavior and share some tips on how to create systems to make sure the internet enhances rather than hurts your business.

competing
with
the
internet

W hen it comes to starting a business, especially one that can scale, there may be no more important exercise than to try to envision what will happen to your market in the future.

We are living in an era of retail revolution. You need only look at the trends over the past ten years to see how dramatically the world is changing in this digital age.

The obvious and most profound change that has occurred in the past 30 years has been the introduction and growth of online shopping. As of 2020, www. eMarketer.com estimates that ecommerce represents some 18 percent of retail sales worldwide—and that number is projected to grow to 22 percent by 2024. And in making these estimates, eMarketer specifically excluded food-service sales, travel, event ticket sales, and online gambling—which accounted for billions more dollars in revenue.

In the U.S., according to eMarketer, ecommerce is slightly less popular, accounting for about 14 percent of retail sales in 2020. Nevertheless, it now boasts a 92.4 percent market penetration rate in the U.S.—so at least nine out of ten U.S. consumers are comfortable with online shopping. And, according to Statista, 75 percent of online shoppers worldwide buy something on the internet at least once a month, if not more often.

What's more, according to *Chain Store Age*, of top U.S. ecommerce companies, Amazon alone accounted for approximately 38 percent of total online retail sales in 2020, with Walmart's 5.8 percent coming in a distant second; eBay was third at 4.5 percent. So if you are planning to start a retail business, your biggest competitor is likely not the store down the street, but the online behemoth with its headquarters in Seattle.

Given that Amazon is now the world's largest internet company, your planning must account not only for where it is today, but also where it will be in the future. Amazon Prime, for example, boasted 200 million members worldwide as of March 2021, who pay an annual fee for expedited delivery. But Amazon Prime is much more than just a delivery option. Prime Music and Prime Video are now dominant players in the home entertainment industry as well. Prime has also launched restaurant delivery services and one-hour delivery in some markets and will sometimes deliver to car trunks, in homes, or inside people's garages. Prime Pantry, another extension of the service, will deliver nonperishable groceries—and Amazon's acquisition of Whole Foods Market in 2017 instantly gave it one of the country's largest brick-and-mortar grocery channels. And that is just one of more than 80 acquisitions by Amazon.

So before getting into any business, an entrepreneur would be well-advised to ask themselves a single question: "Is Amazon coming after me next? And if they are, how can I use service, quality, or a proprietary product to compete with (or leverage off of) them?"

No marketing discussion would be complete without addressing the critical role mobile internet plays in ecommerce—both when it comes to marketing and sales. And, of course, online reviews must be top-of-mind for any business owner, and we'll discuss those below as well, including the systems your business needs to have in place to respond to unfavorable reviews.

the m-commerce effect

The internet intelligence firm eMarketer estimates that in 2021 over 50 percent of retail ecommerce in the United States will be done using a mobile platform—and that number continues to grow. I refer to this as the Mobile Commerce Effect, or M-Commerce Effect.

This trend toward online shopping, especially when combined with the ubiquitous nature of the smartphone, has changed the way consumers shop. It used to be that if you wanted to buy a widget, you went to the nearest widgets store, bought one, and went home. Now if you go into a store and see a widget, your first instinct is probably to pull out your phone and check the prices on that same widget—which can be delivered to you the following day for free (if you are a Prime member). Sometimes you can even get it the same day. Moreover, while Amazon is now collecting sales tax on the products it sells directly (because it has distribution points in almost every state), it does not collect sales tax from its million-plus third-party vendors, who are responsible for more than half the sales on the site.

So as a consumer, you can go into a store, touch and feel and experience the quality of a product, and instantly compare prices at multiple other stores—perhaps having it delivered to your home at no cost other than your Amazon Prime membership, possibly tax free, without having to haul it to your car.

The net impact of the M-Commerce Effect is that almost anything you can buy at retail is forced to compete with what is on the internet. And ultimately, that tends to commoditize any product that is not entirely proprietary to you. Prices and margins continue to be squeezed as retailers are forced to compete with the buying power of a $1.5 trillion company.

The bottom line is that you cannot compete on price, so your selling proposition must be based on something else. What is left? A store can be a convenient place to consider the many options provided in a particular type of product—but that requires stocking a large selection of competitively priced merchandise. Likewise, it can give the customer an opportunity to access the shopkeeper's expertise, but again, there is nothing to prevent them from doing this and then buying online. A physical location provides a convenient place to pick up and return merchandise—but given same-day delivery services, you could argue that both pickup (in this case, delivery) and return (going back to the post office) are often more convenient with online shopping.

So as a potential store owner looking to develop a scalable model for growth, you will need to build in another reason for initial and ongoing purchases. Perhaps you can assemble a wonderful selection of merchandise by developing a system around the purchasing function. Perhaps you can appeal to a specific consumer by developing systems for providing selection around products for those who are hard to shop for (small- or large-sized clothing, for example) or for those who feel a need to try before they buy. Companies like Nordstrom, The Ritz-Carlton, and Disney have made a name for themselves by systematizing a high level of customer service. Golf and bicycle retailers, among others, have carved out specialized niches by systematizing the process of product customization. Fun and engaging shopping experiences that sometimes use technology in the form of touch-screen enhanced mirrors and other tools can be systematized to create a buzz that will keep customers returning while bringing in new business.

But whatever you do, you need to account for the M-Commerce Effect when you are designing a business for growth.

harness the power of reviews

Whether you are selling a product or a service, social media impacts your business. And while this makes sense intuitively, one need look no further than Amazon's own numbers to confirm the importance of having a good online reputation. According to a 2018 Feedvisor study, almost 90 percent of Amazon users refuse to purchase any product that has fewer than three stars.

But you don't need statistics to understand the power of a referral. Think about your own buying behavior. For those who can remember times before the internet (those few remaining dinosaurs among us), when you were making a purchasing decision of any magnitude, the first thing you did was ask someone's advice. Your garage door broke? Ask your neighbors for recommendations. Need to start a diet? Ask your newly thin friends how they lost the weight. Need a good recipe? Call your mom. Need a divorce? Talk to someone who got one.

Today, though, if you want an "expert" opinion, you go to Google and check how many stars a company has, or go to Amazon and read product reviews. You go to Tripadvisor or Manta or Foursquare or Angi, formerly Angie's List, to get the opinions of others who might be in a similar situation. And there are other, more controversial sites, like Yelp, that have a reputation for highlighting negative reviews to strong-arm companies into advertising with them.

Want to know what other "influencers" think? Go to Facebook and see what your "friends" are saying. Or check out Instagram or YouTube or Twitter or Pinterest.

Your business's reputation is now the sum total of your history, captured online, once and forever. Your online reviews on social media and review sites may never be taken down. And, of course, this has especially significant implications for a startup business: You're much more likely to stub your toe when you first open your doors than later on when you've refined your systems. But when people read reviews from five years ago, it is unlikely they will take that into account.

Moreover, unscrupulous competitors can easily post false but anonymous reviews that could be damaging to your reputation. And there are people who are paid to endorse products and businesses as social media influencers—a very few of them earning literally millions of dollars a year. Both Kylie and Kendall Jenner of the Kardashian family, for example, are rumored to get paid $400,000 per sponsored post, while their sister Kim Kardashian West is said to get $500,000 to share a post with the more than 100 million followers who might care what she has to say. By contrast, older sister Kourtney makes a mere $250,000 per post—making it a trifle harder for her to put bread on the table.

Because the vast majority of new business owners cannot afford to hire the Kardashians to promote their product or service, you will almost certainly be relying on your own clients and customers to do that on your behalf. But you should bear in mind that many people who post reviews are often either disgruntled customers or, worse still, unscrupulous competitors hiding behind the shield of anonymity. Moreover, some of the more popular review sites have rigged their processes in a manner that disproportionately weights unfavorable reviews while, in some instances, not even showing favorable reviews.

Assuming that you will not perfectly execute every day forever, your online reputation management system will need at least three separate components:

1. A system for addressing customer/client concerns before they escalate to the point at which your company ends up a target of online vitriol

2. A system for identifying and responding to negative reviews quickly and in a way that will not look defensive, but will instead project an image of caring responsiveness and professionalism

3. A system for proactively encouraging positive reviews from your customers/clients

There are, of course, online reputation management companies that make a living dealing with these issues. For a fee, these companies might start by developing a survey tool that would be sent to your customers at the end of your engagement to ask for a rating. If the customer gave you a four- or five-star rating, they would automatically be redirected to links that would ask them to write a review—thus encouraging positive reviews. On the other hand, if a customer rated the experience at three stars or lower, they would be redirected to someone who could address the problem before the customer left a negative review. And while some review sites have rules governing this practice, such a system can take care of two of the three elements listed above.

These online reputation management companies will often go a step further, monitoring all review sites and providing automated "thank you" replies to positive reviews that slip past their systems or automated "we would like to contact you to resolve the issue" emails for reviews that are less than stellar. Some of these companies will help you get negative reviews removed if they violate the site's terms of service. Given that these professionals can be relatively affordable, this might be the easiest solution.

But if your digital footprint (or your budget) is too small for professionals, these three steps should comprise *your* system for managing your online reputation. Let's explore what that can look like next.

surviving a reviewer attack

You could be providing excellent customer service, delivering a top-notch product, and acting as a recognized leader in your space when—SURPRISE—a scathing online review appears. If your monitoring systems are in place, you should learn about it very soon after it is posted, and this early notice is the key to survival. In the worst-case scenario, you find out about it when a potential customer brings it to your attention.

You can probably name people in your personal life who look for opportunities to complain. But unlike the obnoxious uncle whose audience is limited to those at the Thanksgiving dinner table, today's business complainers can literally shout their insults to a worldwide audience. To make matters worse, opinions voiced online live on forever in retweets, screen captures, and video footage.

If these attacks come from legitimate customers whom you can identify, they are actually much easier to address (more on that below). Unfortunately, they often come from a competitor, who can disparage your business in an anonymous review. This type of attack can create a lot of extra work and angst for your business, but how you respond can also help you rise above it all. You can see some examples in Figure 6–1 on page 117.

Michelle Obama is known for the phrase "When they go low, we go high." Your strategy in surviving an attack could wisely follow that advice.

As salespeople for their ideas, politicians face negativity from many different angles—from town halls, rallies, the press, and certainly social media, but the ones who thrive do not get rattled by the negativity because they are confident in their offering, buoyed by their successes, and know how to speak to their core audience. As a business owner, surviving online attacks will require you to have the focus and poise of a politician.

I hope that this discussion does not send you cowering to a corner and afraid to boost your online footprint. Or, worse yet, running to downplay your social media presence. That is absolutely not my advice. It is absolutely essential to develop and promote your business's online presence, especially with the help of "free" social media channels. You need to encourage your customers and fans to review your business, write testimonials about their experiences, and confidently share their comments. To do that, you need two systems: one to encourage positive reviews and one to promptly deal with negative reviews when they come your way.

In addition to monitoring your social media and review sites such as Yelp, you should take advantage of other "positive" opportunities

---

Attack Example (likely not from a customer)

Whatever you do, don't hire Chicago's Finest Carpet Cleaners. This company is terrible. Their employees brought buckets of dirty water into my house and the carpets smelled like mold when they were done. A few of my neighbors used them too and have the same complaints.

—Peter, Springfield, IL

Response

Dear Peter, You must have a different company in mind. Chicago's Finest Carpet Cleaners uses a waterless cleaning process. We also do not service clients in Springfield, Illinois. Please feel free to call us at xxx-xxx-xxxx and perhaps we can help clear up any confusion. We are also happy to help you find a carpet-cleaning business in your area.

Attack #2

That's BS. I am sure I have the facts right. You are just trying to cover up for your terrible company.

Response

Dear Peter, Our service area and cleaning methods are clearly listed on our website [include link to website and area served page]. As noted above, we would be happy to speak with you and help you find a reputable carpet cleaner in your area that is certified by the IICRC as we are.

FIGURE 6–1—**ATTACK EXAMPLES**

for exposure. For example, one of our former clients, ShelfGenie, boasts about its participation in the National Association of Professional Organizers and the "Best Home Organizing" awards it has received from that organization. Perhaps you operate in an industry that produces newsletters, blogs, trade shows, and podcasts. Contributing authentic (meaning not self-promotional) content through these avenues can boost your company's exposure and increase your credibility. Reposting such content on your website and social media channels boosts your credibility as well.

Look for industry accreditations and awards, as these can help boost credibility and drown out the naysayers. For example, The Joint Commission, which accredits and sets standards for health-care organizations, offers a Gold Seal of Approval in the health-care industry—which BrightStar Care posts proudly on their website. Whatever that Seal of Approval is in your industry, strive to attain it and, as allowed, post it on your website and marketing materials.

Look for public relations opportunities as well (either in-house or through an outside firm). Public relations can be a credibility builder, as can media mentions of your brand, founders, or key management personnel.

And, of course, have a system in place to encourage your customers to write reviews on the sites you believe drive the most business.

How do you go about determining that? Start by learning how your customers found you, which is often as simple as asking them "How did you hear about us?" I am constantly dumbfounded at the number of business owners who lack basic curiosity about what makes their business work. Beyond that, ask if they read any reviews of your company. Maybe they saw you on OpenTable or Angi or Yelp or some other review site. It would be a little over the top to ask them to review you on each of these sites, so pin down which one is most important to your audience.

Then ask for reviews! It is amazing how much you can accomplish sometimes just by asking. Train your people to ask as well. But be aware of appropriateness and timing. If you own a restaurant and you just made a customer wait an hour for their reservation, asking for a review will just make the situation worse. But if a couple just had a wonderful meal and you served them a complimentary dessert—that's when you ask for a favor. Circumstances matter . . . but you can have a system in place that creates the appropriate circumstance.

How you ask also matters. If the person who has just done a great job painting your garage tells you they get evaluated based on how many positive reviews they receive and that they are three reviews short of earning their bonus, and then says "I know it is a lot to ask, but would you do me this favor?" chances are you'll take a few minutes out of your day to write three or four sentences for them. Of course, the implication here is that you have a system in place that provides an incentive for your employees to get good reviews, requires a sign-off on the job or some other reason to put them in front of the customer at a time when they can ask, and trains them how to ask.

And over time, those positive reviews add up. In fact, a lot of companies out there have developed systems that are even more powerful. One repair company I hired told me they would send me a $50 refund if I gave them a positive review on Yelp—which was more than enough incentive for me to spend ten minutes online. And sure enough, I got a nice crisp $50 bill in the mail the following week. Was that a little over the line? Maybe. But they had done a nice job, and I would have given them a good review, had I taken the time to do it—so they were really just paying for my time. So it was easy enough to justify to my reptile brain.

Whatever you do, get your customers invested in your success. If you have 100 great reviews and two negative ones, the voices of the positive reviewers will drown out those of the negative reviewers very quickly.

Another thing you should do is create business pages for the various social media platforms to help manage your online reputation and increase brand awareness while creating a gateway for inbound links and visits to your website—thereby improving the results of your SEO efforts.

The rule of thumb on social media, of course, is "out of sight, out of mind." So you will need to continuously boost visibility and engage your audience with quality content to remain relevant. Social media users have gone far beyond the younger, more internet-savvy users to include older demographics, professionals, and others who use the internet to network and stay informed. Encourage and respond to positive reviews on social media sites, and in the long run, if you are providing good customer service, these will outweigh the bad.

One more thing about social media as it reflects on your marketing budget: Though these sites are typically free of charge to use, they are not truly "free" when you factor in the hours required to monitor and update content on these sites or manage paid keyword advertising.

There are a number of tools available to systematize your social listening, such as Google Alerts, Sprout Social, Synthesio, and Brandwatch. Having an online reputation strategy in place for sourcing and managing online reviews will also help with search rankings. Authority and trustworthiness are a strong indication of your business's credibility—especially when it comes from customers rather than from you. (Review content also generally contains keyword/service-based mentions.)

A response to a negative attack needs to be swift, genuine, and handled with integrity. For a mature, well-funded business, this can be handled by a trusted PR firm. But for many small businesses, the founders must also assume this role.

Just about every marketing expert will tell you that speed is of the essence in replying to a negative post. When you first start, you may only be able to respond within 24 hours, but long-term, your goal is to reply to most posts even faster—generally within a few hours. As your business grows, you may need to use a software program for autoreplies, but these are only recommended for numerous repetitive reviews and comments (e.g., "We apologize for the delay in your pizza delivery. The storms in Dallas are slowing us down a bit. Know that your pizza will be delivered hot and fresh just as soon as we can safely get to you"). If you were to use one of these autoresponders, your system would have to alert you to posts that required a more personalized response. Most small businesses should provide custom replies.

Respond quickly, but don't prioritize speed over thoughtfulness. Even in the smallest companies, it's a good idea to run your response past a trusted advisor or two for a quick check on tone and content. Remember, you're not just speaking to one unhappy customer—you're speaking to every potential customer who reads your response. So try not to let your emotions or the heat of the moment get the better of you—a defensive or argumentative response will not serve your purposes. And because many online responses stay "live" indefinitely, consider what your words will look like years from now. In 2024, a "Covid-19" excuse for missing an important delivery window might not seem as reasonable as it did in spring 2020.

If your response may have legal implications, definitely get your attorney involved. Also keep in mind that although the client can freely post about you online, confidentiality clauses of your client agreement or privacy laws like HIPAA may curtail your response. In these situations, it might be best to reply with something like "Because we value your confidentiality, we think your concerns can best be addressed offline. Please contact us at xyz@xyz.com and we will be happy to address all your concerns."

Keep in mind that sometimes people just want to be heard. If they are truly unhappy with the service you have provided, they have every right to express that feeling. The best-case scenario would be to get them on the phone and really listen to their concerns. Your initial public reply could be something as simple as "Our clients' satisfaction is very important to us and we want to address it as quickly as possible. Please contact us at . . ."

If they do call, let them retell their experience to you without interruption, and when they have finished, ask if there is anything else they think you should know. At the end of the day, you want to provide the best service and product possible. Tell them that, and thank them for bringing the matter to your attention. Then do what you can to try to solve their issue. Be authentic throughout the process. If you really have made a mistake, admit it. If you can turn the negative reviewer into a brand fan after the encounter, it could result in another, more positive post. While it is easy to hurl negativity from behind a computer screen, in a one-on-one conversation, people are generally much more reasonable, especially if they feel they are being heard. They may even take the review down (if allowed by the platform) or add a retraction relating the

Attack Example

Bob's Tile Installation promised us that we would be able to use our new shower the same day they installed the tile. Then when their installer finished, he told us we could not use it for 48 hours. These guys are liars and misled us from day one. I would never do business with them again.

Response Example

Dear customer: Thank you for hiring Bob's Tile Installation for your recent bathroom renovation. We understand that you were probably anxious to enjoy your new shower. All of our staff is highly experienced in tile installation and routinely informs our customers of the required waiting period before using a newly tiled shower. This is so important to the long-term performance of your tile that we even include this information on our website (link) and on all of our customer order forms. We hope you will enjoy your bathroom renovation for years to come.

FIGURE 6–2—BOB'S TILE ATTACK EXAMPLE

positive experience they had with your company once they voiced their concerns.

Again, here is where a system comes into play. Before you engage with the customer, you should have an idea of the value you place on a positive review. Knowing that will give you some guidelines as to how far you should go (or to what extent you should empower your people to go) when responding to a negative review.

Reacting authentically and with integrity does not mean that you always have to be apologetic. If your company or your actions are being misrepresented, you have every right to set things straight and tell your side of the story. See another attack example in Figure 6–2 above.

creating your fortress strategy

In developing your business model, one of the key points to remember is that no matter how innovative your idea is, you will

✳ USE THE INTERNET TO YOUR ADVANTAGE

While this chapter has spent a good deal of time talking about how online retailers and social media channels have made entrepreneurs' lives more difficult, the internet can be your best friend as well—even if you are not aiming to found a tech startup and become a billionaire overnight.

First, the internet allows a small business to sell its goods and services around the world by providing you literally with global reach. Unless you happen to be working out of Crimea, Cuba, Iran, North Korea, Sudan, or Syria, you can set up a free Google Ads account. And your pay-per-click ad running on Google will appear in more than 100 countries (although some may censor your content).

Because you can set whatever Google Ads budget you like, you can become a global purveyor of goods and services overnight with just a website and a credit card. And while you will be competing with companies from around the world, you have an opportunity to reach customers that was never possible before.

The story of the iFranchise Group is perhaps of interest here. The iFranchise Group, which is today the world's premier franchise consulting firm, was founded in my spare bedroom on September 1, 1998. A year later, we had a website (an awful thing I created myself) and began advertising online. By 2001, we had signed our first international client—a sandwich shop in Saudi Arabia named Kudu, which today has some 300 locations in that country.

Could we have signed that client before the internet? Frankly, there would have been no chance.

✳ USE THE INTERNET TO YOUR ADVANTAGE, CONTINUED

As an aside, I like to mention that three days after we officially opened for business in my bedroom, another company whose success was tied to the internet was founded in a garage in Menlo Park, California. While we outearned them for the first three years, that startup (Google, if you haven't already guessed) has since somewhat surpassed us in revenue and profitability. I like telling folks that we outearned Google by $15 million in 2000—although I must admit that Google had losses of $14.6 million that year.

Likewise, while some politicians decry how Amazon puts thousands of companies out of business (without mentioning how they have improved the shopping experience while reducing prices), many other companies can make a living selling their products on Amazon, eBay, Shopify, and other online retailers. These online platforms provide sellers with instant access to literally millions of potential customers. Places like Amazon can handle all the fulfillment for you, including packaging and shipping. And while they take a fee for both listings and sales, those fees are often in the range of 10 percent to 15 percent of the selling price. And considering that you pay no rent for your online store and that they handle the advertising that draws eyeballs to their store, those fees are in line with (or lower than) what you would pay for rent and advertising in a brick-and-mortar store.

eventually have competitors. These come in two different types: those that try to knock off your business model and those that try to migrate their business model closer to yours.

There are numerous examples of this from the world of franchising. Think about some of the frozen yogurt businesses that have grown over the past 20 years. Pinkberry. Menchie's. Red

Mango. Orange Leaf. sweetFrog. Yogurtland. U-Swirl. Golden Spoon. TCBY. Yogen Früz. Each of these franchisors has more than 100 locations. Each of them sells frozen yogurt (often self-serve) with a variety of toppings, with charges based on weight. The flavors and toppings are largely the same.

The earliest entrants into the market—companies like Yogen Früz and TCBY—have had the most success, having opened between 500 and 1,200 locations. But even newer market entrants, like 16 Handles, FroyoWorld, Yogurt Mountain, You Say When Yogurt, Forever Yogurt, CherryBerry, and FroZenYo, have had success through franchising.

But frozen yogurt, as a category, has very low barriers to entry. The machines that are used to dispense the yogurt are not proprietary. A single refurbished machine with a minimal footprint costs less than $4,000, with top-of-the-line new equipment going for less than $13,000. And the newest technology allows a single dispenser to change between eight flavors at the push of a button. Numerous vendors can provide you with yogurt mix (or soft-serve ice cream, for that matter) in a variety of flavors, and many of them would be happy to develop custom formulations for you once you reach a certain size. Add a point-of-service system, some signage, a few tables and chairs, and a toppings bar, and you're in business. In fact, you could open most franchises in this space for between $200,000 and $400,000.

Moreover, because of this ease of entry, the market for frozen yogurt is also vulnerable to encroachment from players in related industries. Cold Stone Creamery, for example, now offers frozen yogurt on its menu. And if McDonald's decided to shift from soft-serve ice cream to frozen yogurt in their stores, they would instantly become the dominant frozen yogurt purveyor. (In fact, when McDonald's introduced Chicken McNuggets worldwide in 1983, they became the world's second-largest chicken purveyor overnight.)

Remember, though, that there are many very successful companies in the frozen yogurt industry. So the world can support businesses despite low barriers to entry that lead to competition. But if these low barriers are a factor for your business, ask yourself how you will compete.

Auntie Anne's, for example, used their site location strategy to compete in a market with relatively low barriers to entry. They made sure to secure the best locations in top malls by developing a highly experienced in-house leasing team. Once mall developers began leasing space to a second pretzel business, Auntie Anne's created a kiosk program that allowed them to open a second store within malls at a much lower cost point. In many cases, this permitted Auntie Anne's to retain their position as the only pretzel retailer in the mall.

Ben & Jerry's has succeeded with their dipping stores largely through innovative marketing campaigns and the creation of proprietary ice cream flavors.

In the pizza space, there are dozens of different players, including local franchisors, that compete in local markets using what we call a "Fortress Strategy." This is the strategy used by a smaller company to go head-to-head with larger national players by focusing all their efforts in a single, smaller market. So while pizza giants like Domino's, Little Caesars, Pizza Hut, and Papa John's dominate the national landscape, franchisors like Aurelio's, Giordano's, Rosati's, and Sarpino's have made their mark by focusing on the Chicago market and building a virtual "fortress" there before expanding outside that area. Jet's Pizza adopted the same strategy in Detroit, and Famous Famiglia did the same in New York.

Likewise, several of the frozen yogurt companies above have created virtual fortresses in smaller local markets. So while they do not dominate the national market, they may have the most prominent brand in a local market. Depending on your goals, this type of strategy can be very effective (and often leads to acquisition by players who feel it is easier to buy you than try to beat you in your local market).

One of the greatest advantages of online advertising is its ability to target with even greater specificity, especially in terms of geotargeting. If you are looking to only expand locally, there's an advertising "select" for that. If you decide five years from now you want to target the same consumer base in a new geographic market, your Multiplier Model will already be established for local marketing—just swap out the market "selects" and you're on your way. With this system in place, you won't have to build a marketing plan from the ground up.

Marketing brings the customer to you. Now let's talk about sales.

selling

In my business life, I often meet entrepreneurs who are "born salespeople" and are very comfortable with the sales process. But one of the things I have always found interesting is the number of people in business who seem to have an aversion to sales.

These people are often extremely focused on the operations side of the business and usually believe that old adage that "If you build a better mousetrap, the world will beat a path to your door."

And again, this chapter is not about how to sell, although we will certainly discuss some of the basics. It is about how to create sales systems.

Unless you are one of those rare people who are naturally gifted at sales, you need a system in place to help you sell. And, more important, if you plan to expand your business, you need that system because the people who will be operating those new locations may not have the same sales gifts you possess.

This chapter will examine both the sales systems that are relatively easy to develop and test and those that are more complex. No matter what you are selling, sales impacts every department in your organization. We'll discuss the importance of knowing your customer and planning the customer experience, the steps involved in the sale, and, of course, the importance of measuring your results.

grow or die

Often, entrepreneurs go into business assuming they can build a nice business model, sit back, and collect the cash, allowing the systems they have arduously built to do the work while they enjoy the fruits of their labor.

But this assumption is dead wrong!

Imagine you have built your Money Machine to a point where it is consistently churning out profits. You have more than enough income to meet your needs and you don't have to work that hard for the Money Machine to keep printing money.

While there's nothing wrong with enjoying the results of your hard work, you need to realize what will happen in the long run if you do not grow your business. Over time, your labor costs will increase, thanks to annual cost-of-living or merit raises. Your rents will go up every year, as your landlord will have built cost-of-living increases into your lease. Insurance costs seem to go up every year, and government regulations may also increase. Shipping and advertising costs will likely rise. The costs of whatever raw materials you use in the production process (the food you prepare in your restaurant, the goods you sell in your retail shop, or some component you need in your service-based business) will also rise.

At the same time, there is more pricing pressure in the marketplace than ever before. The internet has turned once price-stable goods into competitively shopped commodities, based on price and the number of stars they get in their online reviews. And with more and more businesses proliferating, there are likely to be more people trying to knock off your product or service or otherwise compete with you, making it more difficult to raise your prices.

The net result is higher costs without a complementary increase in your pricing, shrinking your margins. And what was once a nice, profitable business will almost certainly become less and less so—even if you keep the same number of clients.

While your primary tool for avoiding margin compression is to continue to grow your revenue, the other alternative is to reduce costs. We often get clients who, among other reasons, would like to franchise to realize certain economies of scale.

The obvious example involves purchasing economies. The larger you grow, the more likely it is you can negotiate better deals with your vendors, but that partly depends on the nature of the product you are buying. If there are no ready alternatives to the product you are purchasing, your vendor will be less likely to negotiate. And, of course, the amount of margin your vendor enjoys (which is often a result of increased competition and substitute products) will also impact your negotiating range.

Other purchases, such as advertising, may also be subject to negotiation. But even if not as you grow, advertising as a percentage of revenue may drop in larger markets, because often a smaller business with less market coverage may be less effective in their advertising purchases.

The bottom line is that if you are not growing your revenue on a regular basis, your business is likely dying a slow (or even a fast) death. You must continue to innovate and grow, or the business will die.

do you want fries with that?

If you have ever eaten at McDonald's, or many of the other fast-food restaurants that have taken a cue from their best practices, you have certainly heard this iconic catchphrase before. I mention it here because the needs for salespeople and sales systems will vary from business to business. Every business relies on sales, and every business needs sales systems. But the complexity of those sales systems will vary considerably based on what the customer is purchasing and who that customer is.

Take Auntie Anne's as an example. While I expect there are occasionally consumers who leave home expressly to buy a pretzel, the vast majority of the purchases at their stores were likely unplanned. These impulse purchases did not require a sales effort in most cases, other than keeping the store clean, the product well-merchandised, and the aroma of fresh-baked pretzels constantly wafting out to draw in buyers.

Of course, once the customer has made their way to the front of the line, there are some sales efforts that take place. The store clerk should do some suggestive upselling: "Would you like some honey mustard dip with your pretzel?" "Can I get you one of our original lemonades with that?" "Would you like a large or an extra-large?"

So if your business has a similarly low level of sales complexity, you should walk through the sales process as a consumer would and think about all the options for add-on sales. In what ways could you or your team best encourage those sales? Are there certain questions, like the "fries question," that you should be training each of your customer-facing employees to ask reflexively as they take orders? If so, what is the best way to ask the question in order to optimize sales and margin? If there are two or more such questions relative to add-on sales, when do you ask for each add-on sale, how do you ask the questions, and in what order? And what are the trigger points your team should watch for at question one to let them know they should abandon further upselling efforts?

If you move out of a fast-food environment into something along the lines of a full-service restaurant, the opportunities for sales begin to multiply, but the process and the rules remain much the same. A server might be trained to offer the option of adding a protein to a pasta dish or a salad, for example. But the way in which it was offered would be almost as important as making the offer itself. Saying "Would you like a protein with that?" sounds wholly unappealing and invites a reply of "No." Asking instead "Would you prefer shrimp or chicken with that?" invites a specific response, sounds more appetizing, and stays away from the lower-margin steak salad on your menu.

Sales systems such as these are relatively simple to develop and test. Simply measure your average ticket and margin before and after implementing the system to determine its effectiveness, and you can get an approximation of the value of adding your "fries question." After rolling it out, you can continue to run a version of A/B testing to optimize your process by doing a before-and-after test of a new or tweaked version of those questions (or entirely new questions).

But always remember that you need to interpret the results through the lens of their statistical reliability. Small sample sizes with relatively small impacts on revenue and assumed margin can easily be a meaningless statistical anomaly. So collect enough data that you can feel comfortable with your findings. And remember that doing these tests as before-and-after tests necessarily creates bias, as you will be measuring different periods of time over which consumer buying behavior may have changed. While a less statistically biased approach might be to implement different systems on randomized on-off days, that is largely impractical for a small business.

As you go deeper into this chapter, we will be dealing with more complex sales systems that are not a part of impulse purchasing behavior. So for those readers whose business ventures are strictly impulse oriented, the remainder of this chapter will have somewhat less relevance.

we are all in the business of sales

If you are an entrepreneur, you are in the business of sales. Maybe people come to you because of your great reputation, but somewhere along the line, a sale needs to be made. And if you are doing a decent job of it, you need to ask for the order.

As we have seen, a sales system can be as easy as a cashier saying "Would you like fries with that?" or "Would you like the value meal?" or "Would you like to try our new special today?" But while those questions all seem extremely simple, a good deal of thought and training went into not only the exact wording of each question, but also the nature of the upsell offer that was being made. For example, in the fast-food business, the upsell offers that are made often involve items with relatively high margins—things like French fries and fountain drinks.

Virtually everyone in your business plays some form of sales role. Your HR person sells potential employees on what a great company you have to work for. Your receptionist sells people on how professional you are. Your production crew sells people on how efficient you are by their very appearance.

So be sure everyone in your organization knows two things. First, they are in the business of sales. And second, be sure they know what they are selling and how.

Perhaps at the local level, building that better mousetrap is enough of a sales pitch. Some entrepreneurs can convince people through sheer force of will—or by the lack of competition in their local market—that their product or service is superior and manage to build a local following.

Other times, people who believe they don't have much in the way of sales skills actually do have a gift for sales. But for some reason, they believe that sales is beneath them or think it is somehow an inglorious profession, the territory of used car salespeople who sell an inferior product at an inflated price.

But when you are building a business designed to grow, sales should start with the premise that you have a product or service that serves a need and provides real value. Moreover, as a salesperson (or anyone working for your business), one would hope that you come to the table truly believing in your product or service. And finally, when looking at your customer, remember that if your marketing has been honest and successful, they have come to you because they *want* to buy. So it is your job as a business owner to convey your product's value proposition to them in a systematic manner. Let's dig into how you can do that.

the four pillars of sales growth

There are, in essence, four ways to increase your revenue for your Money Machine:

1. Sell more products or services
2. Sell your existing products more frequently
3. Increase prices
4. Find more customers

Selling more products or services essentially involves expanding your product line. This may involve developing an "add-on" product that can be sold with your primary product, such as the soft drinks and fries that are sold at the typical burger joint. If there is a synergistic product or service that you are not yet selling, ask yourself what you would need to do to add it and how that might impact your brand image.

On a related note, you could also add nonsynergistic items to your product or service line. In this case, think of the salads that are sold at burger restaurants. In most cases the person who is buying the salad does not want a burger, but perhaps they stopped in because they knew you make a good salad as well.

Or perhaps the salad was ordered by someone who did not want to come to your burger joint at all, but they came because their three friends were going. If you did not have that salad on your menu, it's possible your salad customer would have talked their friends into going to a different restaurant. We call that the veto power. A single veto on your menu, and suddenly you lose four sales instead of one. Remove the veto, and you gain those four sales.

Lastly, you can expand your product or service offering in a way that alters the concept itself. Think of what happens when a burger joint adds a series of breakfast items to their menu. By adding a new daypart, they have expanded the nature of the restaurant's concept to a breakfast and lunch operation.

Your second method of increasing sales is to increase the frequency with which someone purchases your services. Part of the genius behind the membership-based massage model is that it took an infrequent purchase and turned it into a monthly obligation by providing one "free" massage in return for the discounted membership. Another way businesses have increased frequency is by increasing brand loyalty using things like "frequent flier" programs to encourage customers to concentrate their spending with a single airline (or hotel, etc.).

Your third option for increasing revenue can be somewhat riskier—increasing your prices. The laws of supply and demand essentially say that for any product with a ready substitute, increases in price will usually result in decreases in demand. And while there are some products and services where demand is relatively inelastic, price increases can have negative consequences if you spend too much time believing your own press clippings.

Finally, you can increase your sales base by finding more customers. At the unit level, that means you want to find ways to market your products or services to people who are not currently your buyers. A restaurant offering a delivery service might attract people who do not like to eat out (especially in the post-Covid-19 era). Referral programs might help you spread the word about your product and service; an alternative advertising or marketing vehicle might do the trick as well. Imagine, if you will, a business that has been around for years but has never actively participated in online marketing or social media. They could easily find their way in front of a customer base that never knew they existed before.

So one of the keys to sustainable growth is to institutionalize and systematize your quest to conquer each of these sales growth areas so that unit level performance can continue to deliver (or improve) your revenue. These four pillars should be ingrained in the mind of every person in your organization—especially at the management level.

annuity building

When developing your business model, one of the questions you should ask yourself is the degree to which it can provide you with repeat business. One of the great downsides to the franchise consulting business, for example, is that once you have taught someone how to be a great franchisor, they don't need to learn it a second time. There is a constant need to find additional services I can provide to my clients, so they get ongoing value.

If my firm teaches our clients how to do something, then I have in essence made my firm dispensable going forward. If, on the other hand, I have given them something of value but haven't provided the learning I promised, I have failed in my value proposition. So as a consultant, I must find ways to monetize the implementation of my advice. This led to the genesis of TopFire Media, a lead generation firm for franchisors. After all, every franchisor is always looking for leads, and the generation of leads for one franchisor does not create conflicts with another franchisor.

At the other end of the spectrum, the franchise business model itself is the epitome of a business that thrives based on the principle of building an annuity. When a franchisor awards a franchise, they anticipate that they will receive a royalty on that franchise for years, and often decades, to come. Every week (or sometimes every month) their franchisees will write a check for a small portion of their revenue in return for their use of the franchisor's name and system of operations. And it is the franchisor's job to ensure that the name continues to have value by setting and enforcing brand standards.

Likewise, when you build and systematize your business, whether or not you choose to actually franchise, your goal should be to create predictable repeat revenue—essentially virtual annuity revenue streams. And the easiest sale to make is the one you only have to make once—but the customer keeps buying again and again.

Think of the bills you pay every month like clockwork. Perhaps you use a home security service. Unless you move or need to cut corners due to a loss of income, it's likely you will pay that bill every month for years—probably for as long as you live in the home. Likewise, your monthly cable (or satellite) bill is likely to get paid for years at a time with little thought given to dropping the service. Your cell phone bill, with its attached wireless plan, is another bill that might as well be on autopay. And, of course, there are the general utility bills—electricity, water, sewer—that you have little choice but to pay.

Businesses that have this type of annuity built into their model have multiple advantages. Not only do they have predictable revenue streams, but they are thus freed up to focus on new customer acquisition—knowing that each such purchase acts like an annuity for their firm.

While it is difficult to create a business model with that level of consistency, the best businesses will always do whatever they can to encourage loyalty and repeat business among their customers.

When it comes to creating repeat business, look at what major companies have done with loyalty programs. Airlines lock in their most valued frequent travelers with reward programs that provide free trips, seat upgrades, early boarding, and other perks that often prevent buyers from shopping for the most competitive rate or the most convenient schedule. Hotels have instituted frequent guest programs that offer similar benefits. At a more local level, grocery stores, restaurant chains, barbers, and others offer loyalty programs with discounts or other rewards in an effort to increase brand loyalty.

Similarly, when creating your business model, ask yourself why your customers will continue to come back to you time and time again.

In some businesses, there is a natural cycle to the business model. Grass keeps growing, and a homeowner who wants to pay someone else to cut it is unlikely to go shopping for a different service every week. Instead, they are much more likely to sign up for a service once at the beginning of spring and, if they are satisfied with the experience, re-sign the following year. We call this type of business "sticky" because there is a high chance the customer will stick with their initial choice once they have made it.

Other businesses may be slightly less sticky from a contractual standpoint but may be almost as sticky—or even stickier—in practice. Hair keeps growing as well, and while I cannot think of anyone who signs a contract with their barber or beautician, many of us have a personal loyalty (or perhaps just a store loyalty) that can go on for years.

Restaurants, on the other hand, have much less stickiness. People need to eat, but most of them do not eat at the same restaurant every day. If the food, service, and prices are good enough, perhaps the customer will come back again in a week or two. Depending on your dining segment, perhaps 35 percent of your customer base might visit more than twice a week. (And there are people, including billionaire Warren Buffett, who famously chooses one of three different breakfasts, who eat at McDonald's every day.) So if you are a restaurant owner, your goal should be to increase purchase size and frequency—whether by advertising, daily specials, couponing, apps, loyalty programs, delivery, or any other means—all while maintaining quality.

creating stickiness

In business, the term "stickiness" is used to denote a customer's likelihood to continue to use your product or service to the exclusion of those of your competitors. As a business owner, you will want to consider ways you could add stickiness to your concept to generate repeat business.

Fitness businesses are a common example of a business model that illustrates the concept of stickiness. Everything from discount gyms to martial arts facilities to barre and spinning studios have used a membership-based business model to create their own form of annuity. The memberships themselves might obligate customers to pay for a certain period of time or they might provide certain accumulated benefits that make the costs of going to a competitor—commonly called *switching costs*—higher than the value provided by that competitor.

As long as these companies can add more new customers than they lose, the business should continue to grow. Of course, this becomes self-limiting at the unit level. Once they reach 100 members, a fitness concept that has a 10 percent monthly drop-off rate will need to sell 11 new memberships per month to grow. But at 1,000 members, they would need to sell 101 new memberships per month. For most fitness businesses, their equilibrium membership size will rest somewhere between those two numbers—and that's when the owner knows it is time to expand to another location.

Often, you can find success by applying or adapting the lessons learned in one business to a completely different business model.

When John Leonesio was about to open his first Massage Envy location, he looked at the therapeutic massage business and asked himself what made that model's revenue so inconsistent. The answer? People came to get a massage whenever they had the free time to do so, but they did not prioritize it. But what if, instead of paying for the service as needed, they were to pay for the service on a membership basis, the way that the fitness business in which he spent his early career had been run?

For many in the massage industry, it sounded crazy. Prior to Massage Envy, therapeutic massage was done out of high-end salons where patrons made appointments when the mood hit—and when the therapists had openings. But Leonesio believed that if he could get a loyal membership that would return month after month, the business would continue to grow. As long as he had a big enough pool of licensed therapists, he could focus on growing membership at the unit level.

To get people to sign up for memberships, of course, he had to provide them with a benefit—in this case, a "free" monthly massage and access to deeply discounted massages—to give them value for their money. That led to the Massage Envy recruiting strategy, where they focused on therapists who did not have an existing book of repeat business and who would be eager to provide more services (and get more tips) by working at a busier salon.

Not only did this new business model have more consistent revenue, but it was also highly sticky. After all, once a client was owed a few massages, why would they go somewhere else, as long as they were getting good service? Essentially, the client's switching cost—their real or perceived cost of moving their business in terms of money, time, or effort—was greater than the perceived incremental value that could be offered by competitors (in terms of reduced costs or improved/differentiated services).

With more than 1,150 locations open in 19 years, Massage Envy has achieved growth that few businesses ever do. More to the point, Leonesio's innovations have changed the nature of the industry. Today, companies like Hand and Stone Massage and Facial Spa (more than 400 locations), Elements Massage (about 250 locations), Massage Heights (125 locations), MassageLuXe (about 70 locations), The Woodhouse Day Spa, LaVida Massage, and others have all adopted the membership model. And, according to the International Spa Association, in the five years between 2003 (when Massage Envy began franchising) and 2008, the number of locations in the spa industry more than doubled, from 9,870 to 21,000!

In essence, the introduction of this annuity-based membership model revolutionized what was once a highly fragmented market. But Leonesio was not finished. After selling his interest in Massage Envy in 2008, he went on to apply that same membership model to chiropractic services by founding The Joint. Today, The Joint has more than 500 chiropractic offices around the United States and is continuing to grow. And other franchisors such as NuSpine Chiropractic are using this business model with much success.

Of course, you don't need to have a membership model to get repeat business or create stickiness. Think about advertising companies such as Valpak, Money Mailer, or Welcomemat. When you receive their coupons in the mail, how often do you see the exact same companies advertising month after month? And why wouldn't you? As a business owner, if you found the combination of direct mail and digital advertising consistently drove business to your store, why would you ever stop using these services? The cost of switching—potentially investing in an advertising vehicle that did not work—would simply be too high.

In the end, when deciding on your business model, take into consideration your ability to continue to develop business from existing customers and to get them to come back—because that's what will ultimately allow you to grow like a franchise.

begin with a plan

Regardless of the business you are in, you should start with a plan.

Let me start with a disclosure and a confession. First, at the iFranchise Group, we sell plans for a living. So I have a bit of self-interest when I tell people to start with a plan. And second, I am not a big fan of most people's plans. I receive a lot of documents that follow some template of what someone told them a plan should look like. It's often an ivory-tower approach to the world and is neither realistic nor helpful from the standpoint of decision making or tactics.

You can almost always spot a useless plan if it starts with a mission statement. While I have occasionally seen businesses that take their mission statements seriously, in my experience, the vast majority of businesses spend half a day arguing with a consultant over a mission statement and then never revisit it again. By the way, we should differentiate between the mission statement (which is usually aspirational and meaningless) and the core values of a company (which, while they may not find their way into the business plan, are key to developing the corporate culture—more on that later).

So when I say that your business needs to start with a plan, I am not so much a fan of the plan itself (although you should write it down and develop financial projections around your decisions) as much as the planning *process*: thinking through the small decisions that will add up to the system that comprises your operation.

If you are in a retail business, your plan could revolve around a single customer visit. It would start with the visual experience the customer has when they walk in the door to the way your layout encourages them to walk and what your signage draws them to look at along the way. It should include, in an ideal scenario, at what point in their journey they encounter a salesperson, how that salesperson initially engages with them, the questions that are raised along the way, and how the salesperson shepherds them through each part of the sales process, from start to close.

If you are in food service, what will your customer's experience look like? How will they find you? Will they walk in the door? Will they sit down or stand in line? Will they order off a menu, order at the counter, or go through a "make-your-own" line? How will you price your products?

This isn't about developing a plan that will sit on a shelf and gather dust. It is about thinking through the business issues that will influence how you make money. And from that perspective, the planning process is vitally important.

know your customer

Just as you start the analysis of your business venture with your goals, you need to start the selling process by understanding your customer's goals, if you hope to secure the sale. The key to designing your sales system lies in your ability to secure good-quality information.

Did you ever wonder why most grocery stores are willing to give you discounts for using a loyalty card? Sure, part of their reasoning is to "purchase" your return visits to their stores. But a big part of what they are paying for is the information they capture about you with every purchase. What do you buy? How much do you buy? When do you buy it? And some of the discounts they offer allow them to test how brand loyal you are, which helps them know how to stock their shelves and how to optimize their margins.

Modern point-of-service (POS) systems in restaurants and retail stores are similarly designed to provide insight into consumers' buying habits and preferences, so that business owners can correlate those preferences with pricing, promotions, inventory management, and margin decision making. And, because many POS systems can provide advanced reporting based on credit card purchases, they can glean much more information in terms of customer frequency, average purchase size, buying preferences, and contact information— allowing you to design marketing campaigns of interest to your best customers. Address details collected here can help you understand the size of your territory once you are ready to expand to another location by telling you how far people will travel to shop at your store.

As an entrepreneur, the lesson to be learned here is that one of the first things you need to do is set up systems to collect and analyze sales and marketing data from your customers, so you can understand what is driving their purchasing decisions.

Of course, purchasing decisions vary considerably depending on which goods or services you are selling. If you're selling pretzels in a mall, that decision-making process will look very different from the decision to purchase a new automobile. And both of those purchasing decisions will look very different from the decision to hire a janitorial service company for a business. So you must understand some basics about consumer behavior when you are deciding what information you want to collect.

impulse and planned buyers

Generally speaking, your customers will fall into one of two types of buying categories: impulse buyers and those making planned purchases. While a pretzel might occasionally be a planned purchase, where you might decide that it would be a fun date to go for a walk, eat a soft pretzel, and drink a lemonade, usually it falls into the category of an impulse purchase.

Your opportunity to collect information about an impulse buyer is often at the moment they are standing in front of you. As they purchase the pretzel, you might ask them (or train your staff to ask) "Is there anything else we can get for you?" If someone asks for something you do not serve, make a note of it. A comment box would be another way to solicit this information. And, of course, unsolicited comments will certainly come in from social media—whether you want them or not. You can also create your own informal focus groups, where you might ask a group of friends to try various products and give you suggestions for companion products, pricing, promotions, or other enhancements.

When dealing with planned purchases, however, the information you will want to collect is significantly different. Planned purchases may fall into multiple categories. Some, like a home or a car, are more complex purchases in which your consumer must make a high level of commitment to the purchasing process. Some may be more habitual, in which the consumer may view the purchase as more of a commodity, such as putting gas in their car. And the last type might be more of a variety-seeking purchasing behavior, as when consumers seek out a new restaurant to experience something different.

For purchases in which there is a high level of involvement in the purchasing process, some of the questions you should be asking about your buyers should focus on motives—which can be a want, a need, or a pain that they have.

People sometimes make a specific purchase out of "pain"—that is, they are trying to solve some emotional difficulty. That pain might be that their house does not look as good as it could, but they do not have time to keep it up (so their lawn needs cutting). It could be that their carpet is run down and needs to be cleaned. So your first job is to find out what is motivating them.

Your second job is to find out what is motivating them to act *right now*. Why are they looking for someone to cut their lawn now, and not six months or a year ago? Learning that reason will often tell you more about them than almost any other question you might ask. People often buy based on emotions, not logic. In fact, most of the major decisions in your life—your spouse, your job, your home, your car—have been based on emotions. So connect with your buyer on an emotional level.

For example, in the franchise sales process, the buyer's motivation may be to:

- ❋ Be their own boss
- ❋ Get away from an abusive boss
- ❋ Build something that can be passed on to their children
- ❋ Pursue a passion
- ❋ Make more money
- ❋ Have more free time or flexibility
- ❋ Work with friends or family
- ❋ Build something that can be sold

Of course, the motivations for every sale will be different. So just as if you were selling franchises for a living, you need to understand the motives that might be driving your prospective buyer.

Remember the ancient Greek proverb when you are trying to put together the information needed for your sales system: "We have two ears and one mouth so we can listen twice as much as we speak."

obtaining advances

If you have a more complex sales process, remember there are typically multiple steps in the decision-making process for each prospective buyer. The purchase of a car, for example, might involve reading online reviews, visiting several dealerships, taking multiple test drives, getting various quotes on both vehicles and trade-in values, shopping for financing, and finally signing the paperwork. Each of these actions will move the buyer closer to their purchasing decision. And when a salesperson controls which steps the buyer is taking, they can control the sales process and "advance" the sale toward the desired outcome.

If you want to take charge of the sales process, it is your responsibility to track where your prospect is in the buying process and present them with a proactive step that will advance the process. Of course, the nature of the sale you are making will dictate the type of advance. For less complex sales, like those in a restaurant, the advance might be to get your patron to look at the dessert menu. For a clothing retailer, it might be to get your prospect to try on a suit. But for service-based businesses or for businesses with higher-ticket sales and multiple-step sales processes, advances can come in a number of different forms:

* Getting your prospect to set an appointment for an estimate
* Winning a commitment from the customer to review your collateral materials or your website before your next discussion
* Setting up a follow-up conversation with a spouse or partner on a conference call
* Filling out a financial qualification form
* Getting your prospect to review your estimate in a face-to-face meeting
* Getting your prospect to commit to calling some of your references

The list goes on and on, depending on the nature of your business. But to the extent that these steps are a part of your choreographed sales process, each of these advances should give you an opportunity to measure progress.

Again, when it comes to a more complex sale, the key is to track the advances you use, determine what is working, and incorporate those advances into your sales system.

eating the elephant

There is an old maxim in big-ticket sales that says the only way to eat an elephant is one bite at a time. The theory behind this truism, of course, is that if you are trying to sell someone on an expensive product or service, you need to take your time, start with your customer's situation and pain points, and work your way patiently toward a solution for those problems.

But eating the elephant a bite at a time is not without its own problems. Imagine that you are sitting out on an African plain in the hot sun, eating your elephant. A couple of things are going to happen. First, chances are that other predators will find your elephant in short order, and they will get their shot at eating your elephant, too. And even if you manage to hide your elephant from those predators, chances are that before you can finish it, it will go bad in the heat.

So let's imagine a sales scenario where you have built in five mandatory advances. Each of these advances takes time, and the element of time in any sales process will kill some sales. Moreover, each of these advances acts as an additional "sale," as the salesperson will need to, in effect, sell each advance. If their "close rate" on each advance is less than 100 percent, then each advance will result in leakage in the sales process. You can see this process below in Figure 7–1.

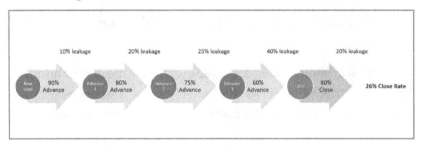

FIGURE 7–1—**LEAKAGE IN THE SALES PROCESS**

With five steps in this sales process, you could anticipate a close rate of about 26 percent. But if you could combine two of these advances into a single step, even if you reduce your advance rate, you might improve your overall close rate, as you can see in Figure 7–2 below.

In this version of the sales process, by combining Advance 1 and Advance 2 into a single step, even though the advance rate was

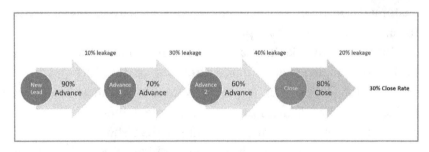

FIGURE 7–2—**AN IMPROVED CLOSE RATE**

reduced to 70 percent, the overall close rate went up to 30 percent. In addition, the sales cycle was shortened, making it less likely for competitors to join the fray. So as you develop and measure your metrics, bear in mind that in some cases, the best metric may involve changing the system rather than focusing on improvement or tweaking existing numbers.

And, of course, the sales process, because of the varying nature of competition, marketing, pricing, and other factors, is probably the most fluid of any of the systems you will develop and will require your most constant and diligent attention.

objections are your friend

One of the things that differentiates those who are good at the sales process from those who are not is their attitude toward objections. Objections, or the "conflict" that is natural in any sales role, are something the best salespeople actively seek out, while those who shy away from the sales process actively avoid them.

Those who are uncomfortable with the sales process typically prefer it when sales appear to be going smoothly. A prospective buyer who does not actively engage in the process will often accommodate them by silently allowing them to feel as if their sales pitch is landing—only to walk out the door and vanish, never to return their calls again.

Objections are a vital part of the sales communication process. If you don't know the customer's objections, you can't overcome them and move forward with the sale. And once that customer walks out the door, you may have lost them forever.

So if your business involves any kind of complex sale, you need to be certain that your system will force anyone involved in the sales process to routinely and aggressively attempt to uncover any hidden objections.

The key to uncovering customers' objections, of course, is simply to ask questions:

* What's preventing you . . .?
* What other information . . .?

* It seems as if you're concerned about . . . Is there something I can do to help you get more comfortable with it?

The questions you ask, of course, will vary depending on what you're selling, the sales modality (phone, face-to-face, electronic, etc.), and the appropriateness of this level of follow-up. Hearkening back to our earlier discussion, if your sales pitch was for an add-on order of fries, a follow-up question about "what other information they need" would be a bit of overkill given the relative size of the purchase.

But if the opportunity is large enough, you should probably be looking for objections whenever you are having trouble advancing in the sales process.

Once you have uncovered it, you will again want to have a system for overcoming the objection. People generally do not respond well to arguments, so simply telling them they are wrong and here's why will usually fail to yield positive results. Instead, start by agreeing with their initial premise, and then turn their objection into a positive. Like this:

* "You are absolutely right, Mary, we are new to this industry, but I think that is an advantage for you. Not only will you be getting in on the ground floor of this opportunity, but we are going to be putting all our top people on this project to ensure that we do a great job for you—because we need customers like you to be our success stories and help build our reputation, so we can build our business."

* "I recognize that we are expensive, John, but we are not expensive because we are gouging you. We are expensive because we use the best material and pay the best people to do our installations. And frankly, paying more means that our costs are higher. But it also means that we can offer the best guarantee in the business, because our product will perform better and longer."

* "I wish we could install it faster, Dr. Smith. But all our installations are customized so that they are an exact match with

our clients' requirements. We could slap together some off-the-shelf equipment for you—in fact, years ago, we used to represent some of those products—but we found our clients just were not happy with them and so we discontinued selling them, even though we made good money on them. We figured we would rather amaze our clients with great results in five weeks than give them decent results in two."

Obviously, the key is to have thought through what these objections are likely to be and be prepared with a good answer for how you will overcome them.

Sales training and effective marketing helped protective coating franchisor LINE-X make the "Top Five Fastest Growing Franchises" in *Entrepreneur* magazine for several years in a row. Our client Scott Jewett, who was the CEO of LINE-X before eventually joining the iFranchise Group as a consultant, employed an experienced sales team and implemented a system to ensure that all leads were diligently pursued. At their weekly sales meetings, they discussed overcoming objections from potential franchisees, but on one occasion they were flummoxed by a prospect.

When reporting on a serious prospect for a master franchise in the Dominican Republic, LINE-X's international franchise salesperson said, "Scott, those guys from D.R. are not going forward. They withdrew their application for a franchise." When he asked why, they told him they "had prayed on it and God said not to buy the franchise." That's an objection no one had anticipated or thought about how to counter. Believing there was no appropriate response other than to respect their beliefs, LINE-X went on with their business.

About six months later, the salesperson announced, "Hey, those guys in the Dominican Republic sent me a contract and a check!" What changed? The salesperson had continued to maintain respectful contact over time, and one day the prospects announced, "We prayed again . . . and God changed his mind."

This story demonstrates that effective sales are process-driven. If LINE-X had given up on contacting them, the master franchise might never have been sold. It also shows how gracefully accepting rejection can pay off.

Just like the A/B testing we discussed as a part of your marketing system, your salespeople should constantly be refining their approach to handling objections. But equally important, in building a system that will allow you to replicate your business, as you come across these objections, you should be documenting sales "scripts" that will allow you to train others to overcome these same objections going forward.

Especially when you are dealing with salespeople, it is usually most effective to have sales meetings to discuss these issues, as the competitive landscape often changes so rapidly that a manual documenting sales scripts simply will not keep up with it. And, as your organization grows, there are low-cost learning management systems (LMS) that allow you to post and share low-budget training videos that can be consumed much more readily than the written word (although it pains me to say it). So take advantage of these tools as you systematize your sales process.

measure your sales results

Generally speaking, when my clients begin measuring the results of their sales process, I tell them to measure everything. The more information you collect from day one, the easier it will be to track this data historically when it comes to measuring any changes you decide to implement. As part of tracking all these systems, I cannot emphasize enough how important it is to note the exact date that various significant events (both internal and external) occurred. As you start to accumulate enough information to begin graphing your data, you will want to insert these dates into the graphs to illustrate the impact that each may have had.

For example, some of the external events that we tracked on our calendar in recent years to illustrate their impact on our world included:

* The 9/11 terror attacks

* The 2008-2009 lending crash
* Each presidential election
* The Covid-19 shutdown

You should make note of similar events so that in retrospect, you can detect if outside factors impacted your results. The kinds of internal events you should track on these graphs would include:

* Changes in advertising or ad themes
* Overhauls of your website
* Use of pop-up advertising or a new ad campaign
* Use of a new landing page or new premium offer
* Hiring of a new sales rep

These dates would not appear on every chart, of course, but only on the charts in which they are relevant. So, for example, if I were tracking the organization's overall time to close, the hiring of new sales reps would likely impact the speed to close. Thus, I would want to show the dates of those hires on that chart to help explain why the numbers may have changed.

From a tracking perspective, some of the standard things you will want to be sure your system can measure include:

* *Conversion ratios for each step in the sales process, based on objective criteria to avoid interpretation errors.* All initial inquiries, regardless of their level of qualifications, would be called leads, for example. If the next step in your sales process is the face-to-face meeting, measure the conversion ratio from lead to meeting. And set your system up so you can track this based on who schedules the face-to-face meeting, so you can track scheduler effectiveness as one variable. (This is based on the assumption that, as you grow, you will need multiple schedulers.) If you close at that face-to-face meeting, you would need a second measurement of face-to-face meeting to close that can be tracked by salesperson in the same way. If there is an intermediate step—e.g., paying for an architectural drawing—track that step as a separate conversion and

then the drawing to final close as the third step. So you would measure a separate conversion ratio for each step of the sales process, which can be tracked by individual salesperson performance.

❈ *Sales-related information by salesperson.* In addition to close ratios, make sure your system can measure other sales-related information that will affect your assessment of salesperson performance. Time-to-close is often a good measure of how well a salesperson or sales organization does at creating urgency in the sales process; this is usually measured in days. Average sale is an important variable that will help you understand if your salesperson is simply taking orders from the low-hanging fruit, or if they are providing a more fulsome solution to your clients. To the extent that average ticket size has a bearing on margin or that the salesperson has an impact on margin, you will also want to track margin performance or discounting.

❈ *Marketing-related information.* You will want to be able to parse this information based on which salesperson made the sale and on where the lead came from. So if leads from print publications had a low close rate, but a much higher average ticket and margin, that might influence future marketing decisions. Likewise, you may want to be able to parse this information based on client demographics. If a certain client type seems to be a particularly good fit for one salesperson and a different client type seems to be a better fit for a different salesperson, there would be some profound implications for the allocation of future prospects. It might even lead to the creation of two separate sales systems using the processes employed by each salesperson.

❈ *Add-on sales.* Lastly, once you have converted the sale, there may still be additional sales opportunities in the future. These may be the responsibility of the account manager, the original salesperson, or whoever is responsible for fulfilling the original client contract. Again, you should track and parse the same type of statistics across each opportunity.

standardize your sales system

If you have a more complex sales process, you should develop a sales system to accommodate it. For bigger-ticket sales, you will likely get a good deal of pushback from old-school salespeople who will tell you that each sale, like each prospect, is unique, and that their sales process cannot be relegated to a system. But ultimately, a complex system that builds in flexibility is still a system—and is a better tool than no system at all.

Remember, this system is designed not for the old-school salesperson, whose knowledge of sales, if we give them the benefit of the doubt, will guide them flawlessly through the sales process every time. The goal is to allow you to expand your business by helping new salespeople understand how to handle prospects, so you can shorten their learning curve and get them up to speed quickly.

Your sales system should, at a minimum, have established standards around several distinct areas that will influence sales and marketing effectiveness. These should be documented in a manual that will allow you to pass this information on from one generation of salespeople to the next. Some of the areas of sales this manual should address include:

* *Data collection.* The standards here should be very specific, although it may be more or less difficult to enforce depending on how the lead comes in. For example, you can have a form fill that demands each and every form be filled out completely before it can be submitted, but that may reduce the number of leads generated—and thus be counterproductive. So while you can certainly ask for all the information, you cannot mandate that it is all collected. (However, it should always include lead source, as best as you can identify it, so you can track marketing effectiveness.)
* *Initial correspondence.* The correspondence you send to a prospect may differ based on the nature of the prospect. For example, you may have some form fills or other questions that categorize prospects based on their need. If you do, you

should have specific correspondence packages prepared for each category.

❋ *Callbacks and additional touches.* How frequently you reach out to a prospect should be part of your system as well. In franchise marketing, for example, studies have shown a positive correlation between the speed of the initial response and the likelihood of closing a franchisee. So the best franchise salespeople set up autoresponders that notify them on their cell phones when a qualified prospect requests information so that they can respond within minutes. Your sales process may require multiple calls and emails, so you need to balance how frequently you contact your prospects. There is a fine line between being perceived as helpful and being seen as a stalker that you do not want to cross.

❋ *Written correspondence.* While written correspondence should not all be boilerplate, there will be some things that you will want said in a very specific way. For example, if you are making claims about your product, you must be sure that those claims are absolutely true and are something you are willing to stand behind. You may want to have certain claims verified by your attorney. Moreover, you may want to standardize some basic letters to make them more effective—both in terms of efficiency and message consistency. The other part of correspondence that should be systematized is a section on how to interact with others in writing. In franchising, we frequently see problems arise when email correspondence gets out of hand or misinterpreted from someone who was not properly trained on how to interact with customers or franchisees.

❋ *Qualification requirements.* If you have standards for qualifying your customers or clients, you should clearly lay them out.

❋ *Sales process.* If there are certain steps in the sales process that you feel will lead to the best overall outcomes, you should standardize those as well, although you may want to leave some flexibility in terms of steps and/or order of operations. For example, in franchising, we often ask a prospective franchisee to come into the franchisor's office for a final interview, called a Discovery Day. For franchisors, this step is designed both to sell the prospect on the franchise and as a final step in the franchisee qualification process. Most franchisors would mandate that step as an on-site visit—but during the Covid-19 crisis, many adapted their Discovery Days to a virtual meeting process.

✳ *Sales "scripts."* While reading from an actual script is rarely the best formula for making a sale, the existence of sales scripts that can be used as training tools will vastly shorten the learning curve for new salespeople. In more complex sales, these "scripts" are likely to take the form of a series of questions directed at the prospect's situation (as opposed to a sales pitch). The answers to these questions will lead the salesperson toward the solution that is best suited to that buyer. These questions likely branch in different directions based on each response, so they are more difficult to script, but they make up a system that will help the salesperson identify how they can best meet the buyer's needs.

✳ *Responses to questions and objections.* Anyone involved in the sales process will almost certainly encounter certain predictable questions and objections. Again, you don't want your salesperson to have a "canned" approach to these, as the response may vary based on the customer's needs. But you don't want a new salesperson to first have to address these questions under "live fire." They should have already seen each and every one of these questions or objections, so that they never have that "deer in the headlights" look when the question comes from a real prospective customer.

✳ *Competitive information.* If your salesperson will ever need to compare your product with one of your direct competitors, provide them with enough information so they can do so in an informed and responsible manner. You want them to be able to respond in a way that will present your company in the best possible light and highlight your competitive advantages vis-à-vis your competitors.

train and train again

Of course, formalizing your sales system in a manual is only half of what you need to do. Once the system is complete, you must train your employees on all aspects of the system. And while it may seem like a big commitment, remember that the goal of the system in the first place is to improve close rates, increase the average order size, improve margins, and get salespeople up to speed more quickly.

Typically, the manual you have created will act as the textbook for your training program. You might require your new salespeople to read a section of the manual the evening before you train them on that section. Then, the following day, you might go through a series of exercises designed to reinforce the lessons in that section. For example, you could have a lecture where you would use a PowerPoint presentation on a particular topic. You might then do a role-playing exercise on that topic, where they would assume the role of the salesperson and you would act as the buyer. Later you might switch roles. You could show them a video from a previous session and ask them to critique it. Then, at a later point, you might have them draft some correspondence documenting the "call" you did, and you could critique that correspondence later. You could give them some flawed correspondence to critique as well, to see if they can spot the types of flaws you would like them to avoid.

Ultimately, you will want to set up a training schedule using different "instructors" (assuming your company is big enough) to cover different material. You should devote as much time to the training as you feel is needed—and then some. In our experience, more training is almost always better, although you must ultimately balance the time spent in training vs. a number of factors such as cost, lost productivity, and the complexity of the subject matter being taught. And if you can incorporate video into your training, even though it can add to the expense, it will improve your salespeople's retention rates. Exercises and other types of training in which they actually "do it" will similarly improve retention.

While you will ultimately need to determine the amount and types of training to be provided, there are really two underlying questions you need to attempt to answer in doing so. First, will the marginal improvement of any incremental training provide you with a positive return on the costs of providing that training? And second, is there a greater value in hiring people with more experience (even at a higher cost) than there is in providing more training to someone with a lesser skill set?

It is worth remembering that we are all programmed to forget—an ironic sentence in and of itself. Psychologist Hermann Ebbinghaus developed what he labeled the "forgetting curve" more than 100 years ago, where he showed that people forgot 56 percent of inbound information in an hour, 66 percent in a day, and 75 percent in a week. But there are things that can be done to improve that. Different types of inputs (reading, hearing, visuals, video, etc.) will help improve memory. Hands-on exercises will improve recall further, as will spaced repetition. So the bottom line is that the use of role-playing and repetition in the training process will at least initially prepare your salespeople for their role. But repeating training on multiple occasions will help to further ingrain the system into your daily business operations.

Of course, an ability to sell without the ability to deliver value makes for a very short-term business model. So now that you have an understanding of how to systematize the sales process, let's focus on systematizing the operations that will deliver value for your customers.

operations

Imagine that you have the world's simplest business model. Even that business model needs operating systems to be competitive in the real world.

To illustrate this, let me give you a hypothetical example.

Let's say you have a lawn-care business. But in this business, you purposely choose not to develop or refine any systems. You don't do any paid marketing. Instead, you use yard signs and word-of-mouth to gradually build your business. When you cut a lawn, you don't take a systematized approach to deliver your services to your customer—if you feel like cutting the lawn that morning, you get up, pack up your truck, ring their doorbell, and say "You want me to cut your lawn again today, Mrs. Jones? Only $50." Sometimes you price it a little higher, sometimes a little lower—usually because you forgot what you charged last time. But you have a winning personality and a pleasant smile and you do reasonably good work, so you continue to get new customers.

Despite your lack of systems, your business prospers. You hire some people to help you. But because you have no systems to guide your hiring, the accounts they inherit are all handled differently.

Some of your employees fail to use the edger when they are going around the sidewalks. Some of them set the mower too low, damaging the crowns of the grass and injuring the lawn. Some mow the lawn even when it is wet, resulting in an uneven cut as the rain wets down some of the blades . . . and causing ruts where the wheels run through the soggy turf. Some of them fail to maintain the lawn mower, causing delays, dissatisfied customers, and increased equipment costs. None of them use precise routes to increase their efficiency, so they zigzag from one end of town to the other, depending on where they feel like having lunch that day. You are performing a service, but you lack a system to help you do it more efficiently and effectively.

In reality, however, every business owner has production systems, no matter how inadequate they may be. They hire when they run out of bandwidth. They cold-call to get new clients. They market by word-of-mouth. They use old equipment to cut lawns in a haphazard manner.

But the more a poor system is duplicated, the faster it will inevitably lead to disaster. If the business model is branded, poor reviews will lead to lower closing rates and ultimately to higher client acquisition costs. And even if it is not branded, the system alone will lead to higher client turnover; higher costs for maintenance, equipment, labor, and travel; and inefficiencies in billing and collections.

The point, of course, is not to provide you with a definitive guide to lawn maintenance, but to illustrate that even the seemingly simplest businesses require systems in order to replicate them.

Ask any franchisor why one of their franchisees failed, and you might get a number of answers. Sometimes the franchisee was a bad fit. Sometimes they were undercapitalized. But the one answer that comes back again and again is that the franchisee simply did not follow the system. Maybe they thought they could do it better. Maybe they wanted to conserve capital by cutting corners. Or maybe they were simply too entrepreneurial for franchising. But "They just would not follow the system" plays itself out in franchise after franchise where there are excess failures.

Sure, sometimes the franchisor has a broken production or operating system—or their system breaks under the weight of changes in the marketplace. But for the most part, franchised businesses succeed because their franchisees follow the systems.

Allan Young, the cofounder of ShelfGenie and other successful franchise organizations, saw that his most successful franchisees were those that followed the system. So he now has a new initiative: He acquires multiple different franchises that all have some degree of synergy (in his case, in the home services segment), and then hires people to run them for him. "As an investor in these franchises, I start by looking at the franchisor's track record," he said. "If they have a track record of success, I simply hire someone to run the operation and insist that they follow the franchisor's systems to the letter."

A great operating system, followed to the letter, is the key to repeated success.

In this chapter, we will look at developing a prototype for the business model and think about whether one or multiple prototypes might work best. We will also look at the business model with an eye toward whether it encourages or inhibits repeat customers. Once established, your systems need to be detailed in a quality control document such as an operations manual and taught to your team—these are covered later in the chapter.

the purpose of the prototype(s)

If you are building a business for the first time, starting the process may seem easy. Estimate the consumer demand for a given product or service. Examine the competition. Decide where to locate. Give some thought to product pricing. Arrange your supply chain. Open the location, and make any necessary adjustments.

But if you are thinking like someone who wants to multiply their business—and you should be—you need to give more thought to the prototype (or prototypes) of the business unit you will be operating. That means thinking about your business as merely the first iteration of many more similar businesses to come. So in making choices for your prototype, keep the ability to replicate your formula front and center in your mind. If, for example, your "prototype" was located inside Disneyland, you might well make great money—but there are only so many locations where you could replicate the traffic and demographics of Disneyland. That would make it much more difficult to use the lessons you learned with your first location when opening subsequent locations.

The first rule of a prototype that is built for expansion is that it should be built in a way that it can operate profitably without your direct involvement.

Of course, for most startup business operations, part of the leverage you bring to the table as the owner comes in the form of the sweat equity you invest. Since most operators will require some form of compensation during the early stages of a business, the logical choice is to work at the location and pay yourself for that effort. Alternatively, if your savings or the income provided by your significant other allows you to operate without a salary, you can still achieve profitability faster by contributing your sweat equity to the business.

But if you are thinking like a franchisor, you need to get out of unit-level operations as quickly as possible, so you can treat each operating unit like a passive investment that can run without your involvement. That means, of course, that this prototype location you are creating must be capable of providing an ROI after paying a market-rate salary for whoever takes over your job.

The second rule of developing a prototype is that businesses looking for rapid expansion should keep in mind what they hope to gain from the prototype. Prototypes need to be built with a purpose: to test one or more hypotheses about a concept that you want to expand. So don't look at the prototype from the standpoint of someone who wants to maximize your return on this individual business. Look at it from the viewpoint of replicating that business.

As a case in point, I have met with companies that are operating in Times Square and with other businesses located in a major Las Vegas casino. Some of the numbers they are able to generate are simply staggering—but they are not really helpful for a new franchisor. There are not any similar markets in the U.S. where someone could anticipate the results you might get in Times Square. And while there are other casinos in which you could duplicate some concepts, there are only a few of them. So while these locations could give you the information you need at a high level (and the exposure they bring to a brand would certainly help with franchise marketing, should you go that route), an aggressive expansion strategy would probably not be possible. In short, they are not terribly valuable for establishing your Multiplier Model. And, in fact, the high level of exposure they would give your brand could work against you, as it would astronomically increase the chances that your concept would be knocked off by someone who spotted it while passing through town.

consider the possibilities with your prototype

When opening a prototype, the first question to address is whether it will "play in Peoria." In other words, will it appeal to a mainstream customer, or does it need a specific demographic to succeed? So when choosing a location, pay particular attention to the surrounding demographics. Who are the local customers? Who are the competitors? And while there are a number of additional questions you will want to address, it is vital to find a niche where you can replicate the business model.

And, assuming you are looking to expand aggressively, this is where the need for multiple prototypes may come into play.

If, for example, you are building a business that involves food service, you will probably want to test various formulas for success: Will it work in a street-front location? a strip center? a mall? in the city? in the suburbs? in a college town? on or off campus?

What's more, you will want to know if you need to change your product mix in each of these different locations. Some locations may be better suited for different times of day (called "dayparts" in the restaurant industry). A food-service operation in a downtown location might do some breakfast business, a robust lunch business, not much in terms of dinner, and nothing at late night or on weekends. The same operation on a college campus could have a big late-night and weekend business but a more limited lunch daypart. And those differences will influence which menu items are your primary focus. The downtown location might have a strong catering business with large lunch orders, and the college location may do a strong late-night delivery business with limited catering.

To the extent that your prototypes are targeting specific customers, your advertising will likely vary between some of these prototypes. Different messages will likely resonate differently with your target audiences. A price-focused message (or perhaps a message focused on healthy or "green" offerings) may be more effective in a college town, for example, while a focus on quality or convenience could be a more appropriate message for an older demographic.

Business economics will change between locations as well. The investment, for instance, may be very different from one location to the next. The prices you charge will likely vary based on your targeted customer, the local competition, and the fixed costs of overhead that you need to cover to turn a profit. Your ability to prepare food on-site and your equipment costs may be different based on the amount of space you can afford to lease.

In short, the prototype(s) you create should be designed to solve these issues if you are looking to expand aggressively. Look at each from the standpoint of return on invested capital and from the availability of future locations when you make your decisions to move forward.

Of course, a risk is associated with developing multiple prototypes. Some of them may not work, and the capital you invest in these prototypes thus may not provide you with an adequate return. In the worst-case scenario, some of the units may fail, depleting your capital.

So an alternate strategy, especially if you are capital constrained or are looking for less aggressive long-term growth, is to build your first prototype and then begin your expansion from there. This is the path that Massage Envy took. They planned for their first location to be the platform from which they would launch their franchise and thus looked to build the first prototype in a location that was readily replicable from day one. That first location looked as if it was already part of a larger network of massage therapy studios, with a space that was bright, open, and professionally designed with high-end touches. When that first unit was successful, they simply had to find similar locations and repeat the process. And because they had built it in a strip mall site with numerous potential matching locations, their business was positioned for ease of duplication.

When I first meet with entrepreneurs who are considering franchising, some of the ones who later become our most successful clients tell me that many of their customers already think they are a franchise. If your customers believe that, you likely made many good decisions as you planned your prototype development.

right-sizing the territory

One of the questions you should address in the process of creating your Multiplier Model is the size of the territory that can be served by a single Money Machine. As an entrepreneur, your first instinct will probably be to build any location you can, regardless of where it might be located. But territory size will be a significant factor in the success of your expansion model.

Often entrepreneurs think that by assigning a larger territory to each location, they are improving their chances for each unit's (or franchise's) success. Their rationale is that a larger territory has more people and thus more potential for revenue. But in fact, this may not be the case at all.

As an example, consider what would happen if a company limited their market penetration of a major metropolitan area to a single location. They have now locked themselves out of expanding further into the territory (or their franchisees, if they are going that route). But they have not locked out their competition. If their competitors open 20 locations in that same market, they will have substantially more visibility, advertising strength, buying power, and ability to service clients on a timely basis. And that could cause the demise of your Multiplier Model.

Amy Reed, cofounder of the pet-sitting franchise Woofie's Pet Ventures, went through this experience early in the growth of her business. "When we first started, a lot of our competitors marketed themselves as having big territories (servicing all of Northern Virginia)," she said. "So we thought that was what we needed to do—to appear bigger than we were, especially being a new company in the pet-sitting space. Within a month, we knew we had to scale back and limit our availability to two towns. We knew that customer service and having a close relationship with our clients and team members was the way to grow our business.

"By scaling back the size of our territory, we grew the business significantly. It seemed contradictory, and it was definitely a bit of a risk, but our instincts told us to do it. It was tough to do, especially as a new business, because we turned away potential clients outside our service area, and you never want to turn away business! But we stuck to our plan, and it ultimately led to the growth of our company. We became the largest pet-sitting company in the metro DC area by scaling back our territory and focusing on the close relationship with our clients and team members."

Just as important, having learned this lesson early in the process, Reed was in a better position to develop a franchise program that would fully saturate markets, to the benefit of all her franchisees.

establishing your brand standards

As a franchisor, perhaps your most valuable asset is your brand. In a typical franchise system, the franchisor licenses two things to the franchisee—the know-how of operating the business and the brand. And while the know-how can be changed relatively easily, what the brand stands for cannot. So while one would normally think of branding as a marketing exercise, creating the brand standards that people will associate with your Money Machine is more of an operational issue.

If, for example, you want to be known for fast delivery, like Domino's Pizza, speed of delivery becomes one of your brand standards. To maintain it, you will need to design your systems in such a way as to be able to deliver your pizza hot and fast. If, on the other hand, your brand standards are focused on a value-based message, like Little Caesars, your operations should be designed to produce a pie at a lower overall cost to the consumer.

The brand you choose needs to communicate a message to your customers. As many business authors have noted, your brand carries a "promise," which your customers will expect you to fulfill. Your job is to try your best to be sure that the execution of that brand promise—which manifests itself in the customer experience—is consistent with the consumer understanding of that promise.

It is important to establish your brand standards early in your developmental process. But to do so, you must first decide exactly where and how you want to differentiate yourself in the eyes of a customer.

Unless you are one of the lucky few that have a truly new and unique product (or service), you will need to make yourself stand out from your established competitors. And even if you do have something unique, something that new rarely has built-in demand—so you will need to educate your consumers as you introduce it.

When a successful franchisor decides to go into business, it is generally because they feel they can meet an unmet need. They saw an area of the marketplace where the current competitors fell short of what they believed the consumer wanted. Or, alternatively, they found a method of meeting a consumer need in a new way that allowed them to make more money selling the same product or service more efficiently.

Take McDonald's, for example. When Dick and Mac McDonald built the original McDonald's restaurant in San Bernardino, California, they were trying to solve a problem. Their prior restaurant ventures had been engineered in much the same way as many restaurants of that era—using carhop service. In fact, dating back to about 1925, when A&W Root Beer became the first American restaurant franchise, carhop restaurants had flourished—with nearly 450 A&Ws alone operating in the U.S. by 1950.

But the carhop model, in which patrons would park at the restaurant and be served in their cars by waiters, posed a number of problems, including higher labor costs and customers who lingered long after finishing their meals. And while Sonic Drive-In still prospers using this model, with more than 3,500 restaurants in the U.S. as of 2021, the McDonald brothers felt they could improve on it.

They focused on delivering a cheap meal with fast service. To that end, they built their prototype as a walk-up facility with no interior dining. Instead of carhops, the counter person both took the order and delivered it. To further increase speed, hamburgers were precooked and held in a warmer, and their kitchen was set up as an assembly line, designed to churn out identical burgers, not customized meals. Perhaps because the kitchen was up front for all to see, the brothers also focused on cleanliness and insisted that their staff was well-groomed and polite.

The McDonald brothers now had an operation that could serve customers many times faster than the traditional carhop business model. And people loved it. When Ray Kroc, who at the time was selling milkshake mixers for Prince Castle, got an order for eight Multimixers, he knew they had created something different. Kroc realized that he had a golden opportunity if he could obtain the franchise rights to the brothers' restaurant.

While much of what happened next is well-documented, one thing for which Kroc should receive more credit is his insistence that each franchisee follow the rigid brand standards that he established. Every burger had to be prepared to exacting standards, and cleanliness was an obsession of his.

Your first step when establishing your own brand standards is to determine what you want to be known for. What will set you apart from your competitors? You must then create, quantify, and document the actual brand standards and how the location will be measured against those standards. You should also set guardrails and penalties in place for those who fail to live up to your standards. You then need to communicate those brand standards, again and again, like a mantra, until everyone associated with the brand knows them and understands how important they are. Only then will they become institutionalized in your business.

Jeff Abbott, a senior consultant at the iFranchise Group, has an interesting story from when he worked as an executive with Taco Bell. One franchisee who attended the co-op meetings had three locations and a well-deserved reputation for running horrible operations. He would not staff properly or send people to train. He repeatedly failed corporate inspections and barely managed to fend off the health department. The franchisor got calls all the time from customers complaining about his operation.

So lawyers at Taco Bell developed a case based on all the terrible reports, terminated his franchises, and took over the stores as company-owned locations, which they would fix up to operate or resell.

Jeff went to the next co-op meeting expecting that the rest of the franchisees would be upset, because the company had disenfranchised one of their own. At the first break, two of them with locations near the former franchisee came up to him, and he braced himself for the worst. But to his surprise, the franchisees smiled, said they'd heard what had happened, and said, "It's about damn time!" The former franchisee's old customers had been coming to their restaurants and complaining about his operation, and they felt he had been dragging down the reputation of the entire system.

That story, and a dozen like it, illustrate just how important the maintenance of brand standards will be to everyone else involved in your brand—from consumers to store operators. Fail to enforce those standards and you do so at your own peril—and at the peril of your business.

understanding the aspects of production

When it comes to production, it is impossible to discuss the systematization of production in terms of specifics without knowing the exact nature of the business. Production at a burger restaurant will look very different from a business in which you are "producing" a service, such as lawn care.

But when creating your production system, there will be certain elements you will likely want to keep in mind regardless of your final output:

* *Speed.* This can often be a function of labor, and therefore, it has an associated cost component. Increased speed often increases price.
* *Quality.* This is often inversely proportional to labor. Increased quality requires increased time which increases price, and vice versa. To the extent that you produce a product, it also involves purchasing and will increase or decrease price based on the quality of the product purchased.
* *Customer service.* This is also inversely proportional to labor. Increased customer service, which is an element of increased quality, requires increased time and increased price.
* *Flair/creativity.* The more your business relies on creativity as one of its component parts, the less it will lend itself to

systematization. If your business model, like some technology companies, relies on constant innovation to thrive, you may find it easier to systematize the hiring of creatives than you find the process of systematizing innovation.

❋ *Inventory.* To the extent that your business requires you to use inventory purchased from others to assemble a final finished product, you will need to incorporate factors such as purchasing, inventory controls, assembly processes, and delivery into your production model.

❋ *Pricing.* Ultimately, you need to be able to sell products to consumers at a price that they are willing to pay—and a price at which you can make a profit.

Not only will some of these issues impact your labor model in terms of who you hire and how many employees you need, but they may also affect your capital investment in terms of the type of equipment you deploy. Consider the Neapolitan pizza franchises that have recently hit the market, which offer their customers the opportunity to create their own pizzas, which are then cooked to order in three minutes. How can they combine quality with speed? Through the use of an 800-degree open-hearth oven that adds substantially to the cost of building out the location.

So the questions to ask as you build your basic business model should revolve around your core customer. Who are they? What are they looking for? Speed? Low price? High quality? High touch?

If they are looking for the lowest price possible and are less concerned with speed, that is one production model. If they are more concerned with quality than with price, your production model will be completely different.

I had a prospective client come to me once to discuss the possibility of franchising their business. This particular prospect had a barbecue restaurant that brought in a couple of million dollars in revenue, had cost less than $500,000 to build, and, according to our initial phone conversation, had food costs in the low 30s and labor costs in the high 20s. At face value, their concept showed significant promise. At our initial meeting, however, their financials showed food costs that were closer to 45 percent and a unit that was losing money.

The owner assured me they had done a food cost analysis on every single line item on their menu. We went through each one, and while he was a little off on a few of them, in the end he had priced out all his items correctly. So I told him, basically, that at least one of six things was happening, and likely more than one:

1. Your employees are not ringing up food and are stealing from you at the register,
2. Your employees are stealing from you out the back door,
3. Your employees are not portioning the product correctly,
4. You are wasting too much food in terms of spoilage,
5. Your vendors are stealing from you by selling you less than they report, or
6. Your vendors have raised their prices and you have not responded or updated your analysis.

Note that each of these issues is easily diagnosed and cured with a proper system in place. Inventory controls and cameras could cure the inventory issue. Scoops and scales could cure the portioning (as could his later observation that there was a great deal of food going uneaten on customers' plates, leading to reduced portion sizes). Proper ordering could reduce spoilage. Scales could help keep vendors honest. And periodic pricing reviews could ensure that food costs remain in an acceptable range.

As it turned out, the owner had not been vigilant on any of the items above and, while he had initially done a pricing analysis, he had not kept it current as vendor prices increased. And while he never did franchise, three months after our meeting, he had instituted systems in all of these areas, substantially reduced his food costs, and was turning a consistent profit.

writing your operations manual

One lesson that almost any business owner can take from the franchise community is the importance of writing a good operations manual that will document your brand standards and the systems and procedures you have in place to help you achieve them. After all, what good are systems if you have not codified them so they can be absorbed and implemented by others?

The manual should represent the accumulation of all the systems that make your business successful and unique—and as such, it is the heart of your business. It should be a step-by-step guide that will help your employees learn what you have learned without having to go through the trial and error (and pain) that usually accompanies small business growth. And, because your business is growing and evolving every day, your operations manual should always be a work in progress, constantly changing to reflect the changes in business practices that you make as your business shifts to meet the requirements of a marketplace that is a constant moving target.

One of the most important systems that you can develop to allow you to expand will be a system to replicate the process of opening your business. All too often, new business owners will document day-to-day operational procedures, but will fail to document the steps that they need to take when it comes to the process of opening a business. And unfortunately, it is this process where some of the most costly, and sometimes most irreversible, mistakes can be made. I have thus provided a generic Pre-Opening Checklist in the Appendix to provide you with an idea of how you might want to document your opening procedures.

know your audience

When writing your operations manual, you must understand who your audience is before you begin. If it is designed for your in-house employees, your manual can dictate higher levels of control over your day-to-day operations than if your audience is an independent contractor franchisee. At the same time, there are things you would not put in a manual for employees. For example, an employee would not need to know how to set up bank accounts, obtain FEIN numbers, find a site, negotiate a lease, hire an architect, secure contractor bids, build out a location, and much of the other startup advice often provided to a new franchisee. And providing that information in your manual would only make it easier for your employees to abscond with your intellectual property and use it against you at some point in the future. In essence, your operations manual should include everything your audience needs to know to maintain brand standards, but nothing they do not need to know.

In addition, given the prevalence and relatively low cost of learning management tools that allow you to provide password-protected, customized content, having an operations manual that can be delivered in modular bites to different employees based on their need to know will further protect your intellectual property.

identify the working parts

For most entrepreneurs, the process of developing an operations manual will evolve as they grow their business. As you develop your first system, if it works, document it, and keep it in a general file of information that will eventually grow into your operations manual. As you put more and more systems in place, begin categorizing them into subfolders you can use to organize your manual. Typical sections in a fully developed manual might include:

* Introductory material
* Pre-opening procedures (depending on your target audience)
* Human resources
* Sales procedures
* Daily operating procedures (usually broken out by position)
* Management of the business/quality control
* Marketing and promotion
* Appendixes
  * Detailed instructions (recipes/curricula/service procedures)
  * Design and branding specifications
  * Forms for use in the operation (referenced in the manual)
  * Software manuals or manuals provided by third-party vendors

Again, you will eventually need to organize this rough grouping of information into a table of contents that suits your business model.

Once you have assembled enough of these systematized procedures to begin filling in the blanks, you should begin developing your internal operations manual. Often the easiest way to do this is to hire a firm that has created such manuals in the past, as this documentation can take hundreds of hours and can distract you from handling more important aspects of your business. NOTE: Before sharing your operations manual (especially HR procedures) with employees, be sure to have your HR attorney (or, if you are franchising, your franchise attorney) review these elements to be sure you are not creating any inadvertent liability in the process.

If you need to create your operations manual but did not have a system in place for gathering the necessary information from the start, developing one from scratch will be somewhat different—and certainly more time-consuming. When we create a manual for one of our clients, we typically use a 12-step process that takes, on average, about three to four months to complete. Our process, which is shown in a very simplified form in Figure 8–1 below, will give you a rough guide as to how a third-party company such as ours might approach such a task.

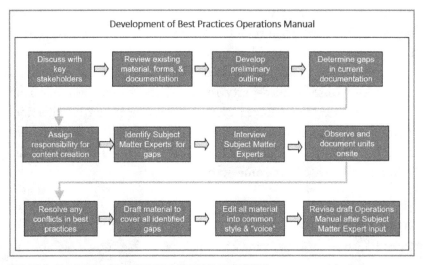

FIGURE 8–1—**BEST PRACTICES DEVELOPMENT**

keeping current

Over time, of course, the systems in your manual are certain to become outdated. And if your manual simply sits on your shelf, it will be of little use to anyone.

In the early 2000s, a large and very successful client asked us to update their manuals. When we read them, some of the documentation referred to "President Johnson." My operations consultant quipped he wasn't sure whether they were referring to Lyndon or Andrew. A decade later, a different person from the same company asked us to help them develop an operations manual using their existing material. When we asked if they had been updating the manual we developed for them ten years earlier, they were shocked to learn it existed.

So part of your goal in systematizing your business operations must be to develop a system that allows for those operating systems to be disseminated to those people who need them. And then to create another system to make sure your systems are regularly reviewed and updated to keep them relevant to the way your business runs. Generally, that means to put someone in charge of tracking operational and procedural changes, making sure that all documentation of these changes passes through their hands, and requiring them to review and update the manual itself on a periodic basis, with specific requirements as to when a red-lined version of the updated manual should be submitted to management for review.

Whether you create and update your operations manual yourself or choose to use a third-party resource, the key to systematizing your business is to also have a systematic approach to the collection, continued refinement, and dissemination of all the systems that make your business what it is. That is the only way to ensure that the systems you create have some accountability.

training your team

Once you have an operations manual, of course, now you need to teach the systems in that manual to whoever will be operating your business units. Without proper training, the manual may end up being no more than an expensive and time-consuming doorstop.

But simply training your people on the information in your manual is not enough. Without a systematic method of presenting your training, every person who goes through the training process will likely have a very different experience. With this in mind, you should start by developing a formal training outline of what needs to be imparted during training, to whom, and by whom. Your training system should be documented in a separate training manual that will serve as a guide for conducting training on the systems the trainee must learn—whether those are skilled technical tasks or operational and administrative activities. Essentially, what you need to develop is much like a "teacher's guide" or master curriculum that will ensure you are training your employees consistently and comprehensively.

Your first step is to create a detailed agenda for each hour of each day of training. Generally speaking, you should divide this training curriculum into different positions within the company—so that the training element necessary for a particular role can be easily broken out and taught as an individual lesson. This agenda should reference the specific elements of the manual that should be covered, under which topics, and the length of each topic. It should also suggest which trainer should conduct each segment.

Relative to the training curriculum itself, you may want to consider outside speakers (e.g., vendors) and/or other resources (videos, etc.), role-playing exercises, hands-on activities, and other teaching methods that will reinforce the systems trainees must learn. Each critical system should have an accompanying quiz or test at the end of the training period so the trainee can demonstrate their competence.

Of course, your training does not need to stop there. You can very easily and affordably develop instructional videos that can demonstrate your processes and systems in a much more robust manner than the written word. These videos, which are often most useful for repetitive tasks that are performed in high-turnover positions, can be housed on learning management systems (LMS) or other password-protected systems that allow access to specific content, even over handheld devices—which allows many employees to do their training on their phones without even incurring an incremental cost to you.

As a final step in developing your training system, create a system to train the trainer—in essence, a system that will allow you to get out of training, so that someone else can train people to train others. Again, train-the-trainer systems are most important for repetitive tasks, especially in high-turnover positions. So if you plan to grow your business, you will need to have someone at each location prepared to train people in those tasks.

keep the lines of communication open

As children, most of us played the game of "Telephone": People gather in a circle, and one person whispers a message to the person next to them. That person then whispers what they heard to the person next to them, and so on around the circle. When the message has made the rounds and returned to the original person, the last person to receive the message says it out loud to the group, and then the first person says what the original message was. Without fail, the two are never remotely alike.

In fact, the more people who play the game, the more errors accumulate in the message. Now consider that in the fast-food industry, annual employee turnover can run as high as 130 percent to 150 percent. So in a restaurant that employs 30 workers, the owner may need to hire—and train—as many as 45 employees each and every year just to keep fully staffed. And if they are doing this without a formal train-the-trainer system in place, after several years the person doing the training may themselves have been trained by someone who is separated from the original training process by five generations of employees. That's a lot of potential errors that could accumulate.

So as part of your quality control process, it is vital to have a system that institutionalizes not just the systems but also the means with which those systems are imparted to new employees, managers, or franchisees. This is a weak link in many of the emerging franchise brands we see. They may have a good process for training new owners, but they fail to provide the documented training systems and processes that their franchisees will need to continually train new employees.

In addition to training, many top franchisors have developed formal mentoring programs to help ensure the success of each new unit. One of our clients, Welcomemat, understood the need to have their more experienced franchisees help new franchisees who were entering the system. A specialty advertising company targeting new movers, Welcomemat has grown from a single location when they started franchising to close to 70 territories today, based largely on their ability to make their franchisees successful.

As they began to scale, they developed what they call the Crown Jewel system. They broke up the country into regions, and each region was named after a "crown jewel"—diamond, ruby, emerald, etc. Then each region was assigned a facilitator from among the more experienced and successful franchisees in the Welcomemat system.

The role of these facilitators was to host monthly regional calls, set agendas, and create a positive structure that would help new franchisees learn the business in their first 12 to 18 months. They were also responsible for rallying other franchisees in the region to help the new franchisee after they had completed their initial training.

The real glue that holds this system together is the way in which franchisees are motivated. If the new franchisee hits or exceeds their 3-to-6-month sales goals, *all* the franchisees in their Crown Jewel region get a cash bonus from corporate. The program has been extremely successful, and the vast majority of new Welcomemat franchisees now exceed their initial goals—while before implementing the program, only a little more than 50 percent of them were hitting those goals.

a system for quality control audits

When it comes to production and operations, one lesson new businesses can take from franchising is its approach to quality control. Typically, for any site-specific business (and even for some that are not), a franchisor will make regularly scheduled visits to each of their operating locations and go through a series of questions and observations to ensure that each operating entity is living up to brand standards. Even if you have only one location, developing that quality control checklist early will give you a tool that allows you to delegate quality control to your manager, so that you can concentrate on growth.

Quality control visits can be either scheduled or unscheduled— but often a mix of both provides the best results. Scheduled visits offer the advantage of ensuring that the key person that you need to engage with is available on the day that you drop by, but also provide advance notice to "clean up their act." So occasional unscheduled visits may provide you with more accurate insight into "normal" operations.

Regardless of whether it is scheduled or unscheduled, the visit should be guided by an agenda of topics to be discussed while you are at the location. Ideally, you should create this agenda in advance with the input of the franchisee or manager—this ensures that you include the topics you both believe are most important to unit-level success. But the ultimate goal of the visit, of course, is to ensure the manager and employees are following the policies and procedures documented in your operations manual.

Some of the agenda items you will likely want to include on every visit are:

* Inspect the premises, equipment, furniture, fixtures, signs, lighting, inventory, supplies, and service
* Observe actual operational procedures for a specified period of time to verify that they are adhering to your standards
* Conduct interviews with employees and customers
* Inspect all books and records related to the operating unit

❋ Review progress toward and achievement of business goals, evaluating past performance in relation to current operations

❋ Create an action plan based on the results of the evaluation and observations—essentially setting new goals and objectives for the operation and mapping out a specific plan for how to achieve the goals

The time spent on an audit like this can vary based on a number of factors, such as the age of the operation, the experience and strength of the manager, whether the operation has achieved strong scores and goals in the past, and the operating unit's stage of development. Moreover, during prescheduled visits, you can provide training on new operational procedures, policies, and marketing plans, as well as continue to develop the in-store operational skills of managers and, if it is a corporate location, your employees.

Even if you only have one unit, it's a good idea to create an audit process early in the development of your Money Machine. First, by creating this process, you will firmly establish the criteria under which your employees will be evaluated. Second, as part of your goal of taking yourself out of day-to-day operations, creating an audit process will allow you to have people other than you take charge of the quality control process—so that your Money Machine can be replicated to units in which you will not be physically present.

create an evaluation form

As part of the unit evaluation process, you will want to design an evaluation form with all the pertinent information you need to properly review the location from a quality standpoint. This form would typically include anywhere from 50 to 100 different areas of inspection (although some businesses have more or less) to make sure that whoever is conducting this quality audit has checked everything that will impact store performance and/or brand standards.

Some of the major categories you might want to consider including in this form, depending on the nature of your business, are:

- ✳ Condition of the exterior
- ✳ Condition of the interior (broken out by area)
- ✳ Staff appearance and professionalism
- ✳ Atmosphere
- ✳ Lighting
- ✳ Displays
- ✳ Merchandising
- ✳ Inventory
- ✳ Restrooms
- ✳ Safety and security
- ✳ Customer service/sales
- ✳ Personnel
- ✳ Financial review
- ✳ Management

Note that if you have a service-based business rather than a business with an actual storefront, your checklist may look different than the one above and your visit may require you to go out on a service call, but that does not eliminate the need for this type of quality assurance audit.

Each of these categories, and perhaps others relevant to your business, would have multiple bullet points under them. You could choose to rate each bullet point on a pass/fail basis in an effort to eliminate subjectivity from your scoring, or on a point scale, or on some mixture of both. Sometimes different weights are used when rating different aspects of an operation because certain elements are more important than others. For example, if you are running a restaurant, food safety is of paramount importance, so you might choose to weight any ratings involving food safety violations much more heavily than those addressing a burned-out light bulb or a dirty parking lot.

Once you have decided how to score your shop evaluation form, your next step should be to determine what constitutes a passing grade. Again, you may have multiple grades or simply a pass/fail score. Regardless of how you choose to rate each individual element, the unit manager (or franchisee) should know in advance how each item on the form will be evaluated and scored.

Independent of your grading system, each form should include a comments section or some other reporting mechanism in which you can spell out areas of improvement in detail, outline action steps to correct any problems and set a deadline to complete them, and put the responsible party on notice. At the end, there should be a place for the manager and the person doing the evaluation to sign off on the form.

This means you will want to complete the shop evaluation form while you are still on-site with the manager so you can point to any areas that may be in need of attention. If the manager has any questions about the results of your inspection, you may want to refer them to the page in your operations manual where the standards are specified. Often, the person filling out these forms will include photos to document the problem—allowing them to assess the improvements when they go back for a follow-up visit.

Finally, you will want to provide your store managers with some kind of financial incentive (or disincentive) for their performance on these inspections. Strong scores, for example, could be one element that is considered when deciding bonuses or promotions. Weak scores may lead to terminations. In franchise systems, failure to achieve the absolute top scores may mean that the franchisor will not consider the franchisee for further expansion. Or, in the worst cases, repeated poor performance may lead to the termination of the franchise.

Ideally, the person conducting the audit will work in a collaborative manner with the manager or franchisee to help the location achieve peak performance and brand standards. If the auditor is seen as little more than a "traffic cop" writing out tickets for bad performance, the result is likely to be managers simply gaming the system. So it is important to build this type of collaborative approach into your training for this role as part of your system for quality control. This often means that you should document exactly how a visit should be conducted in its own manual, to be used by your field team.

Equally important, your scoring system should incorporate the institutional knowledge necessary to tie certain key performance indicators (KPIs) back to their potential causes. For example, when Jeff Abbott worked at Taco Bell, he noted that the cost of goods sold (COGS) at one restaurant in the chain was consistently 2 percent higher than the company target and none of the systems they implemented had solved the problem—while all the other regional stores were right in line.

Taco Bell knew that their systems should generate a predictable result, so they quietly staked the restaurant out all the way to closing. After closing, they observed that the employees were taking a very long time to close the cash register. At the end of the night, closing the register should have taken only a few seconds to run a cash drawer report, count the drawer, and start the end of day report. Instead they were there punching keys on the register for several minutes.

Suspecting that something was wrong with the system, Taco Bell sent in an internal audit team and discovered that the register had a major flaw in its programming: It did not track the totals for refunds rung by the manager. The only way to find that number was to take all those full-day-report paper tapes and go through each transaction day by day to add up the refunds. As it turned out, the general manager and one of the assistant managers were spending those extra few minutes each night ringing in refunds and pocketing the cash. The amount taken was high enough that it was actually considered grand theft, and both of them ended up serving prison time.

Unsurprisingly, COGS returned to normal in that restaurant virtually overnight. A few months later, the register system was modified to track refund totals at the top of the tape, preventing that type of problem from recurring. But if they hadn't been aware of their KPIs, the theft could easily have gone on for years.

Another effective technique in the quality assurance process is to ask your franchisees or managers to conduct their own regular quality assurance evaluations (using the same forms and scoring methods) between the visits that you or your field consultants make. Conducting their own evaluations will keep quality control top of mind with them while you are not there and will reduce the odds that they will develop bad habits.

Ultimately, of course, even the best systems will fail if you do not have a team in place that can consistently implement those systems. Finding the right people and instilling the right culture will thus be a key to consistently applying your systems. We'll discuss that in the next chapter.

people

W hen I started writing this chapter, I thought perhaps I should have a subhead that said "Controls Without Management Are Like a Car Without a Driver."

And then it occurred to me that I was showing my age.

And *then* it occurred to me that this was exactly what I should be saying.

Yes, today we are starting to see cars that drive themselves, and I expect that, sooner than people my age are comfortable with the thought, these vehicles will likely dominate the streets—with cars that require actual drivers relegated to auto museums and Fourth of July parades.

As a business owner, your goal should be to go through a similar process. When you get started, your business will certainly need a driver. But from an aspirational standpoint, your goal should be to create businesses that essentially work on autopilot, with only active monitoring from the driver. You provide some initial input on direction and destination, and the business does the rest.

But in order for your driverless business to work, you will need the right people and the right culture to complement the systems you create. So with this in mind, you will need to develop systems for consistently hiring the right people for your ever-expanding team.

terminal velocity and delegation

To understand the importance of setting up systems that will help you automate much of your business, let's consider the concept that I call Entrepreneurial Velocity.

In fluid dynamics, the concept of terminal velocity is defined as the maximum speed achievable by an object as it passes through a "fluid" (including air). The object reaches that speed limit at the point when the force of gravity is balanced by the sum of resistance (drag) and buoyancy. From that point on the object will continue falling, but it will not fall any faster.

While terminal velocity is a concept that often comes up when discussing skydiving, a similar principle applies to entrepreneurship. When you first get started with your business, you will likely have a six-month adrenaline burn that could keep you going day and night (and might make it impossible for you to sleep). And during the startup phase, while there will be plenty to do for your launch, most businesses will not start out with an abundance of clients—and will therefore not be overloaded.

As you continue to work in and on your business, you will hopefully get more efficient, and the startup tasks that consumed you early in the process will begin to be put to bed. But the time you will spend on the tasks needed to properly scale your business, like facilitating more client work and managing people will continue to increase, until eventually you reach the point at which all the hours in the day are not enough to finish all the work you need to do. And while the mundane and more routine tasks of management, finance, and operations may be your most pressing needs, the creative itch that most entrepreneurs feel may drive you toward fiddling with the business or even starting something new—until you get to the point where the core business begins to suffer.

Again, this is where systems come in. Systems are designed to ensure that your business can deliver a product or service consistently, and to provide your business with an effective means of generating and retaining customers and clients. But one of the key components of systems is to make sure you can delegate tasks to your employees, who, if they follow those systems, can deliver products and services with the same level of quality across the board. This ability to delegate allows you the freedom to focus on the bigger picture—improving systems, evolving the business, and managing people and profits.

The bottom line is that you can only go so far and so fast by yourself. To overcome this speed trap, you can multiply your speed of growth exponentially by providing others with a systematized approach to understanding how to achieve comparable results— thereby duplicating yourself in this process. In order to delegate effectively, you need to be able to trust—and trust does not often come easily to entrepreneurs. But if the systems are put in place, you can overcome those hurdles.

Let's start by airing some unspoken truths, shall we?

* You know more than any employees you could hire about the business you are creating.
* In all likelihood, you can do a better job than any of the employees you are hiring at the job you are hiring them for.

✳ You care more about the quality of the work and customer relations than the employees you are hiring.

There. Feel better?

A lot of entrepreneurs (myself included) start out in business with a real ego problem. Those of us who manage to survive usually have a lot of that ego beaten out of us by the world, the market, our competitors, and our mistakes—sometimes we even gain a little humility in the process. But when we first get started, we have yet to make the mistakes that can teach us humility. And that can result in a reluctance to trust other people that makes managing, and specifically delegation, much more difficult.

So to get to a point where the business can "run by itself," if you are like most entrepreneurs, you will need to overcome any trust issues that you may have so you can delegate with impunity. And to do that, you either need to hire people that are better than you are at a particular task or develop a system that will allow those with less skill to perform at the same level.

hire the best talent you can afford

When it comes to hiring, you have three basic choices: cultivate your own talent internally, recruit a proven performer, or outsource it. Putting the question of outsourcing aside for the moment, how do you decide the price you put on talent?

In many startup organizations, it is difficult to "grow your own talent." Customers may be reluctant to buy from someone who seems inexperienced, making it difficult for younger salespeople to gain the experience your clients are looking for. And even if you can grow your own, these days even a modicum of success can translate to better offers elsewhere—leaving you high and dry.

At the same time, experienced professionals with a track record in other industries may have difficulties transitioning to your industry. And if you hire someone with a track record in your industry, you'll have to pay a premium for their past accomplishments while dealing with potential noncompete clauses and other agreements protecting their former employer's intellectual property and client lists.

Depending on the position you're hiring for, investing in an unproven commodity can be risky. Consider, for example, hiring for a sales position with a relatively long sales cycle. It might take months just to get a feel for how the new hire is performing. And your evaluation of their performance would be complicated by the law of small numbers (which we discussed back in Chapter 5), causing you to make decisions based on short-term performance that might not be representative of their long-term ability to get the job done. A lucky sale or two early on might keep a mediocre salesperson onboard too long, while factors beyond a superstar's control could cause a poor performance that might make you decide to let them go.

The implication of all this is that the more crucial the position is to your company, the more important it is to recruit top talent. Of course, that decision has its own implications as well. Often these people can write their own ticket—with the best commanding compensation packages that are out of reach for most startups.

This brings us to the concept of present value (PV). In layman's terms, present value refers to the idea that you would rather have a dollar today than at some point in the future. If you wait several years to get that dollar, it will be worth less, due to inflation and the amount of money you will have lost because you have not been earning interest on it in the meantime. So PV represents the current worth of that future dollar, once the rate of return has been taken into account.

In applying it here, however, I am equating your hiring decision to a purchase that is anticipated to provide the buyer (you) with a specific ROI. My recommendation is not to hire based on salary, assuming that you have that short-term luxury, but instead to look at the hiring decision as if it were based on ROI. If your new employee will create a stream of recurring revenue for you, you can almost look at it from the standpoint of net present value. And while this is particularly true for sales positions, the general theory would hold for any position in which there is a measurable return in terms of increased revenue, increased margin, or decreased expenses.

This is particularly evident in sales in which there is some form of ongoing "annuity value" to the initial sale. For example, if you are selling contracts for lawn-care services, janitorial services, or advertising sales that might extend for months or even years, the cost of lost sales during the initial period of breaking in a new salesperson goes far beyond the initial sale. It extends over the anticipated lifetime revenue that each customer would bring to the table.

The costs of hiring and training an inexperienced salesperson, even if you believe they can eventually perform at or better than industry average, can thus be measured against the incremental costs associated with the hire by looking at how long it takes to get them up to speed. Using the assumption that an experienced salesperson will become productive faster, you can measure the cost using the chart in Figure 9–1 below.

By extension, there's an argument for hiring superstar talent if you can afford it. Again, assuming a new hire, this is illustrated in Figure 9–2 on page 195.

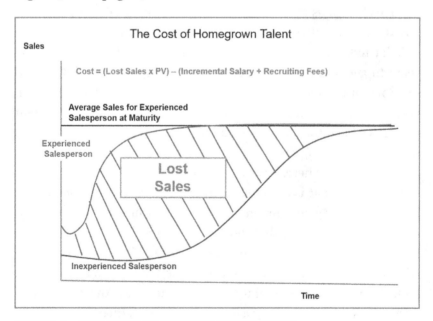

FIGURE 9–1—**THE COST OF HOMEGROWN TALENT**

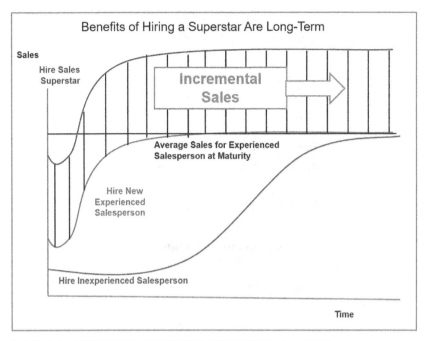

FIGURE 9–2—**BENEFITS OF HIRING SUPERSTAR TALENT**

Of course, there are other factors to consider. You may have budget constraints or be unable to attract this more experienced talent. But this theoretical framework gives you a basis for measuring the value of experience in certain positions in your organization.

However, if you do choose to grow your own talent, recruiting and training for certain positions will be of the utmost importance—and you will need to develop a system for ensuring that the people you recruit have the requisite skill sets. And, of course, it will be imperative to gauge culture, fit, and integrity.

in-house vs. outsourcing

From the standpoint of creating a business that will run without you, perhaps your most important decisions involve the people who will implement that system. And one of the first choices in many startup businesses is whether to hire employees or subcontract to third-party or outsourcing firms.

Outsourcing has become one of the most dynamic trends in the past 20 years and looks as if it will only continue to grow. But before you decide to outsource, let's look at its advantages and disadvantages as they apply to your business.

Outsourcing portions of your labor force, wherever you can, has numerous advantages:

* First and foremost, it allows you to pay for labor only when you need it, saving you money on labor costs when times are leaner.
* It can help you pare down overhead and investments in infrastructure by reducing office space, lowering your fees for things like payroll and accounting, and decreasing other related costs.
* It often allows you to hire better-qualified people on a part-time basis than you could afford to hire on a full-time basis.
* It provides you with much more flexibility, allowing you to gear up fast when demand increases and scale back when demand declines.
* If you lose an outsourced resource, generally the outsourcing company has someone else ready to fill the position, allowing work to go on without disruption.
* The people to whom you outsource are already well-trained, bringing a skill set to the table that you may lack.
* It transfers at least some of the employment risk to the outsourcing company.
* It allows you to focus your efforts on the aspects of your business that are most critical to your success.

At the same time, there are several key factors that argue against outsourcing:

* On a "cost per piece" basis, it is almost always more expensive than a fully utilized employee, as the outsourcing firm has to cover its overhead and make a profit.
* When you outsource certain functionalities, you fail to develop any in-house expertise in those areas. If they are vital to your

success, you have abrogated your responsibility to build those
core competencies internally.

* It comes with a built-in lack of control. While you may be able
to outsource to great people, they will generally operate with
greater autonomy and will not report directly to you in the
same way as an employee. If the outsourcing firm changes its
priorities, there may be little you can do about it.
* Outsourcing companies may use particular software or
other platforms, which may cause data-retention problems
should you decide the relationship isn't working and switch
to a different company.
* In some cases, longer-term contracts may provide less flexibility to modify your strategy should things not work out.
* If outsourced workers are deeply involved in your processes,
it may be more difficult for you to protect your confidential
information or strategic intent.
* If your outsourced resources are not local, you may have
communication problems, slower delivery of services, or other
hidden costs like travel expenses.
* If the outsourcing company is having problems they don't
want their customers to know about, such as financial difficulties, you may not hear anything until the day they close their
doors—leaving you high and dry.

So as you begin to build your staffing model, you will want to
take these considerations into account.

Generally speaking, there are two things you will need to do
here. First, you need to think about the nonfinancial issues that will
impact your business. Some of the questions you should ask yourself
might include:

* How important and proprietary is the intellectual property
that I will be developing as part of my business model?
* How great is my need for confidentiality?
* How variable do I think my need for this type of resource
might be?

- ✻ How easily could I find and train someone for this particular skill set?
- ✻ How important is this skill set in delivering value to my customer?

Second, if you are still on the fence about outsourcing once you have answered these questions, you should develop a financial model that will measure the costs of servicing your clients using outsourcing companies at various levels of sales vs. the costs of doing so using employees.

This is the kind of financial modeling referenced in Chapter 3 where you should use sensitivity analysis. In the vast majority of situations, there will be a point at which the higher variable costs associated with outsourcing will indicate you should bring any functional responsibility in-house. The only real questions you need to answer are 1) will you ever get to the point where the incremental financial savings of bringing something in-house is significant, and 2) does the trade-off in value favor in-house or outsourcing in your situation?

systematizing culture

One of the things many great companies have in common is a strong corporate culture. They have established core values of the brand and the company, and those values actually mean something.

When you are starting a business, it is all too easy to consider your culture as something of an afterthought. You are busy enough with the day-to-day tasks that need to get done just to keep the lights on. But as you grow, defining and systematizing that corporate culture becomes increasingly important to developing a sustainable company.

Over the course of my career, I have been involved with companies that have built a great culture and companies that have failed to do so. And unfortunately, when a company fails to create its own corporate culture, the internal culture often turns toxic.

Those toxic corporate cultures can manifest themselves in many ways. Low productivity. High levels of turnover. Poor morale. No sense of team spirit or pride of workmanship. Disharmony among employees. All of which will ultimately lead to poor performance and a low quality of work—which will ultimately be reflected in a poor customer experience.

A number of things contribute to a toxic culture, of course. But at the top of the list is always leadership. Leaders who are short on praise, trust, and transparency tend to engender these toxic environments. So in your efforts to systematize a healthy corporate culture, you must be careful to avoid developing an environment that leads to micromanagement.

So how do you go about systematizing culture? Despite what some people may think, it's not as simple as buying a Ping-Pong table and choosing an open floor plan. It has to start at the top. And everyone in management must continually promote the culture to their team. The fastest way to kill a company culture is to see leaders who do not embrace and model it themselves.

define your cultural values

Before systematizing your culture, you must define your organizational goals and values. What do you want your company to stand for? What do you want to achieve as a business? Define them as clearly as possible in a way that will allow you to easily communicate them, again and again, to the people you hire.

Ray Kroc, the founder of McDonald's, once famously said, "If I had a brick for every time I've repeated the phrase Quality, Service, Cleanliness, and Value, I think I'd probably be able to bridge the Atlantic Ocean with them." Constant repetition will institutionalize these standards. But only when you find your employees extolling the importance of these brand standards to new hires will you know that these values have become a part of your corporate DNA. So how do you systematize that next step?

Neighborly, a multiconcept franchisor franchising more than a dozen different brands in the home services space, is another company known for its strong values. Their employees are "urged to follow and know by heart and with heart" their 15-point Code of Values that is summarized by their three core values: Respect, Integrity, and Customer Focus.

focus on personality

Perhaps the first and most important aspect of instituting a corporate culture involves the people with whom you choose to surround yourself: your employees, your contractors, and your franchisees (should you choose to go that route). Your decisions on people will, more than any other, influence how the world sees your company, as they will represent your brand to the world.

Our client Famous Famiglia Pizza strives to bring a touch of New York City to every store with a little East Coast attitude from their employees. When they hire, they look for outgoing people who aren't afraid of a little back-and-forth—and then they train them to banter, NYC-style.

Another client, Topgolf, hires for personality and then trains for skills. They believe personality is at least 51 percent of the job, so their interviewing/hiring process is much more in depth than at most food or entertainment venues. "We can teach them how to do the job. We want to know if they will execute based on our culture" was a common refrain among Topgolf executives.

Topgolf believes in hiring for personality, so people who are interviewing for various positions are invited en masse to what the company calls X-Factor day. They play music to get people dancing and having a bit of fun so they can see which ones hang back and which ones get into the spirit of it. They then break into groups, where they are asked to create a Topgolf activity. The goal is to determine who among the candidates are the natural leaders and who allow others to take the lead—allowing Topgolf to better understand who among the applicants will perform best in their respective roles.

Sometimes it's difficult to quantify exactly what you are looking for in your hiring process, as Nothing Bundt Cakes cofounders Debbie Shwetz and Dena Tripp learned. Knowing that franchisee success was the key to *their* success, when Nothing Bundt Cakes first started selling franchises, they tried to figure out which attributes to look for in potential franchisees. As Debbie put it, "So we started by listing out the skill sets. Did they need to have baking skills? No. Would women be better than men? Not necessarily. Did they need to be good at accounting? No, they could hire that out."

On and on they went, until they finally stumbled on the attribute most likely to lead to success. "They had to be fearless," Debbie said. "When you open a Nothing Bundt Cakes, you need to go out and call on the businesses in the neighborhood, give away free cakes, and promote the brand to everyone in those offices. And if you are afraid of doing that, you are going to have a difficult time."

The problem was how they could judge fearlessness. They obviously couldn't just ask—who would say "No"? So they developed an extensive screening process in which they assigned their prospective franchisees various projects, including finding every cake distribution point in their territory and trying each one.

"You could always tell who took the assignment seriously," she said. "When they were finished with the steps in the process, the final step was for the franchisee to put together a PowerPoint presentation on why they would be the perfect franchisee. Then, as a final step, during Discovery Day, we would ask them to sing us a song. Some folks would hesitate, would question us, or would clearly be embarrassed. And some would pop right up and get into it. In fact, one woman jumped up and started singing 'The wheels on the bus go round and round . . .' complete with all the dance moves—and she is now one of our top-performing franchisees."

Today, Nothing Bundt Cakes has some 400 locations in the U.S. and is beginning to expand into international markets. And, nine months into the pandemic, Debbie informed me that only one store had closed since the company was founded. "We tracked it," she said. "The franchisees who were the most fearless were almost always the most successful."

create a cultural system

Your people are the raw materials of your culture. Hire the wrong people, and you are destined to fail. And if you find that you have the wrong people, do not let them infect your organization. If they do not fit, move on from them as fast as you can.

Once you have gotten the values and the people right, it is your job to systematize the inculcation of those values. And while simple repetition might seem like enough, if you want to be sure that they become a part of your corporate DNA, you will need to translate them into action.

Our client College H.U.N.K.S. Hauling Junk & Moving is a great example of bringing values to life by creating a system within an organization. At College H.U.N.K.S., the company has four core values:

* Building leaders
* Always branding
* Creating a fun and enthusiastic team environment
* Listen, fulfill, and delight

They have also developed a 22-page document that they provide to those in "Hunk Nation" that explains the importance of culture and goes into detail about their purpose, mission, brand promise, and vision—as well as their core values. But they don't just pass out this document and forget it.

Instead, every day at 11:11 A.M. (they chose that time because it was easy to remember and it broke up the day), they hold a "daily huddle" with the entire company. When they first started, there were only two or three people in the huddle, but today, there are 20 to 40 people, depending on the day. They continued the tradition even during the Covid-19 lockdown, using Zoom meetings for the huddle. At the beginning of each meeting, they start by doing a core value review.

After that, they ask someone to share at least one core value story—a practice they say they learned from Jim Collins' book *Good to Great*. So people understand that they might be expected to share examples of times that the core values have been lived, either at work or in their daily lives. One or two people volunteer a story. Then they review numbers, or talk about priorities for the upcoming day, important announcements, and other business.

On Monday, they discuss all four of the core values—and on each subsequent day they highlight one particular core value. Now almost everyone comes prepared with an example of how they or somebody on their team has lived one of the company's core values—even though they cannot get through all the examples in a single meeting. It is so automatic that it never gets lost in the shuffle of day-to-day operations. According to Nick Friedman, their president and cofounder, "We think that living the values is what defines 'living the culture' . . . and the culture drives behavior, and then behavior drives results. That's the system we have put in place."

When College H.U.N.K.S. began franchising, they recognized the importance of maintaining these brand values. So while their franchisees often do their huddles first thing in the morning instead of at 11:11, the process continues at their 200-plus franchised territories today.

"Culture doesn't happen overnight. It takes everybody living the core values and not just the owner talking about it," Friedman said. "We want core values to be shared by everyone and not just with everyone."

This is the genetics of success. It's not about developing and enforcing policy. It's about inculcating habit into your organization until it becomes a part of your brand's DNA, so that by the time an employee has been with the organization for a while, they no longer have to think about how to react in a particular situation. It becomes reflexive.

establishing accountability

There are really two keys to being able to trust the people in your organization. The first, of course, is hiring great people, which we have already discussed. The second is to be sure that you have established systems that clearly identify the role that each person plays relative to any task that needs to be performed.

Depending on the size of the business you are building, the issue of delegation may be fairly simple. When you're starting out, the business might consist of just you and one other person—in which case you have an easy binary choice. But as the business grows, delegation becomes more complex. Different people bring their own skill sets to the table and have varying overall responsibilities within the organization—and they need different levels of information about what other people in the company are doing so they can optimally deliver on those responsibilities.

One way this has been systematically handled by organizations, especially as they grow, is by using a Responsibility Assignment Matrix (RAM, a name used interchangeably with the RACI Matrix, based on the acronym below). While these matrices come in a number of different formats, they typically involve breaking responsibilities into different levels of control. Employees are given roles in association with various functional assignments, usually with some variant of the following:

* *Responsible (R)*: The individual or individuals who will be charged with completing the task, although they may delegate parts of the job to others.
* *Accountable (A)*: The one person who will ultimately sign off on the completion of the task by the Responsible individuals. The Responsible report to the Accountable.
* *Consulted (C)*: The Consulted are used on the project to help facilitate its successful completion. Think of them as subject matter experts.
* *Informed (I)*: The people who are updated on the project's progress, often after the fact. They are not consulted on completing the work, but are kept informed as progress is made.

Using these four categories, you can break down more complex tasks into their component parts until there is general agreement as to what needs to be done by whom to ensure that nothing falls through the cracks. The typical format would be a matrix along the lines of what you see in Figure 9–3 on page 205, which shows a Responsibility Assignment Matrix for a hypothetical landscape design company.

Responsibility Assignment Matrix
Sample Landscape Design Company

	Scheduler	Salesperson	Designer	Expediter	Contracting	Foreman	Crew	Purchasing	Billing	President
Sales Process Coordination	R	A								
Quote Preparation		R	C		A			C		
Contract Negotiations		A	C		C			C	R	I
Licensing and Material Procurement				A		R		R		
Landscaping Performed	R	I	C		I	A	R		I	
Final Quality Review with Client	R	A							I	I

FIGURE 9–3—**RESPONSIBILITY ASSIGNMENT MATRIX**

Of course, this is just one possible format you can use, and you can certainly go into much more detail (or less detail), depending on the complexity of your business and the talents of your staff. The key is not so much what organizing method you use, but whether your team all has a crystal-clear understanding of everyone's responsibilities and authority. Without that, there will almost certainly be a vacuum into which confusion will create chaos.

inspect what you expect

No discussion of any production process is complete without referencing W. Edwards Deming, who is often referred to as the father of total quality management (TQM). Deming and statistician Walter Shewhart were two of the founders of a systematic approach to business management, which focused on applying statistical analysis to production processes to identify areas in need of improvement.

While Deming focused mostly on large-scale production, his methods have since been applied to everything from sales processes to service. It was his belief that more than 90 percent of the problems encountered in any production process were not caused by workers, but could ultimately be laid at the feet of either management or the system managers employed.

Deming created what he called a four-point "System of Profound Knowledge" that would allow managers to identify and solve problems with quality. And while a detailed understanding of his work is beyond the scope of what we could hope to cover here, it is worth pointing out that the first two points were "appreciation for a system" (all inputs, outputs, and processes, from beginning to end) and "knowledge of variation"—that is, understanding the root causes behind differences in quality in that system, along with statistical measures for studying those variations.

As a small business owner, you too will have production processes, whether that is producing meals in your restaurant, well-manicured lawns for your lawn-care clients, better health care for your patients, or improved fitness and a certain exercise experience for your health club members. But regardless of the business you are in, you should look at these "production processes" from your customer's viewpoint so you can reduce the number of "defects" produced in that system.

So it is in your best interest to start by learning where those defects can occur. Again, depending on the nature of your business, there will be variations, so each of you will need to build your own model. But you should be able to identify the specific "potential improvement points" that might be of value to your customer. You could start by building a general paradigm that looks something like the diagram in Figure 9–4 on page 207.

Overall, you want to be sure that your marketing is consistent with the quality of your deliverables, that your product or service meets or exceeds demands and is delivered on a timely basis, that customers are treated professionally, and that they ultimately feel they received good value—while at the same time generating a reasonable profit for yourself.

But within each of these potential improvement points, you must determine the factors specific to your business that might influence your ability to deliver on that potential improvement point, knowing, of course, that each of these influencing factors may affect other potential improvement points as well. Take, for example, ensuring that your product meets or exceeds customer expectations. One input that might prove to be a potential

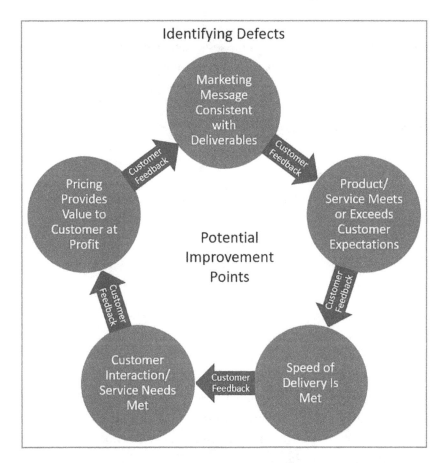

FIGURE 9–4—**POTENTIAL IMPROVEMENT POINTS**

improvement point could be the quality of the unfinished inventory used in the production process. But changing that might have an adverse impact on pricing, profit, or the consumer's perception of value. Alternatively, to improve speed of delivery, you might need to increase your inventory or hire more employees, either of which would increase costs—again potentially impacting perceived value, profits, or both.

And, of course, the type of factors affecting potential improvement points will vary considerably depending on the nature of your business. Outside suppliers will have a huge impact on retail and restaurant businesses, but less so on service businesses. Likewise, location will have an outsize impact on retail and restaurant segments. Service-based businesses may need to be much more attuned to the logistics of delivery and customer interaction than they are to high-traffic locations. But depend on it: Regardless of what type of business you own, your customer will tell you what is important to them.

don't be a fireman

Of course, simply identifying the problem doesn't improve the process. To paraphrase Deming from an interview he did late in life:

If there were a fire in the building and we were to somehow put it out, that did not improve the building. It is very important to understand the difference between putting out fires and improvement of processes. We should not be managing defects instead of looking at the system that is producing the defects.

To develop a system to address this issue, Deming developed a cycle of continuous improvement with four distinct steps: Plan, Do, Study, Act. The thought process behind the PDSA Cycle was that once you have spotted a problem in the system, you must change the system to avoid making similar mistakes in the future. Otherwise you will be stuck putting out fires until the fire comes along that burns down your business.

So once you have *planned* how you will fix the problem to deliver greater value to your customer, you must then implement that plan (*do*). But rather than simply continuing to implement, you must at some point step back and take a sample of the results you are generating to determine how well you are executing against the plan. And then, as you *study* that sample, determine 1) if there are problems, 2) the cause of the problems, and 3) how to resolve those problems. Finally, you need to *act* to eliminate the underlying causes of the problems if you are to resolve the issue.

Note that this system, like many others in business, constitutes a cycle that must be constantly repeated, as the actions you take to alter the system at the end of the cycle may cause new problems, meaning that you will need to start the PDSA Cycle all over again.

When you start a new business, you must integrate quality control mechanisms into it from day one. That means you will need to establish ways to measure various aspects of the quality of your deliverables, develop a process for routine inspection and management of those measurements, and create a system for identifying and modifying processes to solve problems when they arise. I have modified Deming's approach a bit to provide a system that takes into account the steps that are necessary when you are building a system from the ground up. That system, shown below in Figure 9–5, provides a simplified version of a quality control process you can undertake when initially designing a system to service your customers.

At the planning stage, focus on how you intend to differentiate yourself from your competitors. We have already mentioned this in

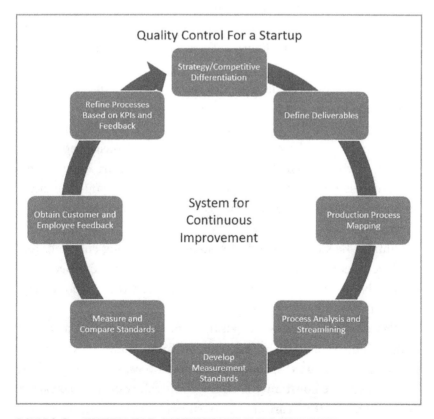

FIGURE 9–5—**SYSTEM FOR CONTINUOUS IMPROVEMENT**

our discussion of the McMillanDoolittle EST model in Chapter 5—essentially you need to pick a position and determine how you want to define yourself: Are you the biggest? the cheapest? the quickest?

Those decisions will have a substantial impact on many of your processes and inputs. For example, if you choose to compete on price, you will need to make sacrifices in terms of the quality and breadth of your inventory, service times, and other factors that might impact your deliverables.

Once you have defined your deliverables, develop production processes that will be as efficient as possible. Regardless of whether you are flipping hamburgers, mapping out routes to service your lawn-care clients, or selling widgets door to door, the more efficient your process (which usually translates into fewer steps), the less opportunity there will be for error and the more efficient your business will be from a labor standpoint.

At this point, it may serve you well to build a process map (such as those shown in Figures 9–4 and 9–5) to help you see any opportunities to streamline your system. Often not only can labor be minimized, but eliminating extra steps can speed the process and improve results as well.

Regardless of the process you create, from a systematization standpoint, you will want to put standards and measurements in place throughout each step of the process to measure effectiveness and progress toward specific goals. This will allow you to identify problems with the process, employees, or any other areas in need of improvement.

Finally, be sure to include a system for obtaining customer and employee feedback. Their collective opinions about the process will need to be factored into the overall satisfaction rating you achieve with your product or service.

Based on an evaluation of all those factors, you will likely want to make adjustments to refine your business model. And because your market, consumers, competitors, employees, suppliers, and the environment are constantly changing, you will want to incorporate this system into the heart of your business as part of your continual

✻ IT IS EASIER TO ASK FORGIVENESS THAN GET PERMISSION

One of the maxims I try to drive home to my staff is that it is OK to fail, especially if you are trying to do something that you believe is in the best interests of the company. And in the long run, it is sometimes easier to ask forgiveness than get permission—a principle I talk about frequently at the iFranchise Group, where most of our people are highly experienced and have a wide latitude to address situations they encounter with their professional judgment.

However, any employee who is taking advantage of this maxim must first understand the company's overall goals and act exclusively in its best interests. Moreover, they must thoroughly understand the brand standards before being turned loose.

Consider, for example, an employee who is working with your best customer. That customer needs a rush order fulfilled, which means you will have to pay a significant amount of overtime. You are not around to make the call, so the employee must decide. Should they turn down an order from a top client? Should they charge the client a premium for expedited delivery—and perhaps even increase your margin? Or should they agree to expedite the delivery without any additional charge, even if that means swallowing incremental costs or perhaps delaying the orders of other customers?

If you have never addressed these issues with your employee, this is an intensely stressful decision. Will it cost them their job if they get the call wrong? If you have given them no instruction on company values and they fear repercussions, they will likely default

✳ **IT IS EASIER TO ASK FORGIVENESS THAN GET PERMISSION,** CONTINUED

to the safest decision—telling the customer it can't be done. Or they may delay the decision (perhaps making potential overtime costs even worse) until you can make the call. In either case, they may have followed your systems, but might have endangered the client relationship in the process.

On the other hand, if they don't fear the consequences of failure, they could be more inclined to say that they can expedite the job. But should they charge extra for it?

cycle of adaptation, if you want to remain relevant to an ever-changing world.

harnessing creativity with centralized control

One of the key elements of the Multiplier Model approach to business lies in the belief that you must be willing to learn from your mistakes. Along those same lines, you must be willing to empower your employees to make mistakes and to learn from them as well.

Often in larger businesses, a culture of fear permeates the organization. People are so afraid that they might lose their jobs—or that a failure might make a permanent blot on an otherwise unblemished record—that they are unwilling to take any "unnecessary" risks. And that likely means they are unwilling to take any risks at all.

While this often allows people who are good at following the rules to advance—and similarly allows what has always worked in the past to continue to work in the future—it stifles innovation. And innovation is what allows small businesses to compete with their larger brethren.

One of the most difficult things to do as a manager, of course, is to give your people the freedom to fail. And it is a difficult line to walk. Sometimes their lack of judgment may seem not to warrant that level of trust—as they will certainly do things that you might not have done yourself.

Importantly, at the same time you are encouraging innovation, you will need to set boundaries as to when your established systems cannot be violated (i.e., your brand standards) and when innovation is allowed, when it is imperative, and how it must be controlled and monitored.

This is an area where franchisors have long-established systems to encourage innovation within the confines of centralized control. Most people by now, for example, know that McDonald's HQ did not invent the Filet-O-Fish, the Big Mac, or the Egg McMuffin—their franchisees did. But McDonald's did not give its franchisees free rein to experiment with its menu. Instead, they maintained control of testing, refining, and ultimately accepting (or rejecting) new menu items for the entire system.

Franchisors to this day continue to use a similar system of soliciting input at the unit level—but making sure they can maintain control throughout the process. Our client Sky Zone provides a more recent example of this.

When Sky Zone, a pioneer in indoor trampoline parks, first started franchising, their customers had to rent shoes from them, much as you would do at a bowling alley, in order to jump. They bought the shoes from China in massive quantities. But after a customer had jumped for an hour, the shoes would come back sweaty and smelly. Employees were charged with spraying the shoes with Lysol to sanitize them, which they did for many years, but the employee experience of putting on gloves and cleaning the shoes was unpleasant and time-consuming—and the customer experience of putting on wet shoes that smelled like Lysol wasn't much better.

Then, when Sky Zone had about 35 franchises, a group of employees in their St. Louis location suggested simply selling the shoes to customers. Sky Zone rejected the idea, as they would have had to charge $30 per pair, which was far too much for an add-on fee. As they brainstormed, though, they thought about letting customers jump in socks. Their fear was that socks were too slippery, creating a safety issue. But then they came up with the idea of putting rubber grips on the bottom of the socks, like the ones you see in airplanes or hospitals. Customers could simply buy the socks (for about $4) and either bring them to their next visit or buy new ones each time.

At the time they came up with this idea, Sky Zone had 35 locations—each of which had already invested in about 1,200 pairs of shoes. But given the improvements it would mean for the customer experience, Sky Zone decided to make the change. Today, Sky Zone sells between 15 million and 20 million pairs of SkySocks every year from their 220-plus locations in 15 countries—putting their brand in dresser drawers across the world and creating a major source of profit for both franchisor and franchisees. And, according to Sky Zone president Jeff Platt, the socks have become one of the most "Instagrammable" aspects of the brand.

Early in the life of a business, when it is still setting up many of its systems, innovation and testing are at the heart of optimizing its systems. But if that level of optimization and testing goes on continually for every aspect of the business, as you get larger and larger, maintaining brand standards will become increasingly difficult. At the same time, if you encourage your employees at the unit level to institutionalize creativity without controls, then your operations will function differently from one location to the next. And then your customers' expectations will no longer be met when it comes to the brand promise.

So while you want to encourage creativity and innovation among your employees, you also need to institute a system to harness that creativity and allow it to be implemented only with centralized control. The key is to establish firm boundaries around your brand standards where lines cannot be crossed without getting prior approval.

pull the weeds or they will overgrow your garden

Try though you might, however, you will make mistakes in the hiring process. It is simply inevitable.

Regardless of the system you put in place for interviewing prospective employees, remember that you are trying to impress them with what a great company you have and they are trying to impress you with what a great worker they would be. In many respects, interviewing is a lot like dating. We're not lying on the couch in our pajamas with our hair uncombed—instead, we have on our Sunday best and give well-rehearsed answers to questions in mellifluous tones.

So sometimes it's hard to discern whether your new hires are truly a good fit in terms of skills, culture, and attitude. That is one of the reasons you should devote as much time as you can to the hiring process in the first place—so you can do your best to make sure you get it right the first time. After all, you are asking people to leave their existing jobs, perhaps relocate their families, and take a chance on you and your business.

But if you do get employees who cannot pull their own weight or, worse, bring a bad cultural fit to the organization, allowing them to remain will ruin your corporate culture, lower your morale, and could ultimately destroy your company.

So if you do hire folks whose work habits or attitude are having a negative impact on your business, as difficult as it is for you personally and as hard as it is on the new hire, it's in the company's best interests (and often in the employee's best long-term interests) to terminate them as soon as you realize the issues cannot be resolved.

Once you have the right people in place along with the systems that will allow you to grow, you will have finally arrived at the point where growth, using the Multiplier Model, is the next logical step. But before we begin to grow our businesses, we should ask if our growth plan does everything it can to mitigate against the kind of problems that could turn your business on its head.

contingency planning

I n business, one of the biggest mistakes you can make is assuming that your business model will hum on uninterrupted for years. Perhaps a new competitor will burst into the market with a different model. Or an existing competitor will come out with an improved product or a reduced price. Or maybe the market will just change in general.

I was rudely reminded of this when, in the middle of drafting this book, there was a worldwide pandemic caused by the Covid-19 outbreak. In the United States alone, tens of millions of Americans filed for unemployment almost overnight as businesses across the country closed their doors. The stock market, which thankfully has come back strong as I write this, at one point had lost more than $10 trillion in market capitalization—not to mention the losses to private industry, the health-care costs, and the long-term costs to taxpayers, who will be paying for the stimulus packages for generations to come. And, while a lack of access to the court systems combined with government stimulus funds has made the number a bit harder to track, many tens of thousands of businesses have closed permanently, and their owners have been financially ruined.

Let me be clear. There are some circumstances in which the world might conspire against you—as during the coronavirus pandemic—and even your best response will not be enough to circumvent disaster. That is part of the risk that each of us assumes as a business owner. But you must do what you can to minimize that risk.

Obviously, everyone prays that something as devastating as the Covid-19 pandemic will never happen again. But, as W. Edwards Deming put it in a TV interview I once watched, "Mr. Murphy was an optimist." Someday when you least expect it, a tornado will drop a house on your world.

In this chapter, we will discuss how rapid recognition of problems, along with contingency planning, can help you survive while those around you fail.

put your mask on first

As someone who has done their fair share of traveling, I have frequently heard the admonition by flight attendants that in the event of an emergency, I should put on my oxygen mask before helping others. And while you tend to zone out during those safety checks after a couple of million miles, there is some wisdom there that we should heed.

If your business is going through a real emergency, your top priority is to make sure it survives. As painful as it may be to lay off employees, take a salary reduction, or make difficult cuts with longtime vendors—all of whom may now be friends—it may be the only option you have to save your business. And that is the only way that you can, in the long run, help those same employees and vendors—despite what it may feel like at the moment.

If your business goes off the rails, remember that time is money. Your expenses do not stop accruing unless you proactively stop them. Your rent, your marketing, and your salary costs will not go away. Your interest expenses will not be deferred. In fact, all your business expenses will likely continue unabated unless you do something about them. The lifeblood of your business is cash.

So you need to recognize that a problem exists before you can get that oxygen mask on—and ideally spot it when the negative trend first materializes.

divining the future

Often, the key to business success lies in your ability to predict what will happen in the future—ideally before your competition does. And a crucial element of this process is trend analysis.

We have previously discussed the importance of analyzing key performance indicators (KPIs) at each pivotal point in your Money Machine paradigm. In creating these KPIs, we were focused on finding ways to improve performance and measure our success in implementing different strategies. But looking at KPIs individually only provides a scorecard of how we have done in the recent past.

To spot future trends, it is helpful to create graphs for any KPIs that have a direct impact on the profitability of your business. In creating these graphs, you should add notes on each indicating when major internal and external events took place (just as we discussed doing for your sales results in Chapter 7). At the iFranchise Group, for example, we have added notes to our long-term graphs for events such as presidential elections, the 9/11 terrorist attacks, the 2008–2010 recession, and of course the Covid-19 pandemic—with further details on short-term graphs, such as the passage of stimulus packages.

If your business is affected by seasonal fluctuations, compare the current year's months with the same months in previous years. If your business is impacted by the weather, you could track significant weather events. Whatever might cause a movement in your KPIs should be noted so that you can better anticipate similar incidents in the future.

Similarly, note any changes caused by internal decisions. If you are tracking website performance, make note of changes to landing pages, your offer, your SEO strategy, and other variables on your trend graphs to measure their effect on performance. If you are looking at salesperson performance, you may want to isolate graphs by salesperson or indicate on your overall corporate graphs when new hires were made. If you changed your compensation structure or added different lead sources, that could factor into salesperson performance and should probably be indicated on your graph as well.

As you begin to accumulate data, you should identify two major numbers for each KPI. The first is a target number. This should be a number that is achievable in a good year, not an ideal that you would love to achieve but never have. Having a target for each KPI will give you benchmarks for a well-tuned Money Machine, and you can always strive to improve those targets.

The other number you should set for each KPI is the break-even. This is the minimum it would take for you to stay afloat when times get tough. So, for example, if "close rate" was one of your KPIs, your target close rate based on performance in good years might be 60 percent. If you know about how many leads you can expect in any given month, the amount of your average sale, and your financial break-even point, you can determine a break-even close rate at which your business could survive. Perhaps that might be 25 percent.

You could do the same analysis for many other KPIs across the board, such as the number of leads you need per month or the size of the average ticket. This would give you an idea of how much pain you can withstand for any one KPI. But problems often occur in groups, so a third number you might want to develop for each is how far below target these KPIs can fall as a whole before you are again at break-even. That leaves you with three different numbers that will alert you to what is going on in your business: a target KPI, a stand-alone break-even KPI, and a group break-even KPI.

With these numbers established, the goal is not to wait until you hit them, but instead to use short-term trend lines to determine if you are heading in the wrong direction and how close you are to the danger zone.

The next step is to determine whether any negative trends are actually trends, or if they are just anomalies. If you were to have one bad month, you wouldn't want to overreact and begin laying off staff or cutting back hours if you knew the following month would be strong. But if it were the beginning of a long-term downward trend, you would be better off taking action sooner rather than later.

Make a practice of regularly asking yourself why the trend changed. Statistics can be your friend here, once you learn the relevant significance of particular movements in KPIs. But even if you are not a statistical wizard, you can still ask yourself "Why?" every time you look at an upward or downward trend in an analysis that you should be conducting monthly, at a minimum.

And when you see things that have a negative impact, begin to catalog what could go wrong. Then imagine some confluence of those events.

if it ain't broke, break it

To create a system to deal with a worst-case scenario, you have to start by picturing the worst-case scenario.

As part of your contingency planning, you need to be constantly thinking about how worst-case scenarios would impact your Money Machine. As part of this process, I encourage you to imagine scenarios that require thinking outside the box—and even then it is unlikely you will come up with every possibility. How many businesses, other than perhaps a handful of those run by Bill Gates' acolytes, really planned for anything approaching the Covid-19 pandemic? Yet there have been a number of disaster movies that speculated about those very similar scenarios.

Aside from global threats from the outside, think about how your competition could harm you. How would you attack your business if you were a new startup looking to compete against it? What about if you were one of the bigger businesses you compete with every day—assuming they really wanted to drive you out of business? Is there disruptive technology that could be brought to bear against you, and if so, how could you respond?

Go through the worst-case scenarios below and ask yourself how you would respond:

* If one of your competitors decided to attack you with a price-war style campaign?
* If one of your competitors attacked you with a very aggressive marketing campaign focused on the quality of your products?
* If an anonymous competitor came at you with an online slander campaign?
* If one of your employees did something scandalous that went viral on social media?
* If someone filed a lawsuit against you that would cost you a huge amount of money to defend?
* If you were the subject of publicity that redefined the way the public thought of you?
* If a competitor came out with a product/service that actually was superior to yours or was as good as yours but sold at a lower price?
* If your top competitors merged to create a new entity with more power or more services than you have?
* If a competitor were to start adding services that you do not offer?
* If something happened in your personal life that distracted you from your business (illness, family illness, divorce, etc.)?

Before Dave Hood joined the iFranchise Group as my partner, he was president of Auntie Anne's. In the late 1990s, the company's more than 600 franchisees were being supplied with the basic mix for their pretzels by a company called Good Food, located in Honey Brook, Pennsylvania. As the brand continued to grow, the management team at Auntie Anne's began to discuss lining up a backup supplier, in the event that something happened to disrupt Good Food's manufacturing. Their running joke was "We'd be out of luck if they ever got hit by a tornado."

It was a costly and somewhat time-consuming process, but the company began identifying and vetting additional suppliers. After about six months, they brought a second mix supplier online in Ohio, with the idea that they would initially be given about 10 percent of the production responsibility. Then, in November 1999, just a few months after making the shift, Good Food was hit by a tornado. They were shut down completely, just before the holiday rush when Auntie Anne's franchisees typically did 40 percent of their business! But thanks to good planning and a little bit of luck on the timing, there was no disruption to the franchisees' business.

So did they get lucky? If a tornado had taken out their entire supply chain right before the busiest month of the year, most people would say it was just bad luck. But people who have the foresight to plan for potential disruptions or disasters know better. Luck—good or bad—has little to do with it. The Reverend H.K. Williams may have said it best when he said, "Remember, if you fail to prepare you are preparing to fail."

Of course, there is more to planning than simply imagining worst-case scenarios and developing tools to spot them when they are approaching. You need to develop and implement plans to respond appropriately and in enough time to create an effective solution.

how long is your runway?

If things do head south, the one thing you have to do, and quickly, is act. Sitting on the sidelines and waiting for things to turn around on their own will only burn your time and money away—and those two resources must be hoarded in difficult times.

The process is fairly straightforward, albeit gut-wrenching. Think of it in terms of measuring how much speed you need to achieve to take off before you reach the end of your runway. You presumably have capital in the bank, accounts receivable you can count on, and new sales you can make—that is your fuel. But you also know that you will be burning fuel, in terms of salaries and payables, as you head down the runway. Your job is to either fix the plane while it rolls down the runway or lighten the load so that you have enough fuel to take off and sustain you in flight. If you fail, the plane crashes, killing you and everyone else onboard.

But remember, as the plane accelerates down the runway, you are becoming increasingly committed to that course of action—your strategy. At a certain point, you will be fully committed. That point of no return usually happens well before the crash—making the timing of your decisions that much more important.

So the first thing you need to determine is your current burn rate, or the amount of capital that you will burn through in any given period (usually measured in months). Every businessperson should have this number tattooed on the inside of their eyelids.

Your burn rate comes in the form of both fixed costs and variable costs. Fixed costs, as we discussed in Chapter 3, are those expenses that you incur periodically regardless of whether you make a sale— these include things like rent, salaries, or other expenses that you are contractually obligated to pay. Variable costs, on the other hand, will go up or down based on either sales or production metrics.

Once you have these basics, you can determine your break-even point by dividing your fixed costs by the marginal contribution of an average sale—which would be expressed as the average selling price minus the average variable cost. Obviously, the more products you have, the more variability your break-even analysis will have. But this formula should give you an idea of the number of sales you will need to break even. Multiply that number times your average sale, and you will know your break-even in terms of dollars.

If you look at current trends, you can then measure the delta of where you are in relation to break-even. And that knowledge, along with some projections on your part, can help you determine how much gas you must put in your tank to get your wheels off the ground. If you find you are undercapitalized, you will need to either raise additional capital or change your plan—both of which are best done earlier rather than later. Simply hoping that things will turn around is a recipe for disaster.

question the status quo

Too many companies fall into the trap of doing things because "that's how we've always done them." Unfortunately for those companies, that type of thinking will lead to their ultimate demise. Today a company needs to be nimble and flexible to keep up with the needs of its consumers. And that means that the system that worked last year may no longer be relevant.

Other businesses will need to pivot, and pivot quickly. As Peter Drucker famously said, "Innovate or die," and in business being prepared to change can literally save your company.

Scott Jewett, who was at the time president of our client LINE-X and has since joined the iFranchise Group as a senior consultant, was in just such a situation in 2001. LINE-X had grown to more than 300 franchise locations in 12 countries. Their franchisees sold a sprayed-on truck bed liner (a thick protective coating used on pickup truck beds), which constituted more than 90 percent of enterprise-wide revenue the previous year. To seek incremental sales and diversify, Scott began pursuing other uses for the product, such as coating the walls of buildings to protect them against earthquake or bomb damage. As part of this process, LINE-X had worked with the U.S. military designing and testing ways to minimize structural damage during bombings.

One week after 9/11, Scott received a call from the Department of Defense asking if his research might help find a way to protect buildings from terrorist attacks like the one on the Pentagon that day. And while 9/11 had caused a big drop in LINE-X's core business, it opened up a whole new revenue source. The application of a single bed liner brought in about $400. But because it was prepared, LINE-X won a contract to use its product to protect the Pentagon and other military facilities that brought in millions.

This pivot didn't just save the company—it was also a media magnet. Discovery Channel, NBC, ABC, and FOX did feature stories on the "bed liner that protects America." Franchisees around the globe found a whole new industry to serve. And some years later, Sco tt helped engineer the sale of LINE-X to a private equity firm for close to $100 million. Having a Plan B or two is always a good strategy against changes in an industry. In this case, it saved the company.

So as you keep an eye out for market shifts that impact your business, ask yourself how you can pivot to take advantage of any new doors that are opening—even as old doors close.

reducing risk with your multiplier model

Once you have completed your contingency planning and have a fully systematized Money Machine, you are ready to begin reinvesting in your growth by duplicating those systems again and again using the Multiplier Model. And while the model does not mandate a franchise strategy, because we are on the topic of risk reduction, we should mention it here.

By its very nature, franchising involves asking a franchisee to make the entire investment in opening a franchised unit. The franchisee will be responsible for signing a lease, hiring employees, acquiring inventory, and making any other investments necessary to start up the business. So by franchising, essentially the franchisor is off-loading some of the risks associated with growth, in exchange for a reduction in per-unit profits. But since the franchisor is also making virtually no investment in opening a location, their ROI is almost too high to be measured meaningfully.

This strategy, as part of a growth contingency plan, allows the franchisor to reduce its risk by spreading it out among various franchisees, who are, at least theoretically, compensated for this risk through their ROI. Moreover, the risk assumed by individual franchisees is by definition smaller and thus more easily absorbed than it would be by a single entity shouldering all of the risk.

As I was writing this book, I was once again reminded of this fact when speaking of a highly successful serial entrepreneur, who I will call Rich. When Rich was in his teens, he started his first business installing tires for a retailer who did not have installation capabilities. He expanded to seven locations before the owner of the tire company saw how much money he was making and bought him out. He then moved to California and began opening and operating full-service tire stores. He had built a successful Money Machine and systematized it so he could take full advantage of the Multiplier Model—and within a decade, he was doing $50 million per year out of the stores that he owned and operated. About that time, one of the major tire retailers bought him out and he retired.

Like most serial entrepreneurs, however, Rich could not stay retired long. He ended up developing a computer service business in 2001, and within nine years, he had nine stores in operation. At that point, he found himself in a position to purchase a specialty electronics store with 14 units in operation that acted as a dedicated channel of distribution for one particular manufacturer/service provider. Within six years, his operation had expanded to 38 locations, again with revenue approaching $50 million. And that was when the manufacturer (who according to Rich fabricated an excuse and provided no opportunity to cure) pulled the plug on his distribution license, leaving him with 30 days to get out of 38 locations. Needless to say, Rich took the company into bankruptcy and sued the manufacturer, but a life's work—and a thriving business—was gone overnight.

Rich is now planning to franchise the computer service business. "I wish I would have franchised the last time," he said. "I would have diversified my risk and the individual franchisees would have been in a position to pivot where I could not, given the magnitude of the problem."

When the Covid-19 pandemic hit in 2020, many of the hardest-hit companies were those that had not used franchising as part of their expansion strategy. California Pizza Kitchen, Ann Taylor, Lane Bryant, Brooks Brothers, Le Pain Quotidien, Dean & DeLuca, and Pier 1 Imports all filed for bankruptcy during that year.

In 2020, GNC declared bankruptcy and made an announcement that it would close between 800 and 1,200 stores. And while GNC had about 1,000 domestic franchises going into the year along with nearly 2,000 international locations, it is likely the biggest weight dragging down the company was the more than 3,000 corporate-owned locations they had at the beginning of the year. Krystal, which also filed for bankruptcy, had taken a 15-year hiatus from franchising before 2020.

Bar Louie, before its bankruptcy, had 110 corporate locations and 24 franchises. After they exited bankruptcy, they had 50 corporate locations and 23 franchises. Most franchisees simply tightened their belts, as painful as it must have been. But the corporate stores almost took them under.

Of course, franchising does not prevent bankruptcies. But this kind of risk diversification is something to consider before hitting the gas on your Money Machine.

hitting the gas

At some point, hopefully, you have a Money Machine that will work with you or without you. You have the systems in place that mean you can trust it to produce profits on a consistent basis, so at this point, it's up to you as to whether you want to grow that business—and how.

So what's next?

One of the biggest problems I have encountered over the years with entrepreneurs is rooted in the nature of entrepreneurial thinking itself. Most entrepreneurs never saw a rule they didn't want to break, or a problem they didn't think they could solve—and make money doing so. That ability to see a solution where most people see problems is what allows entrepreneurs to change the world—and what makes them so fun to do business with. But it can also be their worst enemy. Before they have changed the world with their first solution, they are often on to the second, third, or fourth.

Like the old saying goes, if you chase two squirrels, you end up catching neither. And two squirrel syndrome has derailed more entrepreneurs than perhaps any other problem out there.

That second squirrel demands your time and attention—and if you are building systems to deliver the value proposition at the heart of your business, your time is already stretched thin. The second squirrel demands your capital, in the form of legal work, branding, hiring contractors and employees, product development, A/B testing, and so on. The second squirrel will force you to devote resources to its brand that could otherwise be spent on the first squirrel. And the second squirrel will suck your creative juices dry.

Yet time after time, we see entrepreneurs who have the first squirrel by the tail let it get away so they can chase the second.

If being a creator is where you find the fun in life, then maybe squirrel chasing is the game for you. But if you want to make money, your best bet is almost always to take the working Money Machine and duplicate it. In this chapter, we will discuss how to do just that.

knowing you are ready for the multiplier model

First, while you may be confident in your ability to expand, you will never *know* that you are ready to replicate your Money Machine in a new venue until you have done it the first time. You may have calculated the ROI for your first Money Machine and determined that the returns are stellar. If that is the case, you may be ready for the Multiplier Model right out of the gate. Companies like Massage Envy, Nothing Bundt Cakes, and Fuzzy's Taco Shop (as well as McDonald's many decades ago) started their franchise growth plan with just one successful prototype in operation.

But many businesses are not that fortunate. Even if we take a systems approach to developing our prototype, we may find that the returns from the first operation are not enough to justify the risk. Obviously, this would be true if the location were losing money. But it might also be the case if the location were making a decent return, but not enough to justify additional investments.

At that point, you face a decision. Should you sell the business and try something different? Close it down and take your lumps? Initiate your aggressive expansion plan based on the changes you have made in your head? Or open a new prototype location to test the refinements to your Money Machine?

Obviously, your circumstances will dictate your approach. If, for example, you believe that the mistake you made in your first Money Machine involved location or size, the most conservative approach might be to open a second location to test your theory rather than launching into more aggressive expansion (where either you or your franchisees would be betting on your theory). So you will need to do a gut check to see how certain you are about your next iteration of your Money Machine.

From an ROI standpoint, the second unit is often where you want to focus on reducing the size of your investment. Because the investment is the denominator in your ROI equation, improvements there will have a disproportionately larger impact on your returns and will make aggressive expansion more feasible.

But regardless of whether you decide on expanding aggressively or building a second version of your Money Machine, remember that opening the second location is often the hardest. It comes at a time when you have the least experience, the leanest staff, and the least capital. When you opened your first location, you could probably devote yourself to it full time. Now you likely still have managerial responsibilities at the first that take up your time.

let your goals drive your aggressiveness

Once your Money Machine is ready for growth, like every entrepreneur, you will see opportunities, and you will have to decide whether to take them or sit on your hands.

I strongly advocate you make sure that the business you are growing, and the plans and tactics you follow, are designed to meet your personal goals as a business owner. Ultimately, businesses should not be designed to grow any faster than you need them to grow to achieve your goals. So start with the end in mind and reverse engineer to get where you need to be.

So when you set a goal, make it tangible and specific. Don't take the easy way out by saying that you want to grow fast while maintaining quality. If you want to eventually sell the business, ask yourself how much you want to sell the business for and why?

Note: This is not a question of value. Don't start by asking how much your future company will be worth—because that assumes a certain growth plan. Instead, ask yourself what kind of lifestyle you would like to lead, and then figure out how much money you will need to live that lifestyle. Are you willing to sell your business to lead that lifestyle? And if you are how much will you need to sell it for to achieve that goal?

Alternatively, perhaps you want to achieve a certain level of income or pass your business on to your heirs. Regardless of the goal, figure out what you want and work backward to see what you need to get there.

For example, if you wanted to sell your business for a certain price, try to anticipate what kind of valuation you might get on your business. Divide that multiple into your desired sales price to determine the revenue you will need to achieve to meet your goal.

Then run the numbers. Start by asking how much you could afford to reinvest in your growth. How much are you willing to risk in leverage? How much are you willing to reinvest? Then use those assumptions and your assumptions relative to the cost and profitability of your Money Machine to see if you can simply add new corporate locations to reach your goals.

If you cannot do it with corporate locations alone, then you have a couple of options.

First, you can change some of your assumptions relative to risk. For example, you could assume that you would take on more debt. Now, assuming that your initial growth model didn't already have you taking on a maximum debt load, that increased debt load would allow you to grow the business with less equity capital. But that would mean you would need to be comfortable with a greater degree of risk—and that you had the ability to procure that incremental debt in the first place.

Alternatively, you could bring in additional equity capital—in essence, another investor in your business. While that would reduce your risk by spreading it out, you would give up some level of control to your new equity partner. Even if you retain majority control in the business, a minority partner has some rights; you will need to involve them in key decisions and may not have the absolute autonomy you enjoyed in the past. Moreover, because you will have diluted your ownership interest, you will need to adjust your goals upward to offset the effects of their equity. And again, there is the question of whether you can obtain the equity at a valuation you are comfortable with.

And finally, you can revise your goals. Perhaps you are willing to stretch out your time frame for achieving your financial goals or even reduce them. If these alternatives are acceptable, you may not need to look at growth options involving third-party distribution.

don't get run over by a freight train

One of the mistakes we see again and again in the franchise world involves companies that grow too fast. Unfortunately, we have had some clients that have grown faster than their ability to manage that growth. This problem can be particularly exacerbated by the franchise strategy, because in franchising you are not limited by capital constraints—as your franchisees provide all the money when opening a new location.

Peter Ross, cofounder of our clients Senior Helpers, Doctors Express (now called American Family Care), and other franchise concepts, once fell victim to fast growth syndrome himself. As he points out, it is important to set your own agenda for growth—and not fall victim to the enthusiasm of others.

"When I first started out in franchising, it was very easy to fall in the trap of selling multi-unit franchises," he said. "If you are working with franchise brokers or an outside franchise development team, they love multi-unit sales. And while we did see increased cash from these multi-unit sales, the outside franchise development team and franchise brokers were actually making as much or even more in some cases from the sales commissions.

"If I could do it all over again, I would have limited the number of units a new franchisee could buy to two initially—at least until they proved their success. In the case of Senior Helpers, with the exception of a small number of multi-unit owners, the initial territory almost always outperformed any additional units we sold. It takes time for the additional units to open, and sometimes they never open."

Today, Senior Helpers has more than 300 locations and American Family Care has another 200-plus, so Ross overcame some of these hard lessons. But other franchisors have not been so fortunate.

One well-known franchise growth story is that of Curves, the women's circuit training fitness franchise. The company sold 6,000 franchises in their first seven years of franchising—at one point it had more than 10,000 franchisees in 39 countries, with almost 8,000 in the U.S. alone. As far as I can tell, that is the fastest growth ever achieved by a franchisor. But some 14 years later, Curves now has only 367 locations in the U.S. And while taken in a vacuum, 367 would be a fantastic rate of growth over a 20-year time frame, compared to where they were, the number stands as a testament to what can befall a company when its growth outstrips its ability to support its franchisees.

One key to controlled growth, of course, is having a system in place to methodically replicate your business in exacting detail.

❋ A SYSTEM FOR REPLICATION

When I first visited Japan many years ago, I remember hearing about how McDonald's opened its first restaurant in the Ginza district, which at the time was considered the most expensive commercial real estate in the world. As the story went, the rent was so high that they could not afford to let the location sit for a single day without using it. So Den Fujita, the founder of McDonald's Japan, rented a warehouse and hired his construction team a month in advance to practice construction again and again in the warehouse, so that on the day they took possession of the actual site they could transform it as efficiently as possible. When the day finally did come, they swarmed in, and with an efficiency that might even have astounded the folks at McDonald's, they transformed the newly leased property into an operating McDonald's in 24 hours! Now that is a system!

prepare for the end game from day one

Regardless of the growth option you choose, you should begin preparing your business for the end game from day one as a part of your planning process. If, for example, you plan to eventually sell your business, a number of factors can influence the sale price.

One of those factors might be timing. Prior to the Great Recession, for example, there was a buying frenzy in the franchise marketplace, when smaller franchise companies were commanding selling prices in excess of ten times their earnings. But a year later, after the recession had hit, they were lucky to get six times their earnings—or were simply unsellable. So having timing flexibility— either to jump when the timing is right or to stand pat when it is not—will always hold you in better stead.

Aside from the broader market trends, if you were approached by a company or a private equity firm buyer but seemed unprepared, it might easily chill the sale—or at least reduce the price the buyer might have paid.

Even if your goal is to hold onto the business, having everything systematized and having successors in place will allow for a smooth transition if you are no longer able to lead the company for some reason.

As cofounder and chairman of ShelfGenie Franchise Systems, Barry Falcon found out the importance of systematizing the "exit" process the hard way. Falcon, who led the board decision to approve the sale of the company, felt certain their house was in order, having previously sold Concrete Craft, a different franchise company where he was the CEO and partner.

As Falcon put it, "Looking in from the chairman perspective, we had financials, happy franchisees, and business was growing. So I thought selling the company would be a piece of cake. Boy, was I wrong! As I dug into the process, I found that our accounting was really a mess, systems were not in place to close the books on a timely basis, and we had as many as 17 different entities at one point. It took us well over a year to get the financial reporting cleaned up to a place that a quality of earnings (QoE) process would be accurate."

Falcon's advice, along with that of many similar business owners, is to keep your financial systems squeaky clean from day one. Have audits or QoE reports performed annually and make sure you have a documented process for closing the books by the 15th of every month. The cost is minimal when you compare it to missing an opportunity to sell when the time is right and multiples are high.

you can only coast downhill

One of the things that often comes up when I meet with entrepreneurs is their desire to perfect a business before expanding it. Perhaps they need a new POS system or want to add a breakfast item to their menu or a new product to their shelves. Maybe they need to create a new website or update their marketing campaign.

But perfection is the enemy of progress.

These entrepreneurs, who often see their businesses as their babies, are driven by the desire to create—and to make their baby the most beautiful one on the block. So perfecting the business becomes very personal for them.

But waiting to perfect the business before you expand is a fool's errand. While they are refining their business, someone else might be developing a similar concept—perhaps even based on observing that entrepreneur's "imperfect" one. Or worse, someone else may have already knocked off the entrepreneur and is in the process of expanding.

We mentioned in Chapter 1 that the McDonald's menu has radically changed over the years to meet the needs of their customer base. But it wasn't just their menu that evolved. On the marketing side, there was no Ronald McDonald until 1963—and today, they employ hundreds of clowns to play that role in hospitals, and some claim that Ronald comes in second only to Santa Claus among American children. Of course, when McDonald's started, there was no TV advertising and obviously none online. On the operations side, there were no drive-thru windows—which may account for more than half of a typical store's revenue. There were no POS systems, because the computers available at the time cost more than the store and were the size of a typical bedroom. I expect most of the kitchen equipment used back then is long obsolete. No online ordering. No ordering kiosks in the stores. And Uber would not deliver to your door, because it hadn't been founded yet.

One of the hallmarks of any successful business is constant innovation and evolution. But if that innovation stands in the way of growth, the business is doomed to stagnation and eventual death. For those of you who plan to perfect your business as a first step, I have news for you. You will never get there. Perfecting a business is an impossible task, if only because your market, your suppliers, and your consumers are continually changing.

Your job as an entrepreneur is not just to work on the business model. It has to be to do that while also growing the business. You must take on both of these responsibilities simultaneously to be truly successful. Otherwise, you have done no more than buy yourself a job.

Don't get me wrong. You shouldn't try to expand the business model before it is working. If the business model is not yet profitable and providing a reasonable ROI, you are not ready for expansion. The business must work before you start growing it. Replicating a broken business model is just a recipe for faster failure. Likewise, if the business model needs a major overhaul to maintain its profitability, due to the emergence of competitors or other changes in the market, you may need to prioritize those changes first.

But if the business model is working and providing a good return, you should not prioritize tweaking the model. Instead, focus on where you will be investing your growth capital. And, unless you are capital constrained, allocate some of it to concept innovation and some to growth—even if that just means setting aside some capital in a savings account to begin funding your further expansion.

choosing a growth vehicle

Once you are ready to grow your Money Machine, your next decision will be to choose a format for that growth. You may end up deciding to add some corporate locations, franchise, or bring in a third party in some kind of equity arrangement. To choose your growth strategy, you need to look back to your goals. Remember, your business should be a vehicle through which you can meet your personal and financial goals—it does not have goals of its own. So you don't have to grow the business because there is a demand for growth. You don't have to grow for any reason other than to meet your goals.

So if your goals are to spend more time with your family and your business is already providing you with the standard of living you have always aspired to, ask yourself if the time you will spend away from your family and the financial risk you will incur in expansion are worth the effort of additional growth. And they may, in fact, not be. If that is the case, you may want to focus on your existing business model so you can maintain and harvest its profits.

But if you do want to expand, ask yourself where you want to be at some point in the future. If you have partners in the venture, have a heart-to-heart with them. Don't focus on issues like valuation or what you think you can achieve. Instead, set a goal that reflects what you would like to get out of the business. Perhaps you would like to sell the business for X amount by Y date, or you would like to earn Z amount every year by working only ten months per year. Whatever the goal, be specific in terms of the financial reward you are looking for and the time frame in which you hope to achieve it.

Then you will need to develop a financial model to determine if you can achieve those goals through organic growth. Take into consideration the amount of capital you have to invest, the amount of risk you are willing to take on (in terms of debt financing or leases executed), and a conservative case for revenue and profitability, to see if it's possible to meet your growth goals. You might want to do some sensitivity analysis to see if you will still be able to meet those goals in a worst-case scenario.

Assuming that you can meet your goals through corporate expansion, you could choose to end your analysis right here. While there are other reasons you might opt for franchising, joint venturing, or a third-party infusion of capital (largely questions of risk reduction), most people in this situation will choose the corporate growth strategy. But if you do not have enough capital, you need to look at other options—or alter your underlying assumptions. For example, you could:

* Stretch out the timeline so you have a longer runway to achieve your goal.
* Alter your assumptions about risk—perhaps you could invest more of your own money or take on more leverage in the form of debt.
* Reduce the scope of your goal to something that is more attainable, given your risk tolerance and your capital position.

❋ Alter your assumptions about the underpinnings of your business model, although counting on best-case scenarios is risky.

❋ Look at alternative sources of equity financing, like an outside partner—although you will then have to alter the scope of your goal to offset dilution.

❋ Look at third-party channels of distribution (such as franchising) to fund your growth with other people's money.

If corporate growth will not achieve your goal, do a second round of financial modeling from the standpoint of some of your other expansion strategies. Those might include bringing in equity, doing joint ventures at the unit level, licensing the intellectual property, manufacturing and selling products, or (my personal preference) franchising. And while it is beyond the scope of this book to do a deep dive on the topic of franchising (I have already written that book), I do have some fairly concise advice on that topic.

the role of franchising

You should never "decide to franchise."

The reason I tell people not to decide to franchise is because franchising is an emotionally charged word for many. Whether they are deciding to franchise or to avoid franchising, it is often because the word has certain specific connotations for them.

Physicians, attorneys, and other professionals who are thinking about some form of third-party expansion will often avoid franchising because of its association with McDonald's and other purveyors of fast food. And, after all, that kind of connotation has no place in medicine, law, accounting, or any other "respectable" profession, does it? When someone studies for their job for many years, they don't want to buy into a system that is associated with the stamp-'em-out culture franchising has become synonymous with.

Others decide not to franchise because somewhere along the line a lawyer may have told them it is expensive or difficult—perhaps because that lawyer once had a bad experience with it or does not understand franchise law. Or perhaps a lawyer told them that franchising is litigious. Likewise, they may have heard from a friend that it was difficult. Or someone they know once tried it and failed. But all these reasons against franchising are anecdotal and largely should not influence your business decision making.

Equally, some people choose to go the franchise route because they have heard of businesses that experienced exponential growth through franchising. They have heard about the Sky Zones of the world, which started with virtually nothing and created a new industry from scratch, or the franchise owners like the College H.U.N.K.S., who started a company in their 20s and were millionaires by the time they hit 30. But again, these success stories on their own are not a reason to franchise.

Your lawyer should never decide your business strategy. Neither should your friends, or the relative success or failure of people you have read about. Franchising is simply a method of business expansion that may or may not meet your needs. Your job as a business owner is to make the best decisions possible for your business relative to your growth strategy. And if that means you decide to create a franchise, then find a good franchise lawyer and be sure to comply with all the laws.

So in making a decision on a third-party channel, start by asking three questions about the nature of your contractual relationship with your third party.

question 1: will they use your name?

For most of you, having brand-name recognition will help drive incremental revenue and allow you to advertise more effectively. And the name is one of the three definitional elements of a franchise. If your third-party channel will be using your brand, you have met the first requirement of a franchise.

question 2: will they use your systems?

Because this book is all about systems, my underlying hope would be that the answer is yes. If a new business owner is buying into your business, they want access to the intellectual property you have developed. That means you will be providing them with your systems, in the form of operations manuals, training programs, and ongoing support, to increase their likelihood of success. Moreover, because they are using your name, you will presumably want to control the quality of their operations, because their quality (or lack thereof) will reflect directly on you. And these components— significant control and assistance—make up the second definitional element of a franchise.

question 3: will you be compensated for the use of your name and systems?

If you intend to take a franchise fee, royalty, training fee, consulting fee, materials fee, advertising fee, bookkeeping fee, or any other kind of fee (except a bona fide markup on goods you sell this third party for resale) greater than $500 during the first six months, you will have triggered the third definitional element of the federal franchise law.

If you have all three elements of a franchise, that simply means that you will need to provide certain disclosures, in a predefined format, to prospective franchisees in accordance with FTC Rule 436 in advance of any sale, and you may need to register the franchise with the state or otherwise comply with state business opportunity laws.

When you make a decision to franchise, what you're really doing is deciding how you want to grow. Start with your goals, and ask yourself if you can reach them in the time frame you have established by following your current growth plan. If the answer is no, then you need to look at more options—bringing in outside equity capital or debt financing, for example. Or you can revisit your goals or underlying assumptions, or look to some kind of third-party channel of distribution.

If you choose that last option, ask yourself if you want that third-party channel to carry a common brand for the sake of promoting its goods or services. If the answer is yes, is it important to you to control the quality of the deliverables associated with that brand? (If you believe that strong systems are at the heart of the brand experience, you will likely agree that some level of control is imperative.)

Assuming that you want a branded third-party channel of distribution over which you will exercise some significant control, the last question you need to address is how to monetize that channel. If you decide to monetize it strictly through a wholesale markup on the sale of products you manufacture and sell to your channel partners, you have chosen a dealership or distributorship model. If you invest in that channel as a partner and only take out profits as a partner without taking any fees, you will have created some form of joint venture. And if you charge your channel partner some kind of fee—whether it be upfront fees, ongoing royalties, consulting fees, bookkeeping fees, or fees for services—then the chances are you have created a franchise.

You may find that you want to incorporate multiple monetization strategies into your channels. But your choice should be the result of good business decisions based on sound financial models and rooted in your goals—not stories you've heard from a lawyer, a friend, or a TV show.

Once you have made your decisions, hold them up to the light of day, show them to an attorney (or a consultant), and determine what you have created. If it is a franchise, that's great. If the ideal structure for your business is something else, then that's great, too. Make the best decision for your business, and then let the lawyers and consultants sort out the paperwork.

a system for franchising

In my first book, *Franchise Your Business* (Entrepreneur Press, 2016), I wrote about the Franchise Sales-Quality Cycle, which in effect is the underlying system that governs all of franchising. Essentially, the system holds that if you start with a great concept (which presumably you have built here) and structure it as a win-win, there are certain predictable steps that will lead to success in the franchise sales process. But successful franchise sales are not enough. You must then take additional steps to ensure that your intellectual property is properly assimilated and implemented at the franchisee level to help them succeed as well. That, in turn, leads to validation in the marketplace, which further reinforces the buying decisions of future franchise prospects.

The Franchise Sales-Quality Cycle, which I have since taken to calling the Franchise Success Cycle, is essentially the paradigm we have developed at the iFranchise Group to represent the system that successful franchisors use to grow their brands: They use the success of their franchisees to accelerate their growth and increase their franchise sales. Figure 11-1, which is shown below, illustrates how interrelated the franchisor's message is with the message its franchisees are delivering to the marketplace as a whole.

On the sales side, the basic system starts with a strong concept and a compelling franchise offer. Next, the franchisor must generate

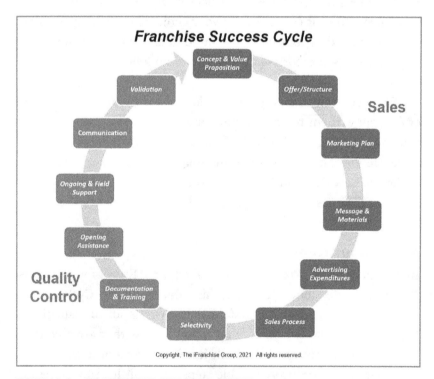

FIGURE 11-1—**FRANCHISE SUCCESS CYCLE**

leads, so they will need a well-designed and cost-effective marketing plan. These leads must be approached with a message that conveys the compelling nature of the offer, using well-designed creative materials, websites, and other communication vehicles. From there, the franchisor will need to establish a systematized sales process, which will yield a predictable number of applications, Discovery Days, and franchise sales (at a relatively predictable cost). Thus, the more the franchisor invests in their franchise marketing plan, the more franchise sales they can expect to achieve.

But if they want prospective franchisees to hear a consistent message across the market (when they call the system's franchisees, read the business press, and look at social media), the vast majority of current franchisees must be doing well and ready to tout the benefits of the franchise system.

As much as you would love to believe that the systems you create will work for anyone, different systems require different skill sets, capitalization, and levels of commitment. So careful franchisee selection becomes an integral part of your success system. From there, you must determine what tools and support you need to impart your intellectual property to your franchisees as effectively as possible. Beyond that, it is your responsibility to continue to communicate with them, maintain good franchisee relations, and encourage their growth and improved performance—so that they will, in turn, say great things about you and about the franchise itself when asked to validate it for the next prospective buyer.

In franchising, success begets success. The franchisees' success creates validation in the sales process and often leads to them acquiring additional units—which, in addition to reducing sales and support costs, allows you to see how they do before signing them up for multiple units. Their success will also help reduce the odds of litigation.

While the components of the Franchise Success Cycle are far more complex than is shown here (and are dealt with in much greater detail in my first book), the important point is that, just like the Money Machine you are building, franchising is essentially a system that relies on predictable inputs to generate predictable outputs. If you start with a great business model, do a good job of marketing it, spend adequate capital, and have a strong sales process, you will sell franchises. And if you are selective in the sales process, meticulous in your support and training, and committed to frequent and transparent communication, you have a good chance of building a network of successful and highly loyal franchisees that will be the lifeblood of your franchise system.

That's why franchising is predictable—and repeatable.

Consider, for example, Neighborly Brands. Originally, lifelong entrepreneur and franchise icon Don Dwyer founded Rainbow International Carpet Dyeing & Cleaning Company, the first of what would become the Neighborly Brands in 1981. By 1990, the brand had grown substantially, and Dwyer acquired the Mr. Rooter franchise, which today is one of the country's largest plumbing and drain cleaning franchisors. In 1992, the company acquired Aire Serve, which today is one of the largest HVAC franchisors in the U.S. And since that time, it has continued to add franchise companies in the home service space almost faster than the ink could dry on the prior acquisition:

* Mr. Appliance—1994
* Glass Doctor—1998
* Portland Glass—2004
* The Grounds Guys—2010
* Five Star Painting—2014
* Mr. Handyman—2015
* ProTect Painters—2015
* Molly Maid—2015
* Drain Doctor—2015
* Locatec—2016
* Window Genie—2016
* Countrywide Grounds Maintenance—2017
* Bright & Beautiful—2017
* Real Property Management—2018
* Mosquito Joe—2018

- Dream Doors—2019
- Dryer Vent Wizard—2020
- HouseMaster—2020
- ShelfGenie—2020
- Precision Door Service—2020

So as of this writing, Neighborly has franchised these brands in nine countries around the world and has accumulated over 4,500 franchises in the process. And I can assure you that their ability to successfully franchise businesses over and over is not just a matter of luck. They have systematized the process of successfully franchising.

And this is not an isolated incident. LYNX Franchising started with JAN-PRO Commercial Cleaning and now has expanded to include Intelligent Office and our former client FRSTeam restorations. Our client Capriotti's just recently acquired Wing Zone, creating a company with revenue of over $150 million. Our client Clean Juice, which won the NextGen award for new franchisors in 2018, acquired Freecoat Nails just two years later with plans to franchise it—and to continue to make strategic acquisitions. Famous Brands owns Mrs. Fields Cookies and TCBY. Yum! Brands owns KFC, Taco Bell, Pizza Hut, WingStreet, and The Habit Burger Grill. Inspire Brands owns Dunkin', Baskin-Robbins, Arby's, Buffalo Wild Wings, Jimmy John's, Rusty Taco, and Sonic Drive-In—for a total of almost 32,000 restaurants. Restaurant Brands International owns Burger King, Tim Hortons, and Popeyes. Self Esteem Brands franchises Anytime Fitness, The Bar Method, Basecamp Fitness, and our client Waxing the City. WellBiz Brands owns three of our former clients: Amazing Lash Studio, Fitness Together, and Drybar, as well as Elements Massage. Realogy franchises Better Homes and Gardens Real Estate, CENTURY 21, Coldwell Banker, Sotheby's International Realty, and ERA in the real estate space. Focus Brands owns Carvel, Cinnabon, Schlotzsky's, Moe's Southwest Grill, and Seattle's Best Coffee. In the hair space, Regis owns Supercuts, Cost Cutters, First Choice Haircutters, and Roosters Men's Grooming Center.

Virtually every hotel company owns and franchises multiple different brands. And Roark Capital Group, a huge private equity player in the franchise space, is currently invested in some 60 franchise companies, including some of those listed above, of which our team played a role in the growth of more than a dozen. And, frankly, I am just skimming the surface with these examples.

In fact, even when entrepreneurs sell their businesses, they often return to franchising. Our client John Leonesio, after spending 23 years in the health club arena, founded Massage Envy in 2002, only to sell the company six years later after successfully franchising that operation, which today has some 1,150 locations. From there, he went on to be the CEO of The Joint, a chiropractic franchise, which has grown to more than 500 locations today. From there, he became CEO of our client Amazing Lash Studio, which now has more than 260 locations. And most recently, he has joined Redline Athletics as their CEO.

Our client Peter Ross had similar success with Senior Helpers (300-plus locations), then Doctors Express (now called American Family Care) with more than 200, and is now starting his his next two concepts. Our client Don Newcomb did the same with McAlister's Deli (450-plus locations) and now Newk's Eatery (130+ locations). Our client Harris Research started with Chem-Dry (about 3,500 locations), added wood refinishing franchise N-Hance in 2003 (which now has more than 500 locations), and most recently added Delta Restoration Services before the company was sold.

One of our first clients Jeff Sinelli founded Genghis Grill in 1998 and was franchising by 2001. He grew the company, sold it, and opened his next business in 2003—Which Wich Superior Sandwiches—which today has almost 350 locations. And he has since acquired and franchised Paciugo Gelato Caffe and is working on new franchise concepts as we speak.

The successful marketing, selling, and servicing of franchises is not about luck. Franchising itself is a replicable system. If you start with a successful business, it is simply a process that allows you to duplicate that success again and again with largely predictable results.

sprint to the mountaintop

Regardless of whether you choose franchising as your growth strategy, one of the questions I hear frequently is "How fast should I grow my business?" But I am obliged to duck that question. People's goals are individual and specific. When it comes to goals, only you can set them.

That said, I will weigh in—only from my personal perspective—on the timeline you have for achieving those goals.

When we talk to franchisors, we generally urge them to slow down when they launch their new franchise program. The reason is simple—when someone starts franchising, they are essentially getting into a brand-new business, and the key to their success is the success of their franchisees. And however you choose to grow, it is much more important to avoid striking out than to hit a home run. A single failure in the early stages of franchise expansion will almost always cost you much more than you would earn from several highly successful locations.

Long-term success as a franchisor depends on carefully monitoring your initial franchisees' performance as they open their businesses. This critical period allows you to evaluate the quality of the systems you have put in place and receive feedback from the franchisees who are using them. Once you have a high level of confidence in those systems through seeing them in action and getting feedback from your early stage franchisees, you can set a more aggressive growth plan in motion.

So avoiding failure at all costs should be the capacitor on your growth.

With that in mind, identify the most important factors in making a unit successful. Is it a question of choosing the best manager or franchisee? How important is the location and site selection process? How important is hiring and training staff?

Once you have determined the success factors, you must decide how you will provide them. Do you need to hire a site selection consultant or firm or develop site selection or business operations manuals? Do you need to establish a system for maintaining consistency in hiring?

The bottom line, as we've said before, is that you should never grow faster than your ability to support that growth. But if you can support it, faster growth helps you stay ahead of your competitors. If you are growing at 100 miles per hour, they will need to grow at 110 miles per hour if they want to pass you. And that extra speed on their part may make it more likely that they will crash along the way.

Ultimately, we each need to recognize that what we all have on this beautiful earth is time. Time that you can spend with your families, with your friends, on yourself, or on your business.

Time is the one asset that is diminishing even as you finish reading this book. And how you spend it, today, tomorrow, and in the future, is what your business decisions should be about.

When you own a business, you do so because you want to create a lifestyle for yourself. But more than that, you want that business to serve your purposes and meet your goals for you and your family.

But I think one of my clients said it best when I asked them how fast they wanted to grow: Sprint to the mountaintop.

You can enjoy the view longer.

sample pre-opening checklist

This Appendix is designed to cover some of the tasks you may need to undertake in the pre-opening process. Please note that it is designed for a generic business with a physical location, so both the processes that it contains and the timelines that are estimated will need to be adjusted for your specific needs.

Sample Pre-Opening Checklist

Task	When to Do
❑ Select professional advisors.	6–9 months prior to opening
❑ Select name for business. • Hire attorney to provide opinion and obtain trademark. • Hire firm to develop logo, letterhead, etc.	
❑ Start looking for a site. • Use demographics to evaluate. • Ensure business licenses are obtainable. • Drive the market to get a feel for "the lay of the land." • Visit competitive locations.	
❑ Once site is selected: • Be sure to have your legal counsel review your lease prior to signing. • Furnish the corporate office with a copy of the executed contract of sale, lease, or sublease.	
❑ Prepare pre-opening budget.	
❑ Estimate construction cost summary for the build-out process.	
❑ Establish a business form. • Consult your tax advisor. • Open a checking account.	
❑ Obtain permits for exterior signage.	
❑ Order "XYZ Company Coming Soon," "Now Hiring," and "Now Open" signs.	

Task	When to Do
❑ Order exterior signage—hang as quickly as possible.	5–6 months prior to opening
❑ Display "XYZ Company Coming Soon" signage.	
❑ Apply for all necessary permits and licenses.	
❑ Develop relationships with vendors and complete applications.	
❑ Obtain a mailing address.	
❑ Develop site layout and design.	
❑ Hire an architect.	
❑ Approve architectural drawings.	
❑ Solicit bids on plans from multiple contractors.	
❑ Select contractor and keep a copy of the final contractor's bid.	
❑ Get required insurance.	
❑ Apply for Federal ID Number.	
❑ Arrange for utilities.	
❑ Research pricing of local competition.	
❑ Ensure that all building permits have been submitted.	
❑ Begin build-out of location and monitor the construction process: • Visit the site daily, if at all possible. • Try to be present for all inspections. • Spend time in and around your site to better understand your location. • Ask contractor for weekly construction updates.	

Task	When to Do
❑ Purchase security/video-camera system.	5–6 months prior to opening, continued
❑ Order equipment, furnishings/fixtures, and other items for your location.	
❑ Set up credit card accounts.	
❑ Research local taxes.	
❑ Review local health department requirements if applicable.	
❑ Place blank applications in the location when construction begins.	
❑ Arrange for all necessary inspections.	
❑ Research local health codes and ordinances, as necessary.	
❑ Finalize number of employees to be hired and establish recruitment plan.	4–5 months prior to opening
❑ Obtain any employee certifications as required in your area.	
❑ Place recruitment ads looking for employees.	
❑ Spread the word that you are looking to hire.	
❑ Interview and hire the employees.	
❑ Research POS system	
❑ Order POS system.	15 weeks prior to opening
❑ Purchase cleaning supplies.	

Task	When to Do
❑ Develop grand opening plans.	14 weeks prior to opening
❑ Develop marketing blitz for your grand opening.	
❑ Order XYZ Company printed materials.	
❑ Finalize menu of products/services and prices.	
❑ Contact vendors and/or suppliers for equipment installation.	
❑ Develop or obtain initial training programs: • The general manager (combined classroom, study, and on-the-job training). • An assistant general manager (shorter version). • Other employees.	12 weeks prior to opening
❑ Post "Now Hiring" signage on the building.	4 weeks prior to opening
❑ Place ads to hire remaining team members.	
❑ Establish supplies of daily paperwork and forms.	
❑ Have phone system installed.	
❑ Arrange distribution by contacting purveyors.	
❑ Order office equipment.	
❑ Research and review OSHA requirements if applicable.	
❑ Order credit card processing system.	
❑ Order menus or other promotional pieces.	

Task	When to Do
❑ Purchase office supplies and set up office.	3 weeks prior to opening
❑ Establish local marketing contacts.	
❑ Order employee uniforms.	
❑ Develop emergency plans and exit procedures; draw maps.	
❑ Establish staffing par levels. • Initially you should hire XX people with the goal of ending up with YY quality employees.	
❑ Establish maintenance and cleaning calendar.	
❑ Establish inventory system.	
❑ Develop an equipment maintenance log.	
❑ Have equipment installed.	
❑ Begin interviews for remaining staff positions.	
❑ Label switches and breakers and check for accessibility.	
❑ Develop emergency equipment shutoff procedure.	
❑ Develop employee filing system.	
❑ Order first-aid kit.	
❑ Make sure phone system is operational.	
❑ Order business cards for management team.	
❑ Meet with vendors.	
❑ Notify suppliers of your projected opening date, location, etc.	
❑ Review initial inventory orders to ensure completeness.	

Task	When to Do
❏ Develop public relations activities.	3 weeks prior to opening, continued
❏ Prepare press kits.	
❏ Establish tentative opening date and notify press.	
❏ Complete interviews and hire remaining employees.	
❏ Prepare employee training materials.	
❏ Develop employee handbook.	
❏ Set training schedule.	15–19 days prior to opening
❏ Hold staff meeting.	
❏ Set up administrative files.	
❏ Have POS system installed.	
❏ Determine POS programming needs.	
❏ Hold a meeting with your managers.	
❏ Begin POS training for all management personnel.	
❏ Call new employees to confirm training dates.	
❏ Assemble new employee supplies: i.e.: • Uniforms • New hire forms • Employee handbooks • Operating policies	
❏ Complete preparations for employee training.	
❏ Finalize employee training materials.	

Task	When to Do
❑ Conduct orientation for new employees, including, for example: • History of XYZ Company • Review of training materials • Completion of employment paperwork • Tour of facility • Overview of training program	15–19 days prior to opening, continued
❑ Conduct employee training.	
❑ Make sure the POS system is working.	
❑ Enter employee data into the POS system.	
❑ Start marketing blitz.	14 days prior to opening
❑ Place "XYZ Company Coming Soon" advertising in local papers.	
❑ Send press releases.	
❑ Begin training for team members.	
❑ Obtain copies of certificate of insurance.	
❑ Order janitorial equipment.	
❑ Obtain banking materials (e.g., deposit slips, deposit bags, deposit stamps).	
❑ Have alarm installed and verify it is working properly.	
❑ Prepare vendor orders and delivery schedule.	
❑ Have remaining equipment installed and working.	

Task	When to Do

❑ Perform trial run of all equipment as soon as it is installed and hooked up.
  • Damage during shipping or other imperfections can affect performance.
  • Improperly functioning equipment should be discovered and repaired as soon as possible so it does not affect the opening date.
	14 days prior to opening, continued

❑ Order necessary cleaning products when construction is completed and equipment is in place.	
❑ Begin review of construction punch list with contractor.	12–13 days prior to opening
❑ Verify with the contractor the status of your use and occupancy permit.	
❑ Finalize grand opening marketing plan.	
❑ Finalize backup suppliers.	
❑ Set up shelving for walk-in and dry storage areas; label shelving.	
❑ Set exterior light timer, if applicable.	
❑ Continue training.	
❑ Review construction punch list items with contractor.	10–11 days prior to opening
❑ Hang interior décor.	
❑ Complete equipment warranty cards.	
❑ Continue training.	

Task	When to Do

❑ Consult your local health department if you are opening a restaurant.
  • Verify with your health department inspector that everything is in good shape.
  • Check to make sure all equipment is working properly.
  • When discussing issues with your health department or any other inspectors, we HIGHLY RECOMMEND you repeat your question twice and repeat their answer back to them, to make certain there are no misunderstandings.
	10–11 days prior to opening, continued

❑ Arrange for installation of fixtures (towel racks, soap dispensers, etc.).	9 days prior to opening
❑ Make sure you have received your certificate of occupancy.	
❑ Stock the first-aid kit and put in its designated place.	
❑ Prepare list of suppliers and service providers.	
❑ Continue training.	
❑ Continue training.	8 days prior to opening
❑ Complete task checklists as necessary for each position.	

Task	When to Do
❏ General contractor should have all punch list items completed.	7 days prior to opening
❏ Place inventory order.	
❏ Continue training.	
❏ Verify that all utilities are in your name or your company's name.	
❏ Verify that all building codes or inspections have been fulfilled.	7 days prior to opening, continued
❏ Verify all services are in place and operating properly.	
❏ Continue training.	6 days prior to opening
❏ Follow up with the contractor regarding final touches.	
❏ Complete all decorating.	
❏ Begin networking by visiting local businesses.	
❏ Continue training.	5 days prior to opening
❏ Cleaning crew should begin cleanup.	
❏ Continue networking.	
❏ Follow up with contractor regarding any open issues.	
❏ Go over last-minute construction details.	
❏ Place any necessary additional orders.	
❏ Double-check POS system programming.	

Task	When to Do
❏ Continue training.	4 days prior to opening
❏ Conduct any necessary late hiring.	
❏ Make sure equipment is in place and operational.	
❏ Organize and prepare for opening.	
❏ All inspections, use, and occupancy permits signed.	
❏ All inspections, permits, and licenses approved and business legally cleared to open.	
❏ Complete schedules for the first two weeks.	4 days prior to opening, continued
❏ Do "practice runs" with employees to help them fine-tune what they learned during training.	
❏ Provide feedback after practice runs and conduct additional training as needed.	
❏ Set up your change fund.	
❏ Continue training.	
❏ Complete a final cleaning of the operation.	3 days prior to opening
❏ Recheck work schedules and make adjustments as needed.	

Task	When to Do
❑ Clean and make final preparations for opening.	2 days prior to opening
❑ Verify that all employees are comfortable with their jobs and know who is working and when.	
❑ Host a "dry run" opening with friends and family.	
❑ Go over employee performance and retrain as needed.	
❑ Complete any last-minute training.	1 day prior to opening
❑ Verify that all employees are comfortable with their jobs and know who is working and when.	
❑ Complete another final cleaning of the operation.	
❑ Employee pep talk and document the day for your archives.	Opening day
❑ Display "Now Open" signs.	
❑ Open the doors.	
❑ Prepare for Grand Opening activities (after a one-month soft opening).	

acknowledgments

O ver the course of my 35-plus years in franchising, I have worked with many of the best and brightest in the franchise world, some of whom I have had the honor of calling my friends and colleagues at the iFranchise Group. Currently, our 27 consultants have more than 800 years of experience in franchising—much of which has come in senior roles with major brand-name franchise companies.

My good friend and partner at iFranchise Group, Dave Hood, the former president of Auntie Anne's, has provided me tremendous firsthand insight into franchise best practices over the course of decades and has had a huge hand in providing input on this book—and for both, I owe him a profound debt of gratitude. I have also learned a tremendous amount from many of the consultants who have worked with me at the iFranchise Group. Leonard Swartz has led six different franchise brands in senior level positions—starting as the COO of Dunkin' Donuts, and later holding senior management positions at Dunhill Personnel, Snelling & Snelling, Adia Services (now Adecco), PIP Printing, and a franchise division of ITT. Scott Jewett, whom I have the privilege of calling a friend, grew LINE-X from its entry into franchising to its sale to a private equity firm after opening more than 700 franchise units. Jerry Wilkerson, who is like a brother to me, stuck with me through thick and thin in the early days, helped introduce me to the franchise world, and showed me the ropes when it was in his best interest to do otherwise. Our partner at TopFire Media, Matthew Jonas, along with Lia Brakel who heads our marketing department, have helped me transition from the stone age in which I grew up into the digital world of modern franchise marketing. Judy Janusz, the COO at the iFranchise Group, has provided the leadership and unwavering commitment to quality that allowed us to build this company, not to mention to find the time to write this book. To all of them, I owe a debt of thanks that I can never fully repay.

I could write another book on all that I have learned from the tremendous team at the iFranchise Group. David Omholt, Barry Falcon, Jeff Abbott, Chris Moorhouse, Cynthia Clarkin, Tommy Clark, Darrell Kolinek, Sunil Dewan, Joanna Meiseles, Gary Prenevost, Charlie Weeks, Mike Baum, Hector Ledesma, Bob Moorhouse, Dan Levy, Jim Green, Joe Bargas, Terry Conroy, Keri DesCoteaux, Ann Anderson, and Emiliano Jöcker have all been a part of my education—as has my brother John, who, along with Judy Janusz, also assumes the occasional role of keeping me in line. And Mohamed Charafeddine along with the magnificent team at iFranchise MENAT have done more than provide me an education on the franchise world outside of North America—they have opened their homes and hearts to me.

I owe a special note of thanks to Lia Brakel, Natalie Lamb, and and Donna Imbery, who, in addition to everything else, directly contributed to this book. And I owe a tremendous debt to my editors, Jen Dorsey, Karen Billipp, and Wyn Hilty, who could add both tutor and cheerleader to the tremendous editorial assistance they have provided me through the process of publishing all three of my books.

It has been my distinct privilege and honor to learn from these people, and from the many others—clients, consultants, and lawyers alike—who have shared their franchise insight and experience with me over the years. To thank them all would take another chapter or two. It is my sincere hope that I'm able to impart some small part of the lessons that they have taught me in this book.

about the author

Author of *Franchise Your Business: The Guide to Employing the Greatest Growth Strategy Ever* and *The Franchisee Handbook: Everything You Need to Know About Buying a Franchise*, Mark Siebert founded the iFranchise Group in 1998. Since 1984, he has been instrumental in the success of numerous national franchisors.

Some of the more prominent companies he has helped include 1-800-Flowers, Ace Hardware, Amoco, Anheuser-Busch, Armstrong World Industries, Athlete's Foot, Auntie Anne's Soft Pretzels, Berlitz, BP Oil, Bridgestone/Firestone, Buffalo Wild Wings, CARSTAR, Checkers/ Rally's, Chem-Dry, Chevron, Circle K, Claire's Stores, Coldwell Banker, Comfort Keepers, Denny's, Einstein Bros. Bagels, El Pollo Loco, FedEx Office, Fidelity Investments, Goddard Schools, Guinness, Häagen-Dazs, Hallmark, HoneyBaked Ham, IBM, Jackson Hewitt, John Deere, Krispy Kreme, LA Weight Loss, LensCrafters, LINE-X, Little Gym, Manpower, Massage Envy, McAlister's Deli, Mobil Oil, Nestlé, Nissan (Saudi Arabia), Oreck, Payless ShoeSource, Perkins, Petland, Phillips-Van Heusen, Pinkberry, Popeyes, Rita's Italian Ice, Ryder Truck Rental, Sears, Senior Helpers, Shell Oil, Sky Zone, Sonic, Subway, Texaco, T-Mobile, Togo's, and the U.S. Navy.

Siebert serves as a partner and member of the board of directors of TopFire Media, a franchise and consumer media company that specializes in public relations, search engine optimization, social media posting, pay-per-click marketing, and inbound marketing. He also serves as a partner in iFranchise Group International, which oversees licensed operations in the Middle East.

Siebert is active in the International Franchise Association, is a past member of the board of directors of the American Association of Franchisees and Dealers (AAFD), and was a member of the board of directors of i9 Sports (a 140-unit team sports franchisor) during its sale to private equity.

Siebert has presented hundreds of speeches and seminars on franchising in cities around the globe. He has been a featured speaker for the International Franchise Association, the International Franchise Expo, the International Franchise Association's Legal Symposium, the American Bar Association, the National Restaurant Association, and at major franchise events in Argentina, Chile, Indonesia, Japan, Mexico, the Philippines, Peru, and Uruguay.

Siebert has also published over 300 articles in dozens of business and professional periodicals. He has been a featured guest on business programs airing on CNN, Fox Business Network, and other programs both in the U.S. and abroad. Siebert is frequently called on as an expert witness in franchise-related cases. He was named to the *Franchise Times* list of "20 to Watch" in franchising in 2002, in 2001 was named the AAFD's Supporting Member of the Year, and received the AAFD Special Recognition Award in 2003. In 2011, Siebert was the subject of a feature article in *Restaurant Franchising* titled "The Franchise Growth Guru." And under his leadership, the iFranchise Group was twice named the best franchise consulting firm in North America, based on a survey of over 700 franchisors conducted by *Entrepreneur* magazine.

index

CPSIA information can be obtained
at www.ICGtesting.com
Printed in the USA
JSHW030148130721
16661JS00006B/6

9 781599 186672